MERLIN POWER

MERLIN POWER

The Growl Behind Air Power in World War II

Victor F. Bingham

T.Eng (CEI), AMRAeS, AFSLAET.

Drawings by Lyndon Jones MCSD

Airlife
England

Copyright © 1998 Victor F. Bingham

First published in the UK in 1998
by Airlife Publishing Ltd

British Library Cataloguing-in-Publication Data
A catalogue record for this book
is available from the British Library

ISBN 1 85310 068 4

Typeset by Phoenix Typesetting, Ilkley, West Yorkshire

Printed in England by Butler & Tanner Ltd.,
London and Frome

Airlife Publishing Ltd
101 Longden Road, Shrewsbury, SY3 9EB, England

Acknowledgements

This book has been a combination from our own records and memories, with the help and encouragement of numerous people over the years. In particular we would like to thank the following, not in alphabetical or preferential order.

Special thanks to Richard Searle and Staff at the Main Library/archive RAE Farnborough. Brian Kervell, Curator of the RAE Farnborough Museum. Handley Page Association. Yorkshire Air Museum. Derek Reed of Pickering Books. Staff of the RAF Museum archives and photographic department Hendon. Staff of the Public Record Office Kew. Staff of the Imperial War Museum photographic department. Group Captain J. Wray DFC RAF. R.K. Page ex-Westland, Handley Page and Folland. David Birch and the Rolls-Royce Heritage Trust. Fred Gibbons ex-77 Squadron. F. Onions ex-RAF and Fleet Air Arm. Gil Appleby ex-Fleet Air Arm, and Dugald McKillop ex-RAF and the Strathallan Museum.

May we thank all who contributed in any way, or loaned photographs for our use. Any opinions expressed are our own, unless otherwise stated.

We would also like to thank John Strickland and Leslie Stedman for help in compiling information and in checking the manuscript; and last of all, many thanks to our wives for listening about aircraft, answering the telephone, and their tolerance.

Dedication

We dedicate this book to Air-Vice-Marshal D.C.T. Bennett, CB, CBE, DSO, FRAeS, who we consider Great Britain's most outstanding civil and military airman. An airman who, during his career, flew many of Britain's Merlin-powered aircraft.

Victor F. Bingham.
Lyndon Jones.

Preface

The Rolls-Royce Merlin is considered by many people to be the most outstanding liquid-cooled reciprocating piston engine of World War Two, and it certainly powered the majority of Allied aircraft in Europe; so we have commenced the text with an abbreviated history of the Merlin engine, from its origins in the Kestrel, through its single-stage conception to its two-speed two-stage final form.

The aircraft powered by the Merlin are numerous, so we have restricted the aircraft covered by this book to those that saw service in the Royal Air Force and Fleet Air Arm, and so have not included experimental and prototype aircraft. In covering these aircraft in one volume it has been impossible to cover in detail the whole history. We have therefore restricted ourselves to compressing the development period, testing, handling and construction of each into one chapter, including a sectioned drawing and photographs, which we felt aircraft enthusiasts would prefer, and appreciate. The sectioned drawings illustrate the construction, equipment layout and installations. No doubt there will be readers who will be critical and opposed to us exposing the weaknesses of their favourite aircraft, but we trust that they will accept that this is a factual book without bias, giving facts and not myths, technicalities not heroics. We trust that it will create further interest, and give as much pleasure to its readers as it has given us creating it.

Aircraft design was, and is, a time consuming business, even under the pressure of war; with years spent on design and development, with a further period to eradicate the faults – or satisfy the Air Staff – before entry into service. In some cases the gestation period has been such that the entry into service corresponds with it being classed as obsolescent! So aircraft design as well as engine design, is usually based on the designs of the past, the constraints of the present requirements, plus a little bit of crystal ball gazing. Some of the aircraft that we have covered were far from one hundred per cent successful, some required further development and some required another type of engine to be successful, for the Merlin did not suit every installation. Some aircraft during World War Two never reached operational status, whilst others did, but should never have done so; nevertheless, if produced in quantity for the British Services, we have covered them in our record of Merlin-powered aircraft.

Victor F. Bingham.
Lyndon Jones.

Contents

Introduction

The aircraft covered in this book were designed during the 1930s and 1940s, a period when the monoplane and stressed skin construction became recognised as the method of the future (the Wellington was to prove the exception); a period which saw the development and peak of achievement of the Rolls-Royce Merlin engine. During the 1920s and early 1930s, most British aircraft manufacturers were kept close to the starvation line by meagre orders, due to the economic climate and tight control – not due to the Air Ministry, but because of the pacifist attitude of the British people and the Governments of this period.

Until 1934 the restrictive limit of the Geneva Disarmament Conference, which laid down a maximum empty weight limit of three metric tons on bomber aircraft, determined that this type of aircraft was weight limited; consequently, development of higher powered engines was also limited. These various limits ensured that British bomber aircraft were restricted in their all-up weight and choice of powerplant; and the Air Ministry Operational Requirements Department, instead of being able to formulate requirements for future equipment, were forced to consider general purpose aircraft of dubious prospects and already verging on obsolescence compared to some of our foreign competitors.

With the casting aside of the limit imposed at Geneva, the maladies of the past ordering restrictions surfaced, firms having insufficient capital to involve themselves with the drawn-out process of design and development, which in some cases took up to seven years. Designs of the past were stretched to save expenditure on costly development; the RAF becoming in the meantime more vulnerable to the expanding nature of the German nation and Luftwaffe. This also brought about revisions to the design and operational requirements of aircraft that were designed to the specifications of 1930–32, such as the Battle, Hampden, Wellington and Whitley.

The standard procurement procedure for the provisioning of the RAF with a new type of aircraft up to 1935 often occupied a period of five to eight years, for the simple reason that one stage in the process had to be completed before the next commenced. Normally, as each year's Air Estimates were prepared, a list of aircraft required by the Air Staff were included, and a specific financial sum allocated to the aircraft in the experimental programme. Then, during the course of the year, the Air Staff would instruct the Director of Operational Requirements (DOR) to prepare a statement for each experimental type required, covering the main operational features; these would include a brief outline of its function, with detailed figures for its performance, armament, engines and crew.

These Operational Requirements were then handed over to the Director of Technical Development (DTD), whose purpose it was to ensure that the aircraft was constructed to these requirements. To fulfil this, DTD prepared a technical specification to cover all engineering aspects; the material to be used, mechanical and wind tunnel tests required, systems, maintenance provisions, engines etc. These technical requirements were then commented on in detail by the various specialist departments covering engines, armament, radio, etc., which meant that this part of the procedure could take anything up to six months. With this completed, the specification was passed to the Director of Contracts for a contract to be prepared. Although a specification and contract would be issued to certain firms, it was a principle that all firms on the Air Ministry's approved list would receive a copy of all specifications.

All tender designs to the specifications were analysed by DTD's staff, who were aided by system specialists. This was then followed by a conference convened and presided over by the Director of Technical Development. This Tender Design Conference then considered the designs, analysed them and placed them in order of merit, so deciding which designs were worth considering further. This normally resulted in two designs being chosen and a prototype of each being ordered; the Air Staff and Air Member for Supply and Research (AMSR) giving their views, with the final approval being the Chief of Air Staff (CAS). With the Air Staff's decision being made the Director of Contracts then gave instructions to place the contracts, and the allocated airframe serial numbers.

Following completion of the above, the next stage in the procedure was the building of the prototype(s), which often resulted in changes in the design (the Fairey Battle being such an example), even in some cases the scrapping of the design. During this period the erection of a mock-up was made, which would then be inspected by specialist and 'user' interests. Any criticisms arising from the Mock-up Conference were then embodied in the design. With the ending of the Mock-up Conference(s) the drawing office of the firm concerned would then concentrate on the detail design and the issue of the drawings to the experimental shop. Following this, the manufacture of the detail parts commenced, followed by assembly of the sub-assemblies, sometimes wings or wing sections being tested in a wind tunnel. Upon completion of each main assembly, the installation of the aircraft's equipment commenced, with some items like engines, propellers, undercarriage units, turrets etc. being supplied by the Air Ministry on Embodiment Loan; while other items such as radiators, fuel pumps and electrical equipment were obtained by the firm on sub-contract.

With the completion of the prototype the first flight was made by the firm's test pilot, quite often without armament or turrets. The firm was responsible for the handling trials as part of the contractor's contract – sometimes taking up to two years to delivery of the prototype to the A&AEE (Aeroplane and Armament Experimental Establishment). At the A&AEE the aircraft was submitted for testing to strictly controlled procedures by expert pilots, who determined if the aircraft conformed to the specifications. Upon all their recommendations, or not, rested the decision by the Air Staff on whether the aircraft type would be developed and go into production.

With the changing political atmosphere in the mid-1930s and the threat of war becoming more positive, the procurement procedure was obviously too drawn out to be effective; so a change was commenced to reduce the interval between the requirements being issued and production commencing. In 1935 the principle of duplicating prototypes was introduced, and was endorsed by the Secretary of State for Air, irrespective of financial limitations. This was intended to minimise design and construction time, which would also mean the flying test programme being shared by two aircraft. But in actual fact the second prototype usually lagged behind the first, as will be seen in this book.

A further change of importance took place in 1935, when in May the Cabinet approved the recommendation that orders for new aircraft types should be placed in bulk before the prototype had flown. Both this and the previous action had immediate effect on the Hampden, Whitley and Wellington. In 1936 four new aircraft types were ordered in quantity before the handling and performance trials had been completed at A&AEE; although these particular aircraft had completed their contractor's trials several months before they had been delivered to the A&AEE. An exception made to this recommendation was the Westland Whirlwind fighter, which was required to complete a handling trial before an order was placed, then further delayed until a handling trial was completed on the second prototype. During 1936–1937 when the design of the B12/36 and P13/36 bombers were being selected, the Air Committee on Supply announced that they wished production to begin within two years to replace all medium bombers not then delivered. This resulted in contracts being quickly placed for the B12/36 and P13/36 bomber prototypes (Stirling, Manchester and Halifax), followed within a few months by production orders. In these cases a relief to the manufacturer had been granted, and the decision to place a quantity order had been taken upon the strength of the designer's drawings and design calculations alone, and was termed 'ordering off the drawing board'.

A Special Order system was also introduced, in which the design and production of a new design was entrusted to the firm concerned, which, in the Air Ministry's view, was at that time best capable of creating the new aircraft required (e.g. the Beaufighter). This trust was based on a fairly good relationship between the Air Ministry and the firms, and that in general the designers made it their business to be conversant with the requirements of the Service. If a firm built a new aircraft design on their own initiative, in the hope that this would interest the Air Staff, this was known as a 'Private Venture'. If the Air Staff were interested, the Air Ministry would purchase the prototype and pay for its development, otherwise, the firm would be the all-round loser. As will be seen in the text of this book, most of Britain's wartime aircraft benefited from these changes in procurement procedures, and in very few cases was the system a failure.

Unfortunately, with every system or procedure there does have to be a decision point, and a person to make that decision; and both in the past and post-war, lack of decision or failure to produce a specification far enough advanced has resulted in the Royal Air Force being denied the aircraft it required – and post-war a lot of this can be laid at the door of our political masters, whose financial restrictions and political thinking goes back to 1930!

Though a self-sealing tank was developed by 1918, due to a desire to make it crashproof as well, no self-sealing fuel tank was installed in British service aircraft at the start of the war in 1939. Armour plate on British service aircraft appeared to be another commodity that was in short supply, and only appeared to be recognised as necessary after the death of numerous well trained pre-war aircrew. When consideration is given to our armament deficiencies in the 1930s the focus is on our 'peashooters' – the Vickers 0.303-in fixed gun of the

1914–18 war was still our main machine-gun in 1937. Though both the Browning 0.300-in and 0.5-in Browning machine-guns as well as other foreign weapons were tested, the riflebore 0.300-in was chosen as the 0.5-in was considered as not sufficiently developed, the 0.300 being bored out to 0.303-in; by 1937 the 20mm cannon was purchased for licence production from Hispano Suiza, but needed development and production of a belt feed, as well as an understanding of its installation difficulties. Many of the Continental countries, including France and Germany, had foreseen the need for more and heavier metal, and had developed the 20mm cannon for a number of years. British failure in the armament field was recognised within the Air Ministry for many years – yet apparently little was done early enough to rectify the situation, and the first experimental installations were not seen in action until the Battle of Britain in 1940, when a number of Spitfires were in use.

Rolls-Royce Ltd, manufacturers of the Merlin, not only developed the engine that powered the aircraft that defeated the Luftwaffe in 1940, but also developed an aircraft cannon and machine-gun, which though not used, gave impetus to the British armament manufacturers. Competition is always a great factor, and Rolls-Royce were always competitive, and 1939–45 showed the Merlin leading the competition.

1

The Rolls-Royce Merlin Engine

A new aero-engine, like most major engineering structures, is usually a combination of cumulative ideas, progressive development of past designs, and a testing and analysis of results from the rig testing of components and full scale engine testing. The Rolls-Royce Merlin engine was no different from this in its conception and design. It evolved no new features such as sleeve valves, swing valves, rotary valves, fuel injection or turbo-supercharging. It was a logical development from a succession of forebears, the most illustrious of which must be the Kestrel and "R" engines.

The Merlin series of engines is considered by many to be the most outstanding liquid-cooled, reciprocating piston engine of World War Two; so to put everything in its correct order and perspective, we have chronicled briefly the history of Rolls-Royce that concerned the Merlin engine. The operative word is *briefly*, for the designs, development, analysis of data, personalities etc. that

led to the Merlin would require many volumes, and this is but one volume that illustrates the British Service aircraft that were powered by the Merlin.

Rolls-Royce was one of the firms selected after the First World War to which contracts would be given, and this selection method determined who should produce aero-engines and who should not. Rolls-Royce would continue producing engines like the Condor and Eagle into the 1920s – these engines all having individual cylinders surrounded by separate cooling jackets.

In 1924, C.R. Fairey (later Sir Richard Fairey) feeling somewhat frustrated with the lack of advancement of engine design in Great Britain, paid a visit to the USA. After touring a number of factories, he purchased the licence to produce the Curtiss D12 engine, having plans to open a factory in England and produce the D12 engine as the Fairey Felix. The D12 engine was the first successful example of a 'V' monobloc cylinder

Side view of two-stage two-speed Merlin Mk 130. (Rolls-Royce)

engine, having cylinder blocks of aluminium alloy into which were fitted 'wet' cylinder liners. In spite of some opposition, the Air Ministry purchased from Curtiss thirty D12 engines, one of which was tested at Farnborough, but no contract was given to Fairey – he was not an accepted aero-engine manufacturer!

The Air Ministry then asked Rolls-Royce, having been refused by Napiers, to undertake the development of a similar type of engine to the Curtiss D12; an example of which was sent to Rolls-Royce by the Air Ministry (at the suggestion of Lieutenant Colonel Fell DD/DTD (Engines)) for a full examination — the year was 1925.

Rolls-Royce's first choice of design in January 1925 was the 1,209 cu in Eagle XVI, this engine having the full financial support of the Government. But by July of the same year Rolls-Royce began the design of the 'F-X' engine, which, like the Eagle XVI, had a gear-driven two-sided supercharger impeller.

The new engine, a 'V' 12 cylinder, known as the 'F-X' (or 'F') engine was of aluminium alloy (Hiduminium) monobloc construction, with a bore and stroke of 5-in by 5.5-in, giving a displacement of 1,295 cu in. The valves, four per cylinder, were actuated by a single overhead camshaft operating through rocker arms. Testing of the prototype began in 1926, and almost immediately faults manifested themselves, so the decision was made to carry out three changes to the design:

(a) Dry cylinder liners replaced with 'wet' liners. (D12 feature).

(b) Fitment of reduction gear.

(c) Due to problems with the supercharger, the decision made to run the engine as a normally aspirated one *(See Note 1)*.

1927 was a year spent on testing, developing and modifying the 'F' type engine, and by the Summer of that year it had completed a 100 hour endurance test at 450 hp at 2,100 rpm. This was the engine that was originally designed to develop 480/500 hp, later to be named Kestrel, that went into production as a normally aspirated engine. It was later scaled up to produce the Goshawk and the 'H' engine, the latter becoming the Buzzard.

As stated previously, one weakness revealed during the testing of the 'F' engine was the supercharger, which was giving such poor results that the Air Ministry advised Rolls-Royce to bring in a

supercharger expert who was leaving RAE Farnborough. This was J.E. Ellor, who became Chief Experimental Engineer on moving to Rolls-Royce.

The first flight of the 'F' engine was made in a DH 9 flown by Hubert Broad. As flight testing continued it became obvious that radiator drag had now reached a serious proportion of the total drag, and a practical and theoretical investigation had to be embarked on to improve the drag factors of both radiators and powerplants. This eventually resulted in 1934 with Rolls-Royce purchasing Hucknall airfield and establishing a flight test centre there. It was originally intended for work in collaboration with airframe manufacturers so as to establish satisfactory engine installations, but led in the end to Rolls-Royce designing, developing and producing complete powerplants.

In 1927, Lieutenant Colonel Fell retired from the Air Ministry and joined Rolls-Royce, and later took over the flight test centre at Hucknall. It was Fell who persuaded Rolls-Royce to build a stretched version of the Buzzard, and develop it into the 'R' racing engine for the Schneider Trophy aircraft, work commencing on this engine in 1928.

The development of the 'R' engine, which produced 2,300 bhp in 1931, achieved a design which attained cylinder mean effective pressures and piston speeds far in advance of previous engines, and so prompted design studies that would result in the Merlin, known in the Works as the PV.12. The PV.12 engine was similar to the Buzzard engine in that it was a scaled-up Kestrel requiring considerable development work and having considerable potential once the defects were eradicated. It was designed to replace the steam-cooled Goshawk, which was a failure, despite having had considerable development carried out on it in 1929–30.

The PV.12 was originally intended by Rolls-Royce to be built as an inverted 'V', to allow a lower sight line over the cowlings, but after the mock-up was shown in 1932, there was apparently considerable opposition to this layout by airframe manufacturers, which caused it to be built as an upright 'V'. Design work on the PV.12 began in early 1933 as a Private Venture (PV), but the Air Ministry were kept fully informed of its development, although no official development funds had been made available.

Some of the development work resulted in re-design of the reduction gear and the strengthening of the block casting. By July 1934 the PV.12 had passed its first type test at a rating of 790 hp at

Hawker Hart modified to accept the PV.12 engine with four blade propeller and larger and repositioned radiator. (Hawker Aircraft)

12,000 feet, with a dry engine weight of 1,177 lb. During the same month work began on a new version incorporating a new cylinder head, known as the 'ramp' head: this had four valves per cylinder and a shaped combustion chamber with two flat ramps of unequal width and inclination. This was intended to give a shortened flame travel and a high degree of turbulence of the charge in the combustion chamber.

The 'ramp' head was completed in October and incorporated on two Merlin Bs: these were built and tested in February 1935, delivering 950 hp on test. The 'ramp' head was used on all Merlins from the B to F inclusive.

The next decision in the process of development concerned the casting of the crankcase and cylinder block, for on the early prototypes these had been cast as a monobloc and had proved unsatisfactory, so it was decided to produce two separate castings for the crankcase and cylinder block, which would improve the casting and simplify the manufacture. This feature was incorporated on the Merlin C, which was tested in April 1935, the PV.12 flight testing being carried out in a Hart suitably modified to accept the new engine *(see photograph above)* and the Merlin C test flown on a Horsley suitably modified. Problems began almost immediately with the cooling system, and after about eight hours

flying the coolant was changed to pure ethylene glycol.

Bench testing meanwhile, of the Merlin B and later models, revealed problems with the 'ramp' head, amongst which were local detonation, cracks in the cylinder head, and exhaust valve fractures; also a Merlin C failed its civil 50 hour type test in May 1935 at a rating of 1,045 hp. Finally a Merlin E passed its 50 hour civil type test in December 1935, but failed its 100 hour military type test in March 1936. There *were* problems.

Emergency measures were now taken in order to get the Merlin in service: it was decided to scale up the standard Kestrel cylinder head to the Merlin size and retain the Kestrel construction (this would be the Merlin G). Work on this began in May 1936. Meantime the Ministry and Rolls-Royce agreed to the Merlin F (an improved E) going into production as the Merlin I and the type test requirements were relaxed. For a comparison of the Kestrel and Merlin engines, *see Figure 1.*

The first Merlin I (model F) when it went on test failed its relaxed type test requirement in July 1936, but fortunately the Merlin G with the Kestrel type head passed its type test with flying colours in the same October, so the Merlin G became the Merlin II; the Merlin I was limited to a production of 180 engines, these being delivered to Fairey for the Battle aircraft!

The Merlin went into production as the Mk II, and the first production engine was delivered in August 1937, producing 1,030 hp at 16,250 feet with a dry weight of 1,335 lb. Very soon afterwards, with the engine in service, trouble was being experienced with coolant leaks from between the liner and the water chamber, as had already been experienced on the Kestrel. This trouble expedited experimental work on a new block with a separate head casting, work on it commencing in March 1938; with the need for mass production of the Merlin for the Hurricane and Spitfire, and a production model established, the two-piece block assembly did not get introduced until the Merlin 60 series, although Packard-built engines incorporated it from the start of production.

Returning to 1935 and the development of the early Merlin engines, work began in the January on a two-speed drive for its supercharger (see Note 2), but difficulties were experienced with this particular type, so Rolls-Royce wisely obtained a licence to produce an established Farman drive. A Merlin with this type of two-speed drive and supercharger was first flown in September 1937, and went into production as the Merlin Series X in December 1938; this engine differed from the Merlin III in having a two-speed supercharger, different reduction gear and a number of small detail differences . . . its dry weight was 1,430 lb.

The next important modification to the Merlin began in 1936, when development commenced on improving the cooling system. One of these developments was the finding that a pressurised coolant system using 70/30 per cent of

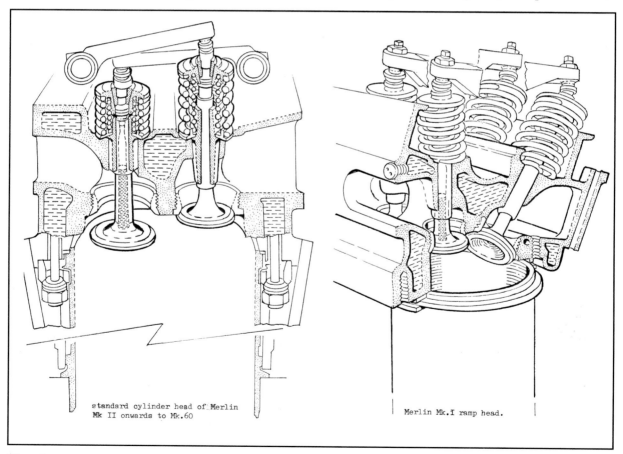

standard cylinder head of Merlin Mk II onwards to Mk.60

Merlin Mk.I ramp head.

Views of two types of Merlin cylinder heads

	Kestrel XIV	Merlin II	Merlin 60	Merlin 140
Cubic capacity.	1295 cu.in	1649 cu.in	1649 cu.in	1649 cu.in
Bore	5.0 in	5.4 in	5.4 in	5.4 in
Stroke	5.5 in	6.0 in	6.0 in	6.0 in
Compression ratio	7 : 1	6 : 1	6 : 1	6 : 1
Reduction gear ratio	0.632 : 1	0.477 : 1	0.477 : 1	0.477 : 1
Nett dry weight	985 lb	1,335 lb	1,650 lb	1,780 lb
Octane rating	87 octane	87 octane	100 octane	100 octane
International rating, rpm	2,750	2,600	2,650	2,850
boost	+3¼ psi	+6¼ psi	+7 psi	+12 psi
bhp	715	990	1,400	1,410
altitude	12,250 ft	12,500 ft	9,250 ft (M)	10,000 ft (M)
Maximum power rating, rpm	3,000	3,000	3,000	3,000
boost	FT	+6¼ psi	+18 psi	+20 psi
bhp	745	1,030	1,705	1,780
altitude	14,500 ft	16,250 ft	5,750 ft (M)	4,500 ft (M)

(M) = MS supercharger gear

Comparison of Kestrel XIV and three marks of Merlin engines

water/ethylene glycol was definitely superior to an atmospheric system using pure glycol. On the pressurised system the cylinder head temperatures (CHT) were lowered at least 70°F (21°C), and the 70/30 mixture did not have such a 'creep' problem as pure glycol. This was first introduced on a number of Merlin VIs, then on all Merlin II, III and X engines, but the first important production with it was on the Merlin XII, beginning in September 1939.

During 1936–37 the Production Department began to complain of an excessive modification rate having serious repercussions on production of the Merlin, and there was a definite indication of this. This high modification rate was due to the demand for Merlins for so many aircraft types (as shown by this book), as well as the continual rate of development of the basic engine.

Once in service another fault in the cooling system began to show itself: this was that under certain conditions the engine lost its coolant and pistons seized. After a certain amount of experiment and searching, it was ascertained that Hispano-Suiza were not experiencing this with their V12 engine, so the possibility of a licence to produce the Hispano-Suiza screwed-in liner-head was discussed, and drawings handed over to Rolls-Royce. Meanwhile Teddington Controls had developed a thermostat device, which partly solved the problem, so the licence was not taken up to produce the Hispano-Suiza patent head.

To study and develop better cooling systems, (see Plate 2 on page 16) radiators and engine cowling,

Rolls-Royce in March 1936 bought a Heinkel He 70. This aircraft was one of the best streamlined aircraft available at that time, and its cabin allowed the accommodation of engineers. The work carried out on the He 70 also confirmed a number of RAE Farnborough investigations and reports.

In 1938, S.G. Hooker (later Sir Stanley Hooker, Technical Director Rolls-Royce (1971) Ltd) joined the company as a technical assistant to J. Ellor. In carrying out an investigation of the Merlin supercharger, he was able to improve the efficiency of the supercharger and the Merlin's output; this was achieved by an increase in the cross-sectional area of the air intake into the impeller eye, and a reduction of approximately one-third of the rotor vane's width. This engine then went into production as the Mk XX (see diagram on p. 17) for bombers and the Mk 45 for fighters, giving an increase in FTH of approximately 3,000 ft above the Merlin III.

In early 1939, Fordair (French subsidiary of Ford America) were requested by the French Air Ministry to negotiate a licence for the production of the Merlin, and so a number of Ford engineers travelled to Derby to obtain a general idea in regard to its manufacture. In their report on the Merlin a number of criticisms were made, two of which were that the supercharger drive was too complicated and required a high degree of workmanship, and that the Rolls-Royce gears were not true involutes, and therefore required special finishing. The latter point would turn out to be the limiting factor in any increase in engine production. How much of this report was

Rolls-Royce's He 70 G-ADZF powered by Kestrel engine. (Rolls-Royce)

political rather than engineering it would be hard to judge, for in the end the negotiations dragged on until German occupation and no engines were produced by Fordair.

When war commenced in 1939, the Daimler-Benz DB601A engine of the Bf 109E fighter had a weight of 1,460 lb compared to the Merlin's 1,375 lb, but also had a displacement of 2,069 cu in against the Merlin's 1,649 cu in capacity. This immediately put the Merlin at a disadvantage, making it necessary for the Merlin to accept higher boosting to obtain equal performance to the DB601A. If too much fuel/air charge is forced in by a high supercharger pressure (boost), then detonation is liable; to eliminate this and to improve performance 100 octane fuel was introduced as standard into the RAF in September 1939. The supercharger efficiency of the Merlin was marginally better than either the DB601A or Junkers Jumo, and with the improvement brought about by Hooker's development, this lead was maintained. One of the problems arriving in the wake of higher boosting was blower surge, this being cured by the fitting of flame traps in the induction system.

On the 24 December 1940 at a meeting at A&AEE Boscombe Down, the view was expressed that the RAF were losing the tactical initiative to the Luftwaffe regarding aircraft performance at altitude, for neither the Hurricane nor the Spitfire were able to reach the altitude performance of the newer Bf 109s. At this particular time the Merlin XX production was slow and the engine difficult to produce compared with earlier Merlins, so requiring an engine developed having the high altitude performance of the Merlin XX, but without the low altitude supercharger of that engine – and so was

developed an engine which was designated the Mk XLV, and raised the Spitfire's altitude by 2,000 ft.

Back in 1936–1937 the RAE* Farnborough had recommended to Rolls-Royce that two stages of pressure ratios should be investigated, but the company wished to avoid the difficulty of the two-stage blower (see Note 3), mainly because at that period the efficiency of the blower was low. Under the combined drive of Ellor and Hooker an increase in supercharger efficiency had taken place by 1939, raising the Mk 45s to 65–70 per cent as against the Merlin IIs 60–65 per cent. Then came a request from the Air Ministry for an engine capable of powering a high altitude version of the Wellington bomber. At Rolls-Royce, calculations were made which indicated that with a two-speed two-stage supercharger and intercooler, the power of the Merlin at 30,000 ft could be doubled, so giving similar power to that of a Vulture engine at that height. From this it was decided to use a Vulture supercharger to feed a single-stage Merlin, and from the test results it was decided that no further performance analysis was necessary, and so the Drawing Office were given the task of producing drawings matching up the Vulture and Merlin superchargers into a two-speed two-stage supercharged Merlin, having flow characteristics similar to the test rig results. Detail design work began in March 1940.

---

* RAE (Royal Aircraft Establishment) Farnborough — renowned for being criticised — also well renowned for its basic scientific research and development, without which the British aircraft industry would be much poorer.

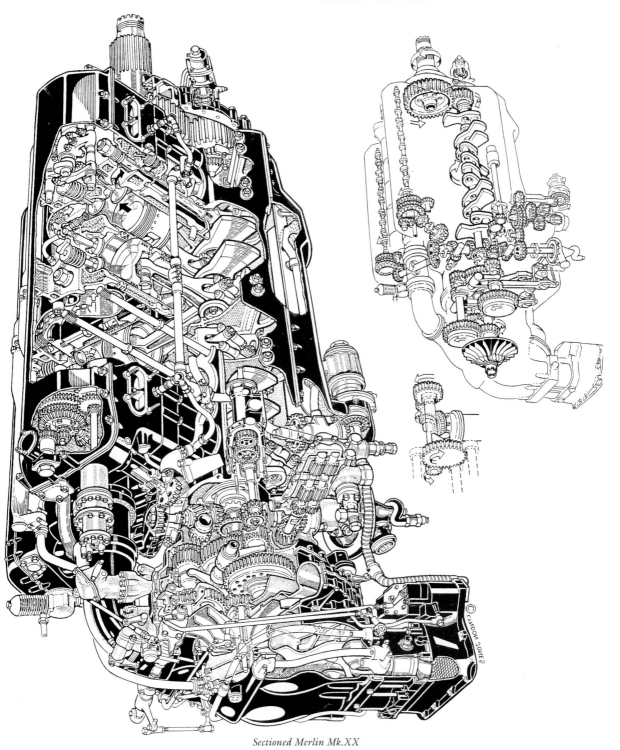

Sectioned Merlin Mk.XX

The engine was designed from the start to use an intercooler after the two-stage blower, but at that period of time there was no intercooler matrix available in the UK of high enough efficiency. The task was passed to RAE Farnborough, who produced a satisfactory design of intercooler having high efficiency and strength, Rolls-Royce developing this design for production. The new engine, designated the Mk 60, had a pressure ratio over the two blowers in high gear of 4.9:1 and an efficiency of 70–75 per cent. The new engine went into production in November 1941, being then further developed into the Mk 61 for fighter aircraft, and hurried into production in March 1942 to power the Spitfire IX, so as to combat the Fw 190.

The demand for Merlins was by 1940 far

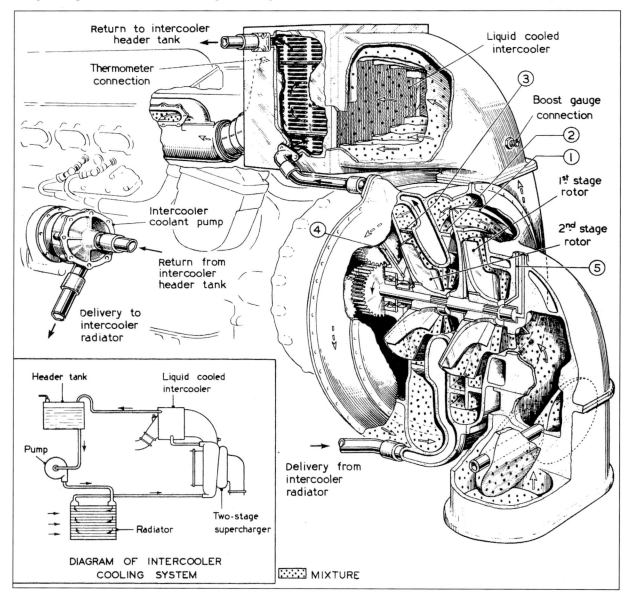

Return to intercooler header tank

Thermometer connection

Liquid cooled intercooler

Boost gauge connection

③
②
①

1st stage rotor

2nd stage rotor

⑤

③

④

Intercooler coolant pump

Return from intercooler header tank

Delivery to intercooler radiator

Header tank

Liquid cooled intercooler

Pump

Radiator

Two-stage supercharger

DIAGRAM OF INTERCOOLER COOLING SYSTEM

Delivery from intercooler radiator

MIXTURE

Diagram of two-speed supercharger and intercooler

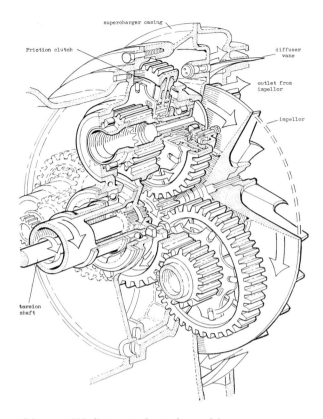

Diagram of Merlin two-speed supercharger drive

well as a number of modifications of other details.

One of the problems encountered with the Merlin, especially with the two-stage marks, was the leading-up of the plugs during flight. This was brought about when low charge temperatures apertained under low power cruising conditions; the low charge temperatures prevented full vaporisation of the fuel, so that small pools of fuel concentrated in the induction manifold, then after building up over a period of time the fuel would be gulped into the engine, causing leading of the plugs and misfiring. To overcome this problem it was necessary to keep the charge temperature above a certain point, and charge temperature gauges were fitted.

During the use of the Merlin in the transport aircraft role there were two methods of engine handling to achieve long engine life. One of these was the cruise control method, in which the power of the engine is reduced as the fuel is used up and the aircraft becomes lighter, so keeping the airspeed constant. The second method is the constant power type, in which the power is maintained constant as the fuel is used up; the aircraft becomes lighter and so climbs higher and speed increases, which gives a shorter flight time. This latter method was the one recommended to BOAC and Transport Command by Rolls-Royce, and had the added advantage in that the charge temperature was maintained high and prevented plug leading troubles.

The 60 series of Merlin included the 63 to 68, and all were two-speed two-stage engines, which followed the same general design of the Mk 60, although some had modified reduction gear casings and some used the Stromberg type carburettor. The Mk 72 and 73 engines also were similar to the 60 series in general design, though they had the intercooler cooling system header tank integral with the intercooler and not attached to the bulkhead.

All the 60 and 70 series engines were based in general on the design of the Mk XX and 60 engines and differed mainly in installation features and equipment, too legion to enumerate. The power output for the series can be illustrated by that of the Mk 66: 2,050 bhp at 3,000 rpm at +25 psi boost at 30,000 ft.

With the introduction of the Mks 113, 114, 131, 134 and 135 engines there was a significant departure from previous Merlins, in that the main lubrication was through a crankshaft end-to-end system, and the carburation system was replaced by a positive displacement fuel pump and single-point

exceeding the capacity of the Derby factory, so as well as the 'daughter' factories being established in the UK, help was sought in the USA. Ford of America was approached but no contract was signed (H. Ford apparently doubting Britain's capability of surviving a combat with Germany). Meanwhile, Packards, who had been involved in aero-engine manufacture for a number of years, made known their interest in sub-contract work, which culminated with the signing of a contract in 1940 for the production of 9,000 Merlins, the engine chosen being the Mk 28. Packards were later asked to produce the two piece cylinder head, and the Mk 66 engine, this then being designated the Mk 266. The engine produced by Packard was relatively the duplicate of the British Merlin, though Stromberg pressure type carburettors and American vacuum pumps were fitted and the fitting of a different supercharger drive mechanism. Packard were also responsible for the development and incorporation into the Merlin of silver-lead-indium bearings, as

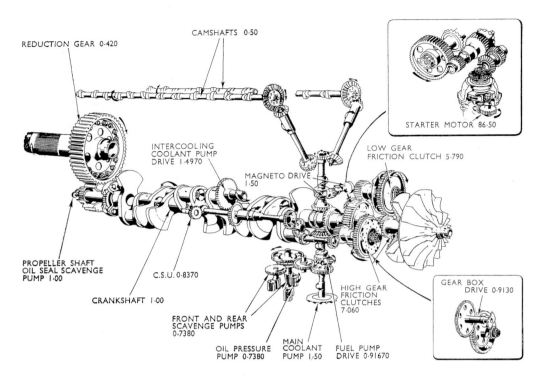

REDUCTION GEAR 0·420

CAMSHAFTS 0·50

STARTER MOTOR 86·50

INTERCOOLING COOLANT PUMP DRIVE 1·4970

MAGNETO DRIVE 1·50

LOW GEAR FRICTION CLUTCH 5·790

PROPELLER SHAFT OIL SEAL SCAVENGE PUMP 1·00

C.S.U. 0·8370

CRANKSHAFT 1·00

FRONT AND REAR SCAVENGE PUMPS 0·7380

OIL PRESSURE PUMP 0·7380

MAIN COOLANT PUMP 1·50

FUEL PUMP DRIVE 0·91670

HIGH GEAR FRICTION CLUTCHES 7·060

GEAR BOX DRIVE 0·9130

Section of a Merlin two-speed supercharged engine gear train

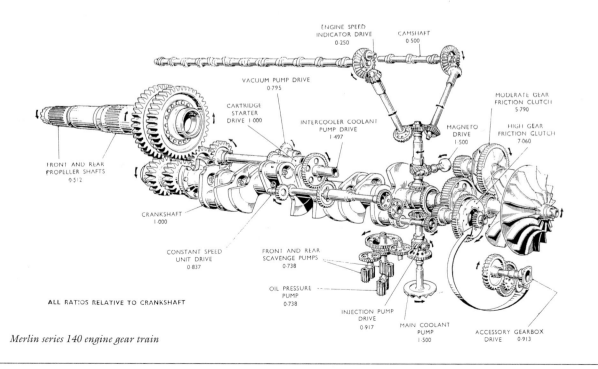

ENGINE SPEED INDICATOR DRIVE 0·250

CAMSHAFT 0·500

VACUUM PUMP DRIVE 0·795

CARTRIDGE STARTER DRIVE 1·000

INTERCOOLER COOLANT PUMP DRIVE 1·497

MAGNETO DRIVE 1·500

MODERATE GEAR FRICTION CLUTCH 5·790

HIGH GEAR FRICTION CLUTCH 7·060

FRONT AND REAR PROPELLER SHAFTS 0·512

CRANKSHAFT 1·000

CONSTANT SPEED UNIT DRIVE 0·837

FRONT AND REAR SCAVENGE PUMPS 0·738

OIL PRESSURE PUMP 0·738

INJECTION PUMP DRIVE 0·917

MAIN COOLANT PUMP 1·500

ACCESSORY GEARBOX DRIVE 0·913

ALL RATIOS RELATIVE TO CRANKSHAFT

Merlin series 140 engine gear train

20

Merlin powerplant of Spitfire LF Mk.9 MH434 at Duxford. (Author)

injection nozzle. The air intake system was also re-designed and incorporated an oil heated Corliss (barrel) throttle. The typical power output of this series is illustrated by that of the Mk 113: for a dry weight of 1,670 lb the power output in high gear (FS) is 1,200 bhp at 29,750 ft (see diagram of Merlin 130 series on p. 22).

These were followed by the Mk 140 engine, which was like the 130 series, a two-speed two-stage engine with single point fuel injection, but the engine drove contra-rotating propellers; its power output in MS gear being 1,780 bhp at 4,500 ft and in FS gear 1,650 bhp at 16,750 ft.

The Merlin's greatest advantages were its high efficiency and its low frontal area, and Rolls-Royce were fortunate in that the Ministry allowed them a relatively free hand in development — providing that their demand for performance requirements were met — and Rolls-Royce certainly provided that. The Merlin provided most of the engine power for the Battle of Britain RAF fighters, the engine power for many Fleet Air Arm aircraft and the engine power for most of Bomber Command heavy bombers.

The Merlin would continue into post-war aviation as the series 500 and 600. The civil range of 620 engines started with the Merlin 102, which was the first engine to complete successfully the post-war British ARB test requirements for civil aero-engines. It was a two-speed two-stage engine with single-point fuel injection and oil heated throttle of the Corliss type. The 620 engine weighed 1,747 lb dry (nett) and at take-off power produced 1,740 bhp at 3,000 rpm at 20 psi boost; and for the installation on the Canadair DC-4M2 Argonaut for BOAC the powerplant had a crossover exhaust from the inboard to the outboard — not exactly a boon for maintenance.

The Merlin doubled its power output over the years without increasing the size of its bore and stroke or frontal area, and its length was increased by only a few inches. Just over 168,000 engines were built in total during its production life. During the first half of the 1939–45 war, all improvements in aircraft speed were achieved by improvements in engine power, and not aerodynamically. The Merlin will be best remembered for its wartime performance, when, during the years 1939–45 it reached its pinnacle of performance and gave to Great Britain supremacy in liquid-cooled engine design during this period.

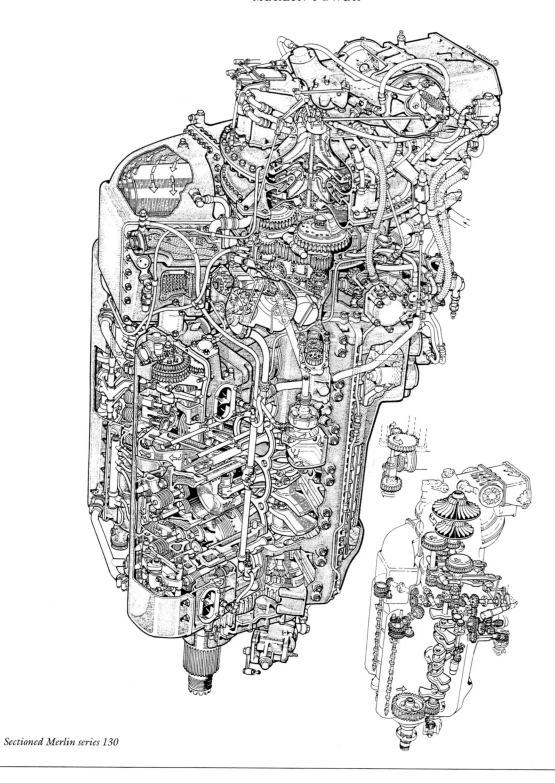

Sectioned Merlin series 130

Note 1: Supercharging

The normal aspirated engine is an unsupercharged one. The function of the supercharger being to force a greater fuel/air charge than normal into the engine cylinders, and unless the engine is to be ground boosted for low level performance (such as racing), it is not normally desirable to use a supercharged engine at full throttle at sea level. So the supercharged engine has to be 'throttled' at sea level to prevent overstressing of the engine. This is achieved by connecting the throttle butterfly to an automatic boost control (ABC), with the throttle butterfly opened sufficiently for take-off performance. As the aircraft climbs and the atmospheric pressure decreases, so does the density of the air inhaled by the engine decrease. To compensate for this, the ABC progressively and automatically opens the throttle butterfly as the aircraft climbs, so as to maintain the boost constant, up to the height at which the throttle butterfly is fully open: this is termed the full throttle height (FTH).

Note 2

Incorporation of a two-speed supercharger to an aircraft engine is so as to incorporate the efficiency of a moderate gear ratio (MS) for take-off and low altitude flight, with the efficiency of a higher gear ratio (FS) for higher altitude. In this way, for take off and low altitude a considerable improvement in power output is obtained, whilst changing into FS gear at a selected altitude maintains the engine power higher.

Note 3: The two-stage supercharger

As the name implies, this is a supercharger having two impellers in series in their separate casings, so as to improve the engine performance at high altitude. In this type the fuel/air charge is drawn into the first stage compressor, then it is further compressed in the second compressor. Unfortunately, with two blowers in series, the temperature of the charge is raised to the point that detonation can occur in the cylinders, so an intercooler is 'plumbed' in after the second stage, so as to cool the charge to an acceptable figure prior to its entry into the induction manifold (from around $200 - 160°c$).

Note 4: Personalities at Rolls-Royce, Derby, 1939

Lord Hives	Technical Director.
A.G. Elliott	Chief Engineer.
Colonel T. Barrington	Chief Designer.
J.E. Ellor	Chief Development Engineer.
A.C. Lovesey	Deputy Development Engineer.
A.A. Rubbra	Assistant Chief Designer.
F. Barnes	Chief Tester.

Merlin Mk 24 installation of a Lancaster showing Morris type radiator. (RAE)

Avro Lancaster Mk.1

2

Avro Lancaster

Without any doubt the Lancaster was the most specialised big bomb carrier of World War Two, and was the only aircraft capable of carrying the 22,000 lb bomb. Its origins began in 1936 with the issue of specification P13/36, which called for a medium bomber of twin-engined configuration and all metal construction; for *worldwide* use; with a possible cruising speed of 275 mph at 15,000 ft at two-thirds maximum power; power operated turrets in the nose and tail, and suitable for operation by day and night at home or abroad.

While Handley Page submitted the HP56 design, Avro submitted the Type 679, both aircraft being powered by the Rolls-Royce Vulture engine. In July 1937 it was obvious that there would be insufficient Vulture engines for both aircraft, so the Ministry requested Handley Page to repower their design with four Merlin engines. This was carried out, and after a re-design which imposed a six months delay, the HP57 emerged.

Avro continued with the Type 679 design, for which a contract for 200 had been placed, which emerged in July 1939 and had its first flight on 26 July. Handling from the first was far from satisfactory, and after its test by A&AEE pilots it was recommended that a larger span tailplane was required as well as an increase in mainplane span. It was also pointed out that longitudinal stability was not up to the required standard.

Even after modification action to the mainplanes and tailplane, it was found necessary to fit a third fin in the central position to improve the directional stability; this was only removed on the Manchester 1A (Type 679) with the fitting of larger and taller fins and rudders. The Vulture engines were also proving a problem, being unreliable, not up to power and requiring excessive manufacturing time. At Rolls-Royce the decision was made as to the choice of engines to remain in production, as it was being found that under the pressure of war that the Derby

Lancaster PN474 ex-82 Squadron, before joining the RAF Memorial Flight. (Author)

Lancaster Mk VII NX739 at Blackbushe. Used by MOS for aerial photography. (Author)

factory was unable to cope with the demand for their range of engines. On operations the Manchester was proving inferior to the Halifax, and once an engine had failed through enemy action or otherwise, the chance of a safe return to base was low.

Meanwhile, Hives of Rolls-Royce had informed MAP that the Vulture was one engine that they intended to stop development on, as active development of the Merlin would yield far better results. Consequently the Manchester was ordered to be dropped from production and the Halifax substituted. This blow to Dobson and Chadwick at Avro caused a decision to be made to replace the two Vultures with four Merlins — a decision forced on Avro by circumstances to adopt the same measures that the Ministry had forced on Handley Page in 1937. So at a meeting with Tedder and Freeman of the Air Staff, Dobson displayed a model of the Manchester with an extended wing with four Merlin engines. The engine powerplants chosen were the Merlin-type fitted to the Beaufighter (see p. 73), which were the ones developed under Lieutenant-Colonel Fell at Rolls-Royce Hucknall, and were close cowled, so obviously unable to cope with hot-high climates.

Avro, very wisely, now ignored the P13/36 specification as well as the hangarage limiting requirement, going for a 102 ft wingspan, which resulted in a wing area of 1,297 sq ft, and built their

bomber for the European theatre of operations. The new bomber, known as the Manchester Mk 3, serial number BT308, was given the Type 683 designation; it .was later renamed the Lancaster. For its flight trials it still had the centre fin, and the tests proved that the new aircraft was not satisfactory in its longitudinal stability, as immediately the aircraft started to take off a swing to port developed that could not be held on the rudders, necessitating the throttling back of the starboard outer engine to counteract this. Further to this, during three-engined flight at or below 120 mph it was found to be impossible to hold the aircraft straight even with full use of the rudders.

During these trials Chadwick took design team members to Woodford, and proceeded to re-examine fully the Manchester/Lancaster airframe; parts were lightened or re-designed as necessary to peel off weight. With acceptance of the Lancaster after modifications and testing, its production went ahead, starting with the 159th Manchester airframe at Avro and the forty-fourth airframe at Metro-Vickers.

This acceptance came about fairly quickly as the second prototype (DG595) joined the first prototype at A&AEE, and incorporated a number of design changes required by the A&AEE and with Avro's quick acceptance and re-design. BT308 had also been fitted with larger fins and rudders, the centre fin removed, and testing resumed in April

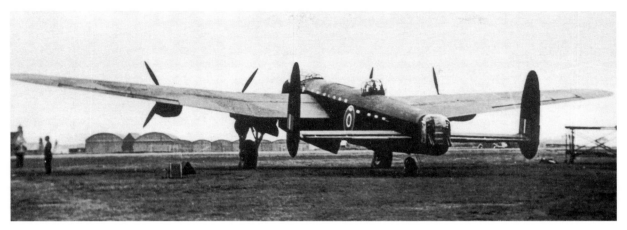

Early type Lancaster I with fuselage windows and no H2S. (Author)

Lancaster Mk VII NX739 of 617 Squadron scrapped 4 July 1957. (P.W. Porter)

1941. The A&AEE then reported rippling and flexing of the wing skin inboard of the inboard engines and tailplane distortion, and required these areas strengthened.

Testing

By the start of September 1941 the Lancaster was being tested at a take-off weight of 55,000 lb, and the modifications that had been incorporated were found to have improved the stability, though longitudinal instability would remain a feature of the Lancaster throughout its life. Then between November 1941 and March 1942 intensive flying trials were carried out at Boscombe Down with L7527, L7529 and L7535. To the chagrin of Avro this did not proceed in a straightforward manner, for L7527 after 17 hours flying had a defect in its undercarriage which resulted in damage to the aircraft. Work was then resumed with L7529, but this had to cease due to wrinkles developing on the mainplane upper surface after twenty-two hours; so then L7535 carried on the work, but after seventy-three hours flying this aircraft crashed. At this stage the A&AEE decided not to do 150 hours on any one aircraft, but to do a further period of flying on L7529 after the wing skin had been stiffened.

Contracts had now been placed with not only Avro (for an initial order for 1,070 Lancasters) but also with the Lancaster Aircraft Group, which included Metro-Vickers and Vickers-Armstrong; with the various companies being responsible for their own production, but the responsibility for notification of modifications and alterations resting with Avro. These modifications over the war years included the deletion of the fuselage 'windows', installation of the H2S blister and equipment, installation of the ventral gun, larger bomb bay doors, different engines etc. — the Lancaster in most cases still being designated the Mk 1.

In September 1941, prototype BT308 was delivered to 44 Squadron for evaluation and crew training. This was followed in the October with the first flight of the first production Lancaster, L7527, production Mk 1s being powered with Merlin XX engines and defended by FN5 front turret, FN50 mid-upper turret and FN20 rear turrets.

With the possibility of enemy bombing severely interrupting the flow of engines of various types, the Air Ministry made the decision to have alternative engines available. On the basis of this decision Avro selected Lancaster 1 airframe DT810 for conversion to Bristol Hercules power: conversion was carried out and the aircraft flew with these engines on 26 November 1941. Altogether only 300 production Mk 2 aircraft were built; this combination, like the Merlin/Halifax combination, was not a 100 per cent success. In 1944 the decision was made by the Air

Staff to standardise on the Hercules/Halifax and the Merlin/Lancaster, and the Lancaster Mk 2 aircraft were withdrawn from operational squadrons, the last one leaving in the September.

The airframe production had by 1942 begun to exceed the Merlin engine supply in the UK, so the opportunity was taken to introduce the Packard Merlin on to the Lancaster. Avro converted two Mk 1 airframes (R5849 and W4114) to Packard Merlins, and designated them Mk 3s, which differed very little from the Mk 1.

By late 1942 and early 1943 the all-up weight of the Lancaster was under review for an increase and the exploitation of the airframe's potential. Trials were being carried out at A&AEE on asymmetric flight at 60,000 lb and on the handling characteristics at 63,000 lb — its handling having been found to have improved with the modifications and as the weight was increased. Trials were also carried out to determine the suitability of its radiators and oil coolers at an all-up weight of 63,000 lb, but even with Morris type block radiators and oil coolers it was considered that the Lancaster 1 was unsuitable for tropical summer use. Also in 1942 commenced plans for the production of the Lancaster in Canada at the Victory Aircraft factory, so a pattern Mk 1 aircraft (R5727) was flown over to Canada, to become the first Lancaster to fly the Atlantic.

Lancaster VII with saddle-type fuselage fuel-tank for Tiger Force operation. (RAF)

During early service on operations a number of Mk 1 aircraft suffered wingtip failures, and this was followed by fin failures, both these faults being rectified generally by the strengthening of the structure and modifying the evasive manoeuvre action. In early 1943 RAE Farnborough were asked to investigate accidents to a number of Lancaster aircraft that had crashed or had disintegrated in mid-air, to ascertain both the reasons and the rectification required; for by March 1943 there were already eighteen squadrons flying Lancasters, and by the end of the war in 1945 over fifty squadrons were flying various marks of this aircraft. A number of these accidents had occurred due to the aircraft's design limitations having been exceeded, because of the Lancaster's known tendency to nose over at high speed, especially in a dive; or because of excessive high 'g' being imposed during evasive manoeuvres. Some may have been due to overloading of the structure, for the Lancaster's all-up weight had been increased to 68,000 lb by 1944, with the same basic aircraft structure. Air Vice-Marshal D. Bennett of Pathfinder Force was one who put it on paper that the 3,000 lb increase in weight had reduced the rate of climb to an unacceptable figure. Further to this, in August 1945 the MAP requested that both RAE observers and representatives from Avro examine wing defects on Lancaster aircraft, which had rendered large numbers of Bomber Command aircraft unserviceable.

Initially, production of the Lancaster was slow, and up to early April 1942 very few Lancasters were available for operations: to the point that for Operation 'Millennium' on Cologne on May 30/31 1942 there were only seventy-three Lancasters as against 131 Halifaxes and 598 Wellingtons. With the teething troubles over and modifications actioned the manufacturers got into their stride and production increased; and Avro, as opposed to some other manufacturers, were quick to investigate complaints and defects, and rectify them if necessary. Though the problem of parachute escape from a crashing Lancaster was never cured. With the one escape hatch right in the nose and access to the second hindered by movement over the main spars, only 12 per cent of aircrew escaped from crashing Lancasters; whereas approximately 25 per cent escaped from both the Halifax and Stirling. These figures were confirmed by Bomber Command research. Against this, the loss rate of the Lancaster was not quite as high as the other two aircraft.

Handling

In regard to flight handling, and ignoring over-enthusiastic and misleading remarks that have been made by various sources, we will summarise the official notes:

At normal loading the aircraft is slightly unstable longitudinally on the climb and at high speed. At all-up weights above 67,000 lb the stability is such that the aircraft tends to wallow. The elevators are relatively light and effective, but become heavy in turns. The ailerons are light and effective but become heavy at speeds above 225 mph and also with heavy loads. The rudders become heavy at high speeds. The aircraft becomes nose heavy as speed increases in the dive, and the pilot needs assistance to relieve the load on the control column.

The Lancaster was definitely lighter on the controls than the Halifax, though it was not as stable as the Halifax and required to be 'flown' if not on autopilot and so was likewise more effective in evasive manoeuvres.

With the development of the big bombs, the 12,000 lb 'Tallboy' and the 22,000 lb 'Grand Slam' the Lancaster with its 33 ft long bomb-bay was the only contender to carry it without major conversion. With an all-up weight increase to 72,000 lb, a Lincoln undercarriage was fitted with increased tyre and oleo pressures, and a Merlin 24 or 224 had to be installed. The aircraft was then designated the Mk 1 (Special). In flight with this model at its all-up weight, the mainplane dihedral assumed a pronounced increased angle –– giving an improvement in stability –– but receiving a recommendation from A&AEE pilots that only experienced pilots should fly this particular mark.

The armament of the Lancaster remained fairly standard throughout its wartime life, being as previously stated; though later on some aircraft had FN64 and FN121 rear turrets fitted. About 1944 a number of Rose-Rice rear turrets mounting two 0.5-in Brownings were installed. Ventral guns were installed early on, as was the FN64 under-turret, but were deleted and only appeared again with the appearance of German night-fighters with *Schrage Musik* (upward-firing) cannon installations, which began to take their toll of Bomber Command aircraft. Even then, if the H2S blister was installed,

Rose-Rice twin 0.5-inch turret with AGLT rear radar of Lancaster. (Author)

the ventral gun installation could not be fitted. On Lancasters modified to carry the 'Tallboy' bomb the mid-upper turret was removed, and on the ones modified to carry the 'Grand Slam' both the mid-upper and nose turrets were deleted.

Modifications were incorporated in a number of aircraft to enable them to carry the Wallis Type 464 bomb, which was mounted in the bomb-bay on external Vee supports. On these aircraft the mid-upper turret was deleted as well as the bomb-doors,

and a certain amount of fairing in of the bomb-bay incorporated to reduce the drag. Before dropping of the weapon it was rotated by means of a Vee belt and hydraulic motor. The Lancaster was used with this weapon to break the German dams, and with the heavier bombs on certain specific targets the Lancaster being the only aircraft so employed.

The Lancaster's strong point was its large capacious bomb-bay, formed by the centre section spars and bomb-beam roof; this was formed into a fuselage which was elliptical in cross-section and tapered slightly throughout its length. The fuselage was constructed in five sections, but was only broken down into four sections when being transported; the construction throughout was of transverse frames and longitudinal stringers, the stringers being recessed into and riveted to the formers; the whole being covered with light alloy stressed skin riveted to the stringers. Two longerons carried the loads transmitted through the floor cross-members, such as the equipment and bomb-load.

The mainplane consisted of three major sections; the centre section constructed integral with the centre fuselage, and the outer planes, port and starboard. Construction was based on two main spars with the load through them partly relieved by lateral stringers and ribs; the ribs being pressed flanged light alloy and constructed in three sections, separated by the spars; the framework was riveted with a stressed skin light alloy covering. Fuel was carried in six self-sealing tanks, two mounted in the centre section, one each side of the fuselage; the other four were mounted in the outer wings. The

Lancaster Mk. 1 308/G flight testbed with early F2 gas turbine in rear at RAE. (RAE)

main undercarriage is attached to and mounted in the inner engine nacelles; and upon retraction of these units, undercarriage doors mechanically linked to them closed over the wheels.

Tailplane construction was on the same principle as the mainplanes; and the fin and rudder shared a similar construction, having spars, ribs, stringers and intercostals, with a light alloy stressed skin riveted on. The tailplane and elevators were built in two sections, with the fins and rudders mounted as end plates.

Large numbers of the aircraft were built having small 'windows' along the fuselage, but as production progressed through the war these windows were deleted. Likewise, the flying control surfaces as with most aircraft of that period, were of metal construction and fabric covered, but about 1943 metal-covered elevators were incorporated to reduce the nose-down tendency of the aircraft. Further changes in line with production, and the demands of Bomber Command for greater range, speed and bomb-load, brought changes in the engines used, with greater power output. The Lancaster started life with the Merlin XX and then had Mks 22, 24, 38, 226 etc.

There is no doubt that the Lancaster was *the* large bomb carrier of World War Two in the European theatre of operations, 7,377 of them being built. Its design was typical of its time, and with it Bomber Command had the means of carrying extra large bombs long distances; its flying characteristics and crew comforts — or lack of them — were typical of the period, but it will be classed by its crews as one of the great aircraft of World War Two.

Lancastrian G-AGWL of Flight Refuelling on Berlin Air Lift 1948. (Author)

Avro Lancaster Mk. 1.

Wingspan	102 feet	(31.09 metres)
Wing area	1297 sq.feet	(120.49 sq.metres)
Length	69 feet 6 inches	(21.18 metres)
Empty weight	36,900 lb	(16,738 kg)
Maximum loaded weight	68,000 lb	(30,845 kg)
Maximum bomb-load	14,000 lb	(6350 kg)
Max speed at height	287 mph at 11,500 feet	(462 kph at 3505 metres)
Service ceiling	24,500 feet	(7470 metres)
Range with max bomb-load	660 miles	(2671 kilometres)
Engines	four 1460 hp Merlin Mk. XX inline	
Standard armament	eight 0.303-inch machine-guns	

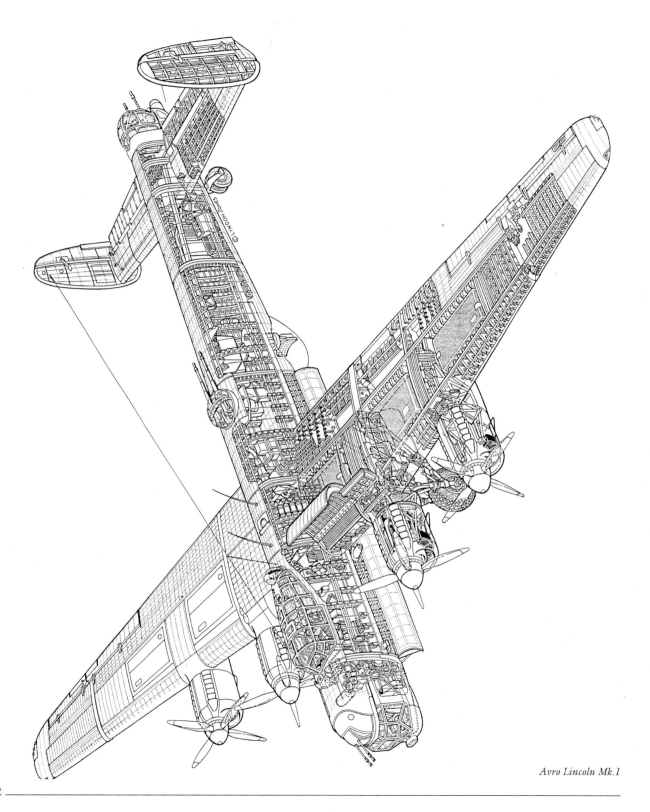

Avro Lincoln Mk.1

3

Avro Lincoln

While this aircraft was an improved development of a proven aircraft, there was no advancement in technology, and in comparison with the modern designs that were taking place or already in being in the USA, the Lincoln was like a dinosaur — maybe an amiable one, but still a dinosaur. Its whole technology had not progressed past the 1939 period, no pressurised cabin, no remotely controlled and sighted rear defence guns, no improved aerofoil. The only improvement was in the calibre of its guns.

Having said that, it must also be recorded that the crews who flew Lincolns (though not in anger) in general liked the beast; it behaved like an overgrown Lancaster, its handling characteristics being listed as follows:

a) elevator, relatively light and effective, but become heavy in the turns.

b) ailerons, moderately light and effective, spongy in cruising speed, but becoming increasingly heavy at speeds above 250 knots IAS, and lose their effectiveness at high altitude.

c) rudders, effective, but become very heavy at speeds above 250 knots IAS.

d) flaps, tend to creep down in flight, requiring periodic checks to be made.

In 1943 the Air Ministry issued specification B14/43 for a Lancaster replacement, and the design that Avro came up with was based on the Lancaster design and development. Avro designated the type as the Lancaster IV when powered with the Merlin 85 engines, and the Lancaster V when powered with the Merlin 68 or 68A engines. Before manufacture of the prototype aircraft was completed the Lancaster IV was redesignated the Lincoln I and the Lancaster V was redesignated the Lincoln 2.

The first prototype, PW925, first flew on 9 June 1944, and the contractors' trials determined that its handling was like a larger Lancaster, although rudder trim was not considered satisfactory. The new aircraft had a new high aspect-ratio mainplane of 120 ft span with a wing area of 1,421 sq ft; with a 78 ft 3 in long fuselage which was based on the Lancaster, and the aircraft's all-up weight had risen to 82,000 lb.

Lincoln SX925 of 97 Squadron. No mid-upper turret and with larger H2S blister. (Author)

The main difference in the wing structure between the Lancaster and Lincoln was that the Lincoln mainplane structure employed no spanwise stringers; so the whole bending load was taken by the main spars. Exhaustive static tests were carried out to prove that the wing structure as designed had adequate strength. The wing structure was thus more flexible than the Lancaster's, and when in steady flight, the wingtip deflected upwards 20 in, and wrinkles occurred on the top surface of the mainplane.

By 1944 Air Marshal Sir Arthur Harris, Commander-in-Chief of RAF Bomber Command, had loudly indicated the need to replace the Halifax and Lancaster in the near future for Pacific operations; not just a straight replacement but an improvement in its technology also. In no way could the Lincoln fall into this latter category. For instance, on 28 March Harris wrote to Portal that Great Britain had no modern long-range bomber being built, and in the event of Bomber Command

Fine view of Lincoln RF570 without mid-upper turret, no front guns. (P.W. Porter)

Lincoln RA657 of Flight Refuelling on flight refuelling trials with Meteor. (Author)

Lincoln RE411 with 20 mm mid-upper turret and H2S blister. Ex-115 Squadron. (Author)

going to the Pacific 'Range of operation will naturally be governed by the range of the new American heavy types'. Instead, the Lincoln was produced and the flight refuelling of the Lancaster considered as a possible alternative!

The standard Lincoln was armed with a Boulton Paul 'F' type nose turret, which was operated from the bomb-aimer's position, where the gunsight and the controls were positioned; the range of operation is 45° each side of the centre line with an elevation and depression each way of 40°. The upper turret was a Bristol B17 which mounted two 20mm Hispano No 5 Mk 5 cannon. The rear turret was a Boulton Paul 'D' turret mounting two 0.5-in Browning guns; the rotation of this turret tended to cause the aircraft to yaw and pitch. The first prototype Lincoln was later fitted with a Martin mid-upper turret for trials.

The first production aircraft was RE227 and large orders were placed, but with the end of the war in the Far East these were cancelled, and the final production figure was 624 of all marks; a number of them being produced in Australia.

In service, one of the main causes of unserviceability was vibration; this was causing failure of the Merlin engine's crankcase/wheelcase and wheelcase/supercharger casing joints. It was assumed that this was due either to the plugs or the propellers. So Lincoln B2 RE230 was despatched to A&AEE for intensive flying trials, which took place between 22 March and 8 June 1945 (200 flying hours). As received the aircraft had Merlin 68 engines driving three-blade Nash Kelvinator propellers. During the first fifty-five hours of flying

there were three engine changes due to joint failures; so the propellers were changed for four-blade Rotol types, which reduced the vibration. Then these were replaced with four-blade DH propellers, and with these the remaining 117 hours were flown and proved satisfactory. No further engines were changed due to joint failures, though one engine was changed due to an engine fire caused by a faulty exhaust manifold. On the airframe side there were failures of the intercostal stringers in the wing trailing edge due to the wing flexing; and the main wheel tyres required changing three times during the trials.

Then Lincoln B1 RE228 was sent to A&AEE for intensive flying trials and investigation of engine vibration; these took place between 27 March and 10 July 1945 and covered 172 flying hours. During the first part of the tests four engines had to be changed due to the engine joints again failing; so the three-blade Nash Kelvinator propellers were changed for four-blade DH type. Though two more engines had to be changed these were due to a blowback and propeller overspeeding, and not due to vibration. Handling of the aircraft on taxying and take-off was straight forward, and flying was similar to the Lancaster 3, though the long nose was considered to restrict forward view. Entry to the fuselage by the fully kitted-up crew was made through the forward escape hatch, as the crew found it hard to negotiate their way through the fuselage around the mid-upper turret.

In July 1945 a brief handling trial was carried out to check the suitability of the Lincoln's oil and coolant radiators; this was carried out on RF337 powered by Merlin 68 engines driving four-blade propellers, and loaded to an all-up weight of 82,000 lb. The tests proved the suitability of the radiators for tropical operation. Official A&AEE figures for the performance of the Lincoln gave it a maximum speed of 310 mph at 18,300 ft, and a range of 3,250 miles with a 14,000 lb bomb-load.

Originally it was intended to use the Lincoln in 'Tiger Force' against Japan, but at the end of the war the Lincoln had only reached the MUs, about one hundred awaiting allocation. The first one for extended service trials joined 57 Squadron at Scampton in September 1945. Afterwards twenty RAF squadrons were equipped with the Lincoln. It was withdrawn from front-line RAF squadrons in 1955, but continued in second-line units for a number of years. The Empire Air Navigation School operated RE364 with nose and tail fairings and known as *Aries II*, later replaced with RE367 known as *Aries III*.

Australia decided to adopt the Lincoln to equip the RAAF and to produce them in Australia, but the first few were constructed from components constructed in the UK. These Australian Lincolns were designated the Mk 30, the first one flying for the first time on 12 March 1946. Twenty of the Mk 30s were modified with an extended nose of 6 ft 6 in. The standard Mk 30 like the RAF version had a crew of seven, the same standard armament and a maximum bomb-load of 14,000 lb. Thirty Lincolns were also purchased by the Argentinian Air Force, twelve of which were refurbished RAF aircraft.

During the Berlin Air Lift in 1949 one Lincoln B2 RE290 was purchased by Air Vice-Marshal D. Bennett for Airflight Ltd; the aircraft was modified to civilian standard and registered G-ALPF; it was then operated by Bennett on the Air Lift. It was afterwards sold to Airtech Ltd, who modified it with a pannier in the bomb-bay that was constructed from two Halifax panniers; in 1951 it was again purchased by Bennett for Fairflight Ltd and was operated on a freight run in Germany, until Fairflight was purchased by Surrey Flying Services, when it was scrapped at Southend in 1952. Two or more other civil Lincolns were also modified with a pannier for use on the Argentinian meat trade, but did not go into regular operation. All these civil Lincolns had their turrets removed and were fitted with nose and tail fairings.

From 1951 to 1957 inclusive 199 Squadron operated Lincolns in the RCM role, and in January 1962 the Signals Development Squadron at Watton was designated 151 Squadron and the last five Lincolns in RAF service served with this unit, being finally withdrawn in March 1963 when the squadron received Canberras. Lincoln RF398 is now held at RAF Cosford, whilst RF342, after flying as a research aircraft registered G-29-1, is now in the Warbirds Collection. In March 1953 a Lincoln of the Air Gunnery School on a training mission over Germany strayed well into Russian air space and, although it turned back, it was shot down on the border, the crew being killed or dying of their injuries.

The mainplane was a cantilever structure with its centre section integral with the intermediate centre fuselage, its spars having top and bottom booms of light alloy extrusions, which were joined by a heavy gauge light alloy web. The front and rear spars in the centre plane had additional web plates bolted to them to form transport joints at frames 6 and 12. The intermediate and outer planes, as opposed to the centre plane, had no stringers; they accommodated two fuel cells, one each side the outer engine nacelle, the nacelles being underslung from the front and rear spars. The stressed light alloy skin was riveted to the flanges and ribs. The centre plane housed fuel compartments, one each side of the fuselage and inboard of the inboard engine nacelles; the total fuel capacity being 2,850 gallons, with an overload capacity of 3,650 gallons. The inboard engine nacelles provide pick-up points for the main undercarriage and house the units on retraction.

The fuselage was similar in construction to the Lancaster, in that it consisted of transverse channel section formers, braced by longitudinal angle stringers, the formers being cut away to accommodate the stringers, to which they were attached by small brackets. The whole was covered with light alloy skin attached with mushroom-headed rivets. The fuselage was constructed in five sections, but when being transported the nose and front centre sections were treated as one. The intermediate centre section was built on the front and rear spars of the mainplane and was integral with the centre section.

The tail unit was cantilever and consisted of a two-spar tailplane with fin and rudder end plates. The tailplane was built in two halves, each having sixteen ribs braced by transverse stringers and a light alloy skin. The elevators were connected inside the rear fuselage by a steel torque tube, which connected to the spars. These were tubular, the spars passing

Lincoln SX972 flight-testbed with Bristol Proteus prop-turbines in outer positions. (Author)

through holes in the sixteen pressed light alloy ribs. Angle section stringers were riveted to the ribs and a 'V' section light alloy section trailing edge and light alloy skin. The fins were based on front, rear and intermediate fin posts, with light alloy vertical stringers and intercostals, a nose stiffening channel and nine horizontal ribs. The rudders were of similar construction to the fins and were attached to the fins by three ball-bearing hinges.

The undercarriage comprised two main units and a tailwheel unit, the tailwheel being fully castoring and self-centring, but not retractable. Each mainwheel unit comprised left-hand and right-hand shock absorbers with top bracing, radius arms, retracting struts and a pair of hydraulic jacks.

The Lincoln airframe was used as a flight test bed for a number of new propeller-turbine or pure jet gas turbine engines; amongst these airframes was B2 RE339 with an Armstrong-Siddeley Python, B2 RA716 with Bristol Theseus, B2 SX972 with Bristol Proteus, B2 SX973 with a Napier Nomad and B2 RF533 with the Rolls-Royce Tyne. This employment was probably the greatest service that the Lincoln did for the British aircraft industry, for apart from operating in Malaya and Kenya it contributed little to operating or technical knowledge — but what it did, it did with very little trouble.

Avro Lincoln 1

Wingspan	120 feet	(36.57 metres)
Wing area	1421 sq.feet	(132 sq.metres)
Length	78 feet 3 inches	(23.78 metres)
Empty weight	43,400 lb	(19,727 kg)
Maximum loaded weight	82,000 lb	(37,272 kg)
Maximum bombload	14,000 lb	(6,363 kg)
Maximum speed at height	297 mph at	(512 kph at
	15,400 feet	4720 metres)
Service ceiling	21,000 feet	(6,400 metres)
Range with max bombload	1470 miles	(2365 kilometres)
Engines	four 1750 hp Merlin Mk.68/68A or 85	
Standard armament	see text	

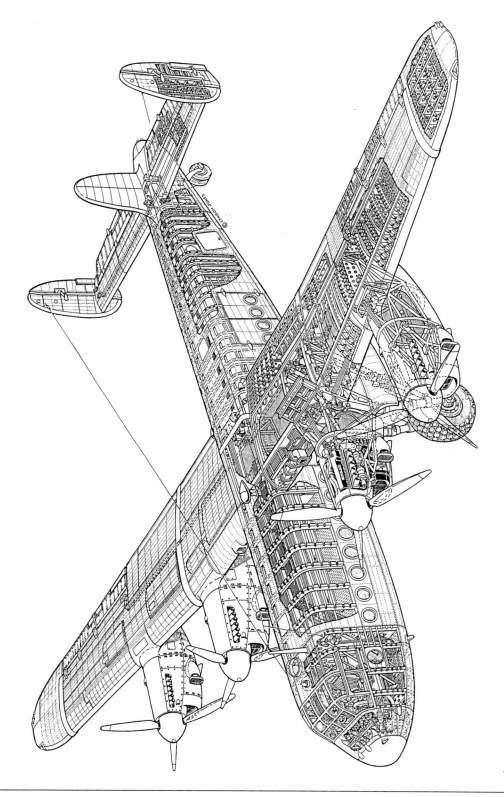

Avro York C.1

4

Avro York

Take Lancaster mainplanes, tail unit and undercarriage, and fit them to a freight car — recipe for disaster? Not in this case, it resulted in the York. Probably not everyone's idea of a transport aircraft, but it did prove to be quite a successful interim passenger and transport aircraft when Great Britain needed one. With its high mounted wing it provided a low platform for the loading of goods from a lorry, and allowed passengers a good view all-round — as well as views of the normal oil leakage from the engine nacelles!

With Great Britain concentrating on the manufacture of war machines, we were at that time dependent on the USA for any transport aircraft, and the most numerous of these was the ubiquitous Douglas Dakota/DC-3. So in 1941 a project originated within the Avro company to use components of their Lancaster airframe for a military transport for the movement of military materiel or personnel. On 9 January 1942 the Air Staff were informed of this Lancaster transport project, and by

23 January the Ministry were asking Chadwick of Avro for more information and detail work on the project. Permission was required for the use of material for the project and for the production of a prototype (in this they were more fortunate than Handley Page with their transport project), and in the process Chadwick went into more detail, as well as suggesting to the Minister that a fleet of these transport aircraft could offset the loss of the Burma Road to China.

On 10 April 1942 the company was instructed to produce four prototypes; two powered with Bristol Hercules engines and two with Merlin engines. The company wished to produce six prototypes, but the Minister would only agree to the production of four, and to this end specification C1/42 was issued. Drawings had been issued to the experimental department for construction of the fuselage on 18 February and on 5 July the first prototype (LV626) took off for the first time from Ringway; having been transported from the Chadderton factory by road.

York C1 MW140 'Endeavour' passenger transport of RAF Transport Command. (IWM)

York C1 MW102 VIP transport of RAF Transport Command. (RAF)

The issue of the specification called for the following:

a) range of 3,000 miles at 20,000 ft with a load of 8,000 lb,

b) 4,500 miles at 15,000 ft with a load of 2,000 lb,

c) service ceiling of 25,000 ft,

d) take-off distance no greater than 1,300 yards,

e) crew of five,

f) to tow all existing types of gliders.

At the same time the company was informed that the four prototypes were to be finished as one for troop carrying, one for first-class passengers, one for paratrooping and one for freight carrying. On 13 July a conference was held to decide on the equipment and layout for the various roles, which was attended by representatives of DOR, War Office and BOAC.

By the start of September estimates were being issued of the York's performance powered with the Hercules and Merlin engines; though the take-off with the Hercules engines was much better, the range and ceiling was not as good as that for the Merlin. So it was felt that the Merlin-powered version should be concentrated on, also because of standardisation. Then Chadwick was informed that the third prototype was to be a 'special York', and by 10 October 1942 he was having to explain to the DD/RDA that he thought the all-up weight would increase to 63,000 lb. This then exploded in the November into a disagreement

between Dobson (Avro) and Rowe over the changes being called for on the York; Dobson claiming that modifications were being called for from various sources and wrecking the production programme (Handley Page had already experienced this with the Halifax). Then Chadwick made a complaint that the decision over the 'special York' was also having a serious effect on production; nevertheless, by 20 December all the structural changes and drawings of the York had been completed, and by 1 January 1943 a proposed programme for the prototype Yorks had been agreed on.

The first prototype was despatched to the A&AEE on 20 August 1942. As first flown this aircraft had two fins and rudders similar to the Lancaster, but inadequate directional stability with the large boxlike fuselage soon resulted — as on the Manchester — with a third fin being mounted on the fuselage, and this became standardised on all Yorks.

In April 1943 the delivery of the 'special York' was made to 24 Squadron; this aircraft was LV633, and had been converted into a special VIP version for the use of Sir Winston Churchill. Amongst the extra features on this aircraft were the extra sound-proofing, special toilet, Merlin 22 engines and square windows (the standard York had round portholes). On delivery of this aircraft to the squadron it was named *Ascalon* and served throughout the war as a VIP transport.

By 16 June 1943 the first of three VIP Yorks had

gone to the hangars at Ringway for assembly, the assembly and flight testing later being moved to newly built hangars at Ringway. The first VIP York was the first production machine (MW100) and was despatched to the RAF later in June. This was followed on 31 July with allocation being made of the first two hundred production aircraft, with five of the first batch going to BOAC. The York production line was later moved to the factory at Yeadon.

The first prototype (LV626) had meanwhile been used for development work after its trials at A&AEE. It was then fitted with Hercules engines to become the prototype Mk 2. The trial installation was completed by March 1944, and departed to the A&AEE in May. During the trials dissatisfaction was felt over severe vibration problems, so the decision was made not to proceed with the Mk 2. The second prototype LV629, had been developed as a VIP transport; while the fourth prototype, LV639, had been allotted for paratrooping trials; but in this role had been rejected. Due to the large square-cut fuselage the airflow around the rear fuselage end became turbulent and thus hazardous for the dropping of paratroops; so the York was never used in the airborne support role.

The construction of the York fuselage was based on a light alloy stressed skin riveted to transverse formers and braced with stringers. The nose section of the fuselage formed the cockpit and extended to the joint at former 1, where the bulkhead separated it from the centre portion fuselage, which extended from this bulkhead to former 29. The intermediate centre section was integral with the mainplane centre section, while the rear fuselage carried the tail unit of tailplane, elevators, fin and rudder endplates and tailwheel unit. The construction throughout was of transverse formers braced with longitudinal stringers to form a rectangular section fuselage, with intercostals bracing the frames and formers below the main floor, the whole covered with light alloy skin riveted to the framework.

The mainplane construction and tailplane construction were similar to the Lancaster, being of two-spar layout. Each spar consisted of extruded light alloy top and bottom booms with Alclad sheet webs, with vertical top hat section stiffeners riveted to the webs. In the centre section the spars had booms which were solid at the engine ribs and outer plane joints, with the ribs in three sections separated by the spars. This centre section, though similar to the Lancaster's, was slightly different to take account of the wider fuselage and pick-up points. The spars' load was helped by the spanwise stringers, to which the light alloy skin was riveted.

The tailplane construction consisted of port and starboard sections, each built up from front and rear spars with sixteen ribs each side: these are braced by transverse stringers with a light alloy skin riveted to the stringers and the ribs. The elevators are of metal construction with a tubular steel spar, pressed light alloy ribs and rolled angle section stringers, which are fabric covered if not modified, and metal covered

Ex-RAF York C1 transport/freighter G-AMUT (MW185) after ferrying to Stansted. (Author)

if modified. The fins and rudders are of similar construction, with vertical stringers, intercostals, light alloy flanged ribs and spars. The fins were metal covered and the rudders fabric covered.

The engines were carried in nacelles similar to the Lancaster, the Merlin engines being T24 or Mk 500s. The inner nacelles formed the attachment point and housing for the main undercarriage units, which retracted to the rear and were covered by main wheel doors, which automatically operated with the undercarriage. The tailwheel was fully castoring and non-retractable, and was fitted with a Marstrand twin-contact tyre.

The control cabin differed to all British built four-engined aircraft of that period in that it had no throttle pedestal; the throttle's quadrant, propeller lever's quadrant, undercarriage lever and flap lever were all positioned in a control panel on the cabin roof; making entry and exit to the pilot's seats easy.

The York's all-up weight at take-off was 68,000 lb, with the average empty weight of a freighter version being 38,700 lb. Fully loaded the take-off was sluggish, and the aircraft needed to be eased off the ground. The all-up weight was later increased to 71,000 lb, and during the Berlin Air Lift the freighter versions were lifting a 16,500 lb payload. The first squadron to be equipped with the York was 511 Squadron at Lyneham, and 24 Squadron received the first two production Yorks MW100 and MW101. Most of the 1940 production were passenger aircraft, which were followed by a batch of freighters. The first production run of 200 commenced with the serial number MW. The last York produced was PE108, which was completed in April 1948.

A description of flight handling of the York can start with the take-off, which was made by opening up the throttles slowly to the take-off position, keeping straight by coarse use of the rudders and differential use of the throttles. The tail had to be allowed to rise of its own accord, then the York was eased off at a speed dependent on its all-up weight — at 50,000 lb the speed was 92 knots (105 mph) and at 65,000 lb it was 105 knots (121 mph). Eased off can be a misnomer, for in hot and high climates the aircraft needed dragging off! Stalling under normal flight conditions and speeds was satisfactory. At the stall pronounced aileron snatch could be felt and usually the left wing dropped, although either wing could drop. The stalling speed with engine 'off' and undercarriage and flaps down at 60,000 lb was 78 knots (90 mph). Recovery from the stall involved a considerable loss of height. With the

undercarriage and flaps down entering the stall, warning was given by rudder and elevator buffeting and a noticeable lightening of the elevator. The aircraft became progressively and increasingly tail heavy as speed was increased. With the aircraft at an all-up weight of 65,000 lb and an engine failure, the aircraft could maintain height on any three engines at medium altitudes, and could be trimmed to fly without footload at speeds down to 122 knots (140 mph). Ailerons were light and effective but became heavy at speeds over 225 knots (260 mph); the rudder also became heavy at high speed. The elevator was relatively light and effective but tended to become heavy in turns.

208 Yorks were built for the RAF, which included five for BOAC, and were the equipment of nine squadrons, six of which operated on the Berlin Air Lift. BOAC's first Yorks seated 12 passengers in the rear cabin, with freight forward — could have been the noise level! — and these were used to inaugurate the first services, then twenty-five more were acquired in 1945–46. Twelve Yorks were purchased by British South American Airways for the Atlantic and South American routes and five were bought by FAMA of Argentina, being operated until replaced with DC-6s.

As well as the 257 Yorks built by Avro, one further one was built by Victory Aircraft Ltd in Canada; this was FM400, but this was the one and only built by them.

TS798 ex-G-AGNV is now held at the RAF Museum Collection at Cosford, while aircraft engineers and fitters of Danair renovated in their own time the company's last York, G-ANTK, which was originally MW232.

The construction of the York closely followed Avro methods, and though the fuselage was new, the remaining structure, apart from the third fin, was pure Lancaster. Obviously, with the high-wing monoplane layout, the control runs were changed, as was some other equipment.

Over fifty York aircraft were built during the war years, which is not only surprising on that fact alone, but surprising that MAP allowed the drain away of strategic materials when the emphasis was on bombers. By the end of production 257 Yorks had been manufactured, at a production rate of approximately three per month. In January 1944 BOAC negotiated for the release of five Yorks for use on civilian routes, and on 22 April of the same year inaugurated the first official route to Moscow.

The crew layout placed the captain in the left-hand seat with the flight engineer or second pilot in the right-hand seat; with the carriage of a second pilot the flight engineer stood between the two pilots — a position guaranteed to alter the flight engineer's face in a crash on take-off or landing! Behind the captain sat the radio operator and his equipment facing forward. On the right-hand side behind and above the second pilot sat the navigator with his back against the crew cabin bulkhead. The noise level in the crew compartment and in the positions at the front of the passenger compartment was still on a par with the wartime bombers, necessitating extra sound-proofing in the VIP transport versions. In the cargo versions and standard models, on the left-hand side of the fuselage just aft of the wings were cargo doors, which allowed cargo to be loaded straight onto the cabin floor. These freight doors (two) were between formers 19 and 23 in the rear centre fuselage, and the area was strengthened by a torsion beam above, between formers 17 and 25, with a beam of built-up channel section longeron below, between formers 18 and 25.

The last major use of the Yorks by the RAF was on the Berlin Air Lift in 1948–49, when they carried nearly 50 per cent of the RAF's total contribution. With the short flight time and a greater proportion of the time spent at take-off power, engine failures increased — and in greater proportion than that experienced by the air-cooled engines.

Quite a number of post-war world routes were opened up by the York aircraft operated by BOAC, BSAA and Skyways; as the years passed the Yorks operated by the RAF were sold off to the charter companies, and soon these were stripped down for cargo work or used as they were on trooping contracts to the War Office. In this condition they were powered by Merlin 500 engines of 1,280 bhp, which gave a maximum speed of 298 mph at 21,000 ft at a take-off weight of 71,000 lb. On 7 October 1950 BOAC withdrew their Yorks from passenger carrying operations after flying 172,000 hours and covering 13,000,000 miles; these Yorks then joined the others used by the British Independents, and carried on flying for another few thousand miles. In the end, as an interim transport aircraft prior to the introduction of the Avro Tudor airliner, it outlasted the Tudor and continued into the late 1950s.

Two civil York freighters loading up at Berlin Tempelhof. G-AMRI nearest. (Author)

Avro York

Wingspan	102 feet	(31.09 metres)
Wing area	1297 sq.feet	(120.49 sq.metres)
Length	78 feet	(23.77 metres)
Empty weight (freighter)	38,700 lb	(17,590 kg)
Maximum loaded weight	71,000 lb	(32,272 kg)
Maximum speed at height	298 mph at	(480 kph at
	21,000 feet	6,400 metres)
Service ceiling	26,000 feet	(7924 metres)
Engines	four 1280 hp Merlin T24 or Mk.500	

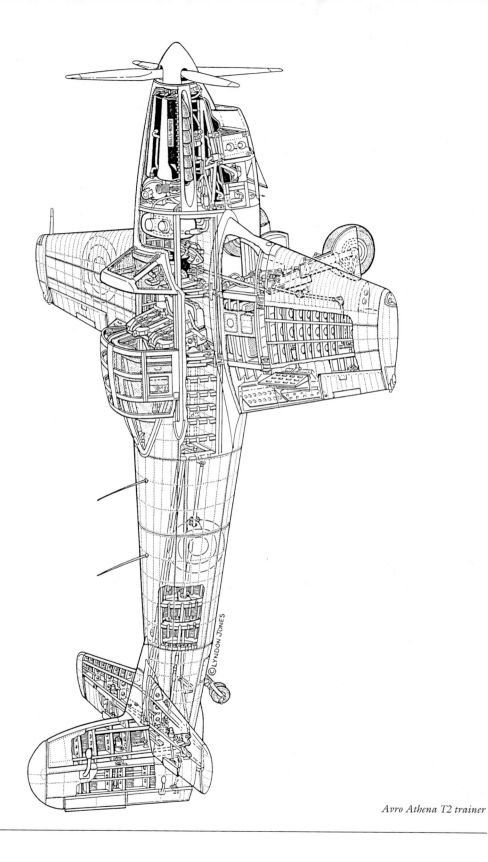

Avro Athena T2 trainer

5

Avro Athena T2

The Miles Master during the course of the 1939–45 war proved the validity of the advanced trainer concept, with an aircraft whose performance would be fairly comparable to the fighter aircraft that the pilot would be flying. With the gas turbine now being the accepted powerplant of the future, the next step was obviously going to be a combination of the two. Further to this, with the Percival Prentice elementary trainer and its three-seat 'clover leaf' arrangement accepted, this also would be considered for the new projected advanced trainer. Yet in the few years after 1945 various changes of policy over the training programmes were made, with the result that specifications were raised and amended quicker than the manufacturers could plan their production. This started with specification T7/45, amongst the requirements of which were the following:

Side-by-side seating for instructor and pupil, with a third seat behind,
Simplicity of control of the fuel system,
Accessibility and ease of maintenance,
Power by propeller turbine.

The Avro design team gave major design consideration to the requirements, and in the case of the fuel system provided one 'on/off' fuel cock. The fuel system was formed by three crashproof tanks with an automatic fuel transfer arrangement, with grouping of components. The fuel tanks were installed between the spars in the centre section, with positions for two drop tanks, one at each outer plane joint. All the services had their major components grouped and available for servicing through hatches or detachable panels.

Rolls-Royce were at this time looking for trade in

Athena T2 VW890 at SBAC Flying Display. (Author)

the post-war world, and were an interested party in the winner of the contract to the specification, as they hoped to supply their Dart prop-turbine to the competitors.

Later on the Ministry had second thoughts and the decision was made to revert to two seats and conventional piston engine power, so specification T14/47 was issued with the powerplant to be the Merlin Mk 35. By now the T1 trainer powered by the Armstrong-Siddeley Mamba propeller turbine, as proposed to the T7/45 specification, had been constructed; as had the Balliol T1, its competitor for the contract.

The first Athena T2 to fly was VW890, which made its first flight on 1 August 1948; fifteen of this mark were supplied to the RAF, serial numbers VR566 to VR580. These were a pre-production batch, and were retained in the RAF mainly on gunnery duties, for the Balliol T2 powered by the Merlin 35 had been selected as the advanced trainer. In regard to the power supply for operating the undercarriage, flaps and dive brakes, Avro carried out a lengthy study of the relative cost, weight, reliability and simplicity of various systems, and were convinced that the pneumatic system offered maximum advantages, particularly in respect of simplified maintenance.

The production T2 had a loaded weight of 8,213 lb, a Browning 0.303-in machine-gun in its port wing, a wing span of 40 ft and a wing area of 270 sq ft. The Merlin 35 drove a DH Hydromatic four-blade D47/435/1 or D130/435/1 propeller, which gave the Athena a maximum speed of 297 mph at 10,000 ft, a rate of climb of 1,830 ft/min and a service ceiling of 29,700 ft.

By August 1949 over 400 hours of development and test flying had been carried out, which was shared between one Mk 1 powered by a Mamba, and two Mk 2s powered by the Merlin 35. A second Mk 1 powered by a Mamba was being built and a third Mk 1 powered by a Rolls-Royce Dart was almost complete. This latter aircraft was fitted with a trial installation of electric actuators for the operation of the dive brakes, flaps and undercarriage.

In early 1950 an Athena T2 G-ALWA was taken by R.J. Falk (pilot) and F. Bassett (engineer) on a three and a half month demonstration tour of the Middle East and India, landing back at Woodford having flown 135½ hours during this period. In India it was handed over to the Indian Air Force, and a number of their service pilots flew the aircraft

on gunnery, aerobatic and dive-bombing trials. The serviceability record of the aircraft was exceptional.

The Athena T2 went to A&AEE for its first trial, which was a handling trial with the C of G aft. The aircraft was VW891 powered by a Merlin 35 engine, the fin of this aircraft was not the finalised form. The trials took place during August and September 1949, and the report stated that the aircraft was generally easy to fly and docile in its behaviour, though attention needed to be paid to the aileron control at low speeds and the large change in longitudinal and directional trim with speed. Dives were carried out from 16,000 ft, and the aircraft had reached a speed of 360 knots by 6,000 ft. VW890 (a three-seater version) had prior to this been to Khartoum in May and June for engine cooling trials.

In October of the same year T2 VW890, which was the three-seat prototype with later designed fin, and VW891 carried out spinning trials at A&AEE. Four-turn spins were made from stalls both in straight and turning flight. There was no consistent difference between the two aircraft, and the response to normal recovery action was considered satisfactory. VW890 with the new fin was found to have a lighter and more effective rudder, and lighter foot loads were experienced, and without rudder overbalance.

During November and December 1949 VW891 was back at A&AEE for trials of the longitudinal stability and manoeuvrability, which were considered satisfactory. Then during January and February VW890 was called upon to carry out climb and level speed, these trials gave the following:

Maximum rate of climb	1,610ft/min from SL to 8,400 ft.
Service ceiling	24,200 ft.
Maximum level speed	257 knots (296 mph)
Maximum cruise speed	207 knots (238 mph)
Max still air range	720 nautical miles at 10,000 ft.

A summary was then carried out by A&AEE covering the handling and performance characteristics of VW890 and VW891 over the period June 1949 and February 1950. This stated that the stall warnings were indistinct, and if the stall was approached gently then the stall was ill-defined, in that the aircraft sank rapidly with some oscillation in yaw and pitch. Any harsh movement of the stick near the stall resulted in the port wing dropping rapidly with little or no warning. On application of

Avro Athena T2 with original fin and rudder 1948. Spin chute under tail. (RAF)

pro-spin controls the aircraft entered spin smoothly and rapidly, however the behaviour in four-turn spins was very erratic, and in every case pitching and yawing oscillation developed.

An engineering appraisal was next carried out, but this was on the third prototype (VW892). A detailed examination was made and many components were removed and refitted, and general servicing checked. The summary stated that the aircraft was easy to service, had good access for inspection, lubrication and for adjustments. The notable exception to this being the tail end of the fuselage where control pivots and joints were not accessible. Against this it was stated that the aircraft should be free from defects and should prove reliable.

The aircraft was of all-metal construction and for ease of manufacture and servicing it was manufactured in five main sections; fuselage, tail unit, centre section and outer wings, port and starboard. The fuselage main section was monocoque and was manufactured in two longitudinal halves, which were riveted together during the final assembly. The fuselage consisted of circular transverse formers to which were attached longitudinal stringers, the formers being cut to accommodate the stringers. To this framework was attached light alloy skinning, which varied from 14 to 22 gauge. The structure was built around four main longerons, two of which formed the side members of the cockpit floor. At the forward end of the fuselage was the firewall, which was a single skin of stainless steel, and above the floor this was backed by a light alloy wall to give additional protection to the systems behind.

Attached to the transport joint at former 22 was the rear fuselage, which had an integral fin and finpost at former 29. Mounted on the rear fuselage were the tailplane, elevator, rudder and tailwheel assemblies. In the rear fuselage were transverse formers which were riveted to two 'T' section longerons and eighteen longitudinal angle section stringers over which was riveted a light alloy skin.

The mainplane had an aerofoil section at the root of Hawker Tempest 18 per cent, and the construction of the centre section was based on two spars, separated by ribs and strengthened by spanwise stringers. The light alloy skin was riveted to the spars, ribs and stringers. The outer wing sections were also based on two-spar construction with

Avro Athena T2 with 2nd stage fin and rudder (1949) with alterations to hood. (RAF)

flanged light alloy ribs and stringers, with a light alloy skin riveted to the framework. The ends of the outer sections were completed by detachable wing tips.

The main undercarriage comprised two main units and a tailwheel unit; the tailwheel was fully castoring and self-centring, but not retractable. Each main unit was a single oleo-pneumatic leg, at the base of which was a stub axle carrying a single wheel, the main unit being mounted on an assembly that was bolted to the upper and lower booms of the main spar at rib 7 of the centre plane. When the main undercarriage retracted into recesses in the underside of the mainplane, two two-piece fairings mechanically moved into position with the undercarriage. The whole unit then was faired flush with the undersurface of the mainplane. The tailwheel was mounted on a Dowty liquid spring shock absorber that was mounted in the rear fuselage structure.

Once cleared for service use, the handling of the Athena T2 was given as generally easy and pleasant to fly, including flying on instruments. The controls were light and well harmonised in the cruising range, but at high speeds the elevator and rudder became moderately heavy. On take-off any swing to the left could easily be checked with the rudder. At the approach to the stall there was slight buffeting, then either one wing or the other would drop, as would the nose. The stalling speed with power 'on' and the undercarriage and flaps down for the approach and landing was 60 knots (69 mph); with power 'off' and flaps and undercarriage up, the stalling speed was 65 knots (75 mph). Spinning could be carried out, but the spin could be rough, with some tendency to pitch; the spin was normally steep and the rate of rotation was high. The trimming tabs were effective at normal speeds, but the elevator trim was spongy, especially at high speed.

Originally seventeen pre-production aircraft were ordered, but the last two were cancelled. The remaining fifteen were delivered between September 1949 and September 1951; some replaced the Harvards at the RAF Flying College, Manby. Athena T1 VM129 was Dart powered and was flown to the RAE Farnborough on 17 September 1949, then to

Athena VM125 powered by Mamba gas turbine on display at RAE Farnborough. (Author)

Rotol Ltd for development flying. The second Athena T1 powered by a Mamba (VM135) flew in December 1949 and was delivered to Armstrong-Siddeley, also for experimental development flying.

The Athena, similar to the Balliol, was a successful aircraft, but was killed off due to a change in training policy.

Avro Athena

Wingspan	40 feet	(12.2 metres)
Wing area	270 sq.feet	(25.8 sq.metres)
Length	38 feet	(11.58 metres)
Empty weight	6,540 lb	(2972 kg)
Maximum loaded weight	8210 lb	(3724 kg)
Maximum speed at height	297 mph at 10,000 feet	(479 kph at 3,048 metres)
Service ceiling	29,700 feet	(9,052 metres)
Engine	one 1280 hp Merlin Mk.35 inline	

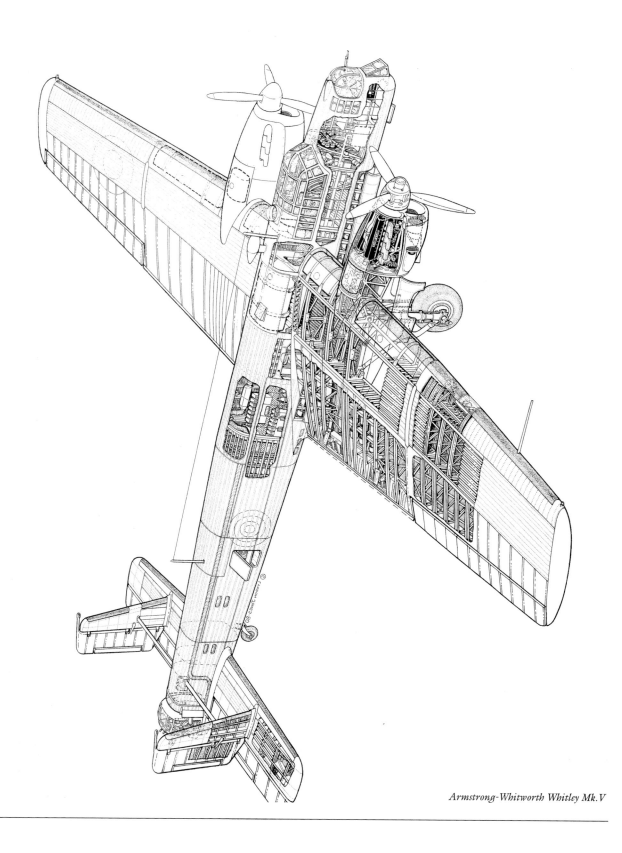

Armstrong-Whitworth Whitley Mk.V

6

Armstrong-Whitworth Whitley IV, V & VII

World War Two began with the Whitley bomber as one of the mainstays of Bomber Command, and although it was overshadowed by the more modern bombers entering the Service, it played an important part when deeds and not words were thin on the ground — a Whitley of No 10 squadron being the first Allied aircraft to reach Berlin, when it penetrated the defences on the night of 1 October 1939.

The Whitley was a direct descendant of the AW23 bomber-transport of 1935, and its wing was a replica of the AW23's, though smaller in span and chord, and on the Whitley was located mid-fuselage as opposed to the AW23's low-wing position.

The Whitley was a design tendered to specification B3/34, which was issued in July 1934, calling for a twin-engined night bomber. It was designed by J. Lloyd as the AW38, and featured a very thick wing in the mid-position, which conferred on the aircraft an ideal position for the bomb-bay, in that it was below the floor level with the bombs totally enclosed — a feature prominent on the world's large bomber designs.

The first prototype (K4586) first flew on 17 June 1936 from Whitley aerodrome and was noticeable for its lack of dihedral on the mainplane. It was powered by two 795 hp Tiger IX engines driving DH three-blade two-position propellers. After an initial amount of test flying and the production of a number of Mk I aircraft, it was found that the lack of dihedral affected the aircraft's stability; so the second prototype, which was powered by two 920 hp Tiger XI engines, was flown with a small amount of dihedral on the outer planes. This second prototype was also to serve later as the prototype Mk II.

When first introduced the Whitley had no flaps, so a large amount of incidence was 'built-in' to keep the landing speed down (necessary in those days for a night bomber), which accounted for the nose down flying attitude which proclaimed it as a Whitley in flight! When flaps were later fitted, no alteration to the incidence angle was made, so the Whitley with flaps had a still lower landing speed at the same weight.

Production of the Armstrong-Siddeley Tiger-powered Whitleys was thirty-four Mk Is, forty-six

Whitley Mk.IV K9055 illustrates the thickness of the Whitley's wing. (Author)

Whitley Mk.1 K7208 converted to Mk.IV prototype with Merlin II engines. (RAF)

Mk IIs and eighty Mk IIIs. The Mk III was produced to specification 20/36, which was issued on 4 August 1936, and introduced the ventral 'dustbin' turret and increased dihedral on the outer planes.

With the Tiger engines the Whitley was obviously under-powered, so it was decided to re-engine the airframe. This took place when a Mk I (K7208) was flown to Hucknall airfield for Rolls-Royce conversion and trial installation. This airframe was flown Merlin powered on 11 February 1938 with two Merlin Mk IIs. When tested by A&AEE pilots a number of recommendations were made, and amongst the things faulted was the noise of the engines and a poor heating system. The latter fault never appears to have been fully rectified.

Further development continued with the Merlin-engined Whitleys, which resulted in the Mk IV powered by two 1,030 hp Merlin IVs being accepted for service, followed by the Mk IVA powered by two 1,075 hp Merlin Xs. The Mk IV aircraft introduced the FN4A four-gun rear turret and also the improved glazed extension bomb-sight window in the nose.

The original gun turrets on the prototype Whitley had been criticised by the A&AEE after the armament and flight trials, for it was found that the AW forward turret was impracticable, as the gunner could not move it against the air pressure in flight. The mid-upper turret was also considered as useless

as the gunner's view and field of fire was too restricted. It was agreed at a meeting at MAP that aircraft should be delivered with these turrets, but without guns, and Frazer-Nash turrets would replace them when developed. It was also decided that the mid-upper turret should be deleted and the position skinned over: and a Frazer-Nash 'dustbin' under turret developed and adapted for the Whitley under-position. This latter turret was developed to house two Browning 0.303-in machine-guns. This was the FN17. On some Coastal Command Whitleys the squadrons fitted flexibly mounted Vickers 'K' guns in the fuselage beam positions. The first Whitley to mount a four-gun rear FN4 turret was a Mk I K7183, which also had the lengthened rear fuselage and went to A&AEE Martlesham Heath in December 1938.

This was followed in January 1939 with Mk III K7243 having its first flight at Baginton with power supplied by Armstrong-Siddeley Deerhound engines. Just over a year later this aircraft crashed at Baginton and was totally destroyed. In December 1939 came a request for the installation of self-sealing fuel tanks, but these were not introduced until September 1940, when they were incorporated on production Mk Vs along with Goodrich de-icing boots on the mainplane leading edge.

Bomb-doors were originally automatically spring loaded to the closed position, but mechanically operated bomb-doors were later installed. Provision was also later made for the installation of two 2,000 lb bombs in the fuselage. On the Whitley Mks I and II the bomb-load was four 500 lb bombs in the fuselage, six 250 lb bombs in the inner bomb-cells and six 112 lb bombs in the outer bomb-cells, but when the 112 lb bombs were declared obsolescent the outer bomb-cells were deleted, only being reinstated when the Whitley V was developed to carry six 250 lb bombs in these positions. Handling trials dropping 'dead' depth charges began at Baginton with Mk V P5104 on 13 March 1941, followed by overload trials to 32,000 lb at Boscombe Down with Mk V Z6640. The first production Coastal Command Mk VII was Z9690, which flew on 1 August 1941.

The Whitley IV & V powered with the Merlin X-engine had a maximum speed of 230 mph against the previous models with Tiger engines of 215 mph, and the bomb-load had increased from 3,000 to 8,000 lb. With the Whitley IV only the last seven of the forty had the Merlin X engines, the remainder having Merlin IV engines. Installing the Merlin engines necessitated a change in the cabin heating, the original Merlin system using heat from the engine radiators. This system was totally unsatisfactory and further experiments were made which resulted in a system where cold air was blown through a Morris heating radiator; from this, ducting took the hot air to all members of the crew except the rear gunner.

The main production version of the Merlin-powered Whitley was the Mk V, which had Merlin X

engines and a 15-in extension to the rear fuselage, the latter item to allow an increased field of fire to either beam for the rear turret. The fins were also modified to improve production, the leading edge being straightened, as opposed to the curved leading edge of earlier Marks.

At the commencement of war in September 1939 there were 196 Whitleys in service as night bombers with the following squadrons, Nos. 10, 51, 58 and 78 squadrons, and shortly after the declaration of war No. 77 squadron was equipped with the Whitley. The Whitley would continue in production until June 1943, and in 1940 was one of the five aircraft given priority ratings for production by the Minister of Aircraft Production.

The Whitley was to score many 'firsts', being the first British bomber to drop bombs on German soil, first to drop bombs on mainland Italy, as well as being the first British bomber to operate over Poland; yet it was in general overshadowed by the publicity given first to the Wellington, and then the new four-engined heavies. It finished its operational career with Bomber Command in April 1942, but appeared out of semi-retirement with Bomber Command OTUs to take part in the '1,000 bomber' raid on Cologne on 30 May 1942.

Whitleys had meantime been transferred to Coastal Command. Numbers 502 and 612 squadrons were the first to be included in the anti-submarine task, their long range helping to close the gap in the North Atlantic, operating from Iceland and the Hebrides, as well as anti-submarine patrols

Whitley Mk.V T4261 'Ceylon'. Looking every bit 'The flying barn-door'. (IWM)

in the Bay of Biscay. Losses on the latter patrols were fairly high, considered as due to weather and enemy action, though the Merlin has been reported as not amenable to the low-slow-flying that was the lot of Coastal Command.

With the success of the anti-submarine patrols it was decided to carry out further development of the Mk V airframe, so a specialised version emerged for anti-submarine use -- the Mk VII -- which introduced an increased fuel capacity, ASV.Mk 2 and 'Stickleback' radar aerials, amongst other things.

A further role that was undertaken by the Whitley began with the Airborne Forces. The Central Landing School (later Establishment) was formed at Ringway in September 1940, and the Whitleys joined shortly afterwards as part of the aircraft establishment. Their role was initially for the dropping of paratroops and the establishment of dropping techniques, both of the paratroops and their equipment. This was followed with the towing of the Horsa glider, the techniques of towing, releasing and handling. The first Whitleys used were of the Armstrong-Siddeley Tiger-powered version. The rear turret was removed and a jumping platform installed in its place: this was later superseded by jumping from a hole in the lower fuselage. This model was not used operationally, and Merlin Whitleys from operational squadrons were used for the first airborne operations.

The first two British paratroop operations were carried out using the Whitley, the first drop being on 10 May 1941 against Mont Vultura (Italy) aqueducts. The second drop was considered to be one of the best executed combined operations: this was against the Bruneval radar station (France) on 27 February 1942 to obtain information on German early warning radar.

With the formation of 38 Wing to provide the aircraft for airborne activities, 295 and 297 Squadrons were equipped with Whitleys to carry out the long-range supply dropping or glider towing role, which they retained until 1943. In the meantime 296 Squadron had converted to Whitley aircraft as well, having previously operated Hectors and Harts on glider training.

From the very first operation, in every role, the Whitley was to operate without benefit of any modern aid: it was to operate with an outdated radio equipment, no de-icing, no windscreen wiper — in fact, little else bar fuel, engines, maps and aircrew guts — yet they were expected to operate across

Germany and also down to Italy, and they did precisely that.

In April 1942 a Mk V was converted to a freighter for BOAC, registered G-AGCF, commencing its trials at Baginton. This was followed by a Mk V BD354 going off to Boscombe Down in June 1942 for take-off trials at an all-up weight of 33,500 lb. Then in September another Mk V T4149/G had RATO units installed under its wings for assisted take-off purposes, and was delivered to RAE Farnborough for trials. A Mk V Z9390 also had a glider towing trial installation fitted at Baginton in the same year, and this aircraft also went to RAE for trials. The most surprising installation of all occurred in April 1943 when a spring tab control was fitted to the rudders of a Mk V Z6649. This was part of an investigation into controls at Farnborough, where Z6649 was destined. One of the last production Whitleys was a Mk V LA951, which was retained by Armstrong-Whitworth and used as a general test vehicle and tug for the AW52G glider, until replaced by a Halifax aircraft. LA951 was the last airworthy Whitley and was pensioned off and scrapped in March 1949.

No one could possibly describe the Whitley as beautiful; functional certainly, and positively strong; it was generally stable, and was easily flown 'hands off', and when coming in to land was 'motored' in. Its very thick wing was indicative of a period when the design of monoplanes considered it necessary.

The mainplane was built around a single main spar which accommodated all bending loads, being particularly strong in torsion. This main spar was an extremely strong box structure, with flanges of spanwise corrugated sheet metal and webs of vertical corrugated sheet metal, all braced internally by tubular bracing ribs. The nose ribs forming the leading edge are of top hat channel section connected to the spar by bolted brackets. The trailing edge was a continuation of the bracing ribs used in the spar, the area aft of the main spar being fabric covered.

The fuselage construction was the usual Armstrong-Whitworth method of light alloy rolled section and pressings for frames and formers, the whole fuselage being built in three sections. The heavy longerons were positioned in the fuselage where the mainplanes passed through, these longerons then continuing approximately two-thirds to the rear. The remaining structure was of built-up frames, which were particularly large at the mainspar pick-up points and the transport joints; then formers and hoop stringers, to which the Alclad sheet was stagger riveted. On the Mks IV to VII the nose turret was the FN16, the rear turret was the FN4A, while on the Whitley IV the mid-under was the Nash & Thompson.

The tailplane construction was a miniature wing, with the main spar going right through the fuselage, being attached at two heavy fuselage frames. The fins were built on to the top of the tailplane to two vertical posts, the front one of 'I' section and the rear one of polygon section. The elevators and rudders were of metal construction, fabric covered.

The under turret on operations was the source of many troubles, for when lowered it caused so much drag that crews were reluctant to lower it. It also was liable to icing-up and therefore could not be retracted once it was lowered, not until warmer air was reached. Its pitiful armament of two 0.303-in machine-guns was hardly worth the complication and trouble, and squadrons campaigned to have it removed.

With the coming into production of the new four-engined heavy bombers, a Whitley was used to test a trial installation of the Merlin 10 and heating system for the Halifax B1, which like the Whitley's heating system was not a great success.

The prototype Mk VII (P4949) was a converted Mk V, and further numbers of Mk V were converted, with a total production run of 146 Mk VIIs. Having ample range and a good load-carrying capability, the Whitley was well suited to the Coastal Command role although the cockpit accommodation was cramped for long-range operation. The Mk VII joined the Coastal squadrons in 1942, although a 502 Squadron Whitley had claimed its first U-boat in the Bay of Biscay on 30 November 1941.

Nicknamed by some the 'Flying Barn Door', it nevertheless performed arduous tasks without modern aids or devices during the build-up of Bomber Command — if it was a flying barn door, it was an extremely strong one.

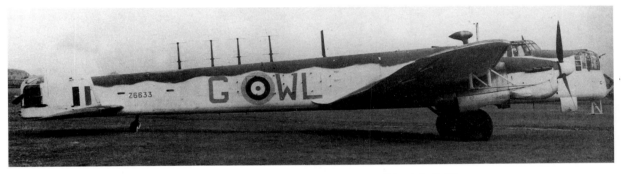

Whitley Mk.VII 'Stickleback' Z6633 of RAF Coastal Command illustrates both types of ASV aerial. (RAF)

Whitley comparison table

	Mk IV.	Mk V.	Mk VII.
Wingspan	84 ft	84 ft	84 ft
Wing area	1137 sq ft	1137 sq ft	1137 sq ft
Length	69 ft. 3 in	70 ft 8 in	70 ft 8 in
Fuel capacity, normal	705 gallons	837 gallons	1100 gallons
Empty weight	17,250 lb	19,350 lb	19,650 lb
Maximum weight	25,900 lb	33,500 lb	33,950 lb
Maximum speed	244 mph	230 mph	215 mph
Cruising speed	220 mph	210 mph	195 mph
Climb to	16 min to 15,000 ft	16 min to 15,000 ft	22 min to 22,000 ft
Service ceiling	17,600 ft	26,000 ft	20,000 ft
Normal range, miles	1250	1500	2300
Engine	Merlin 4	Merlin 10	Merlin 10
Engine power, maximum	1030	1145	1145

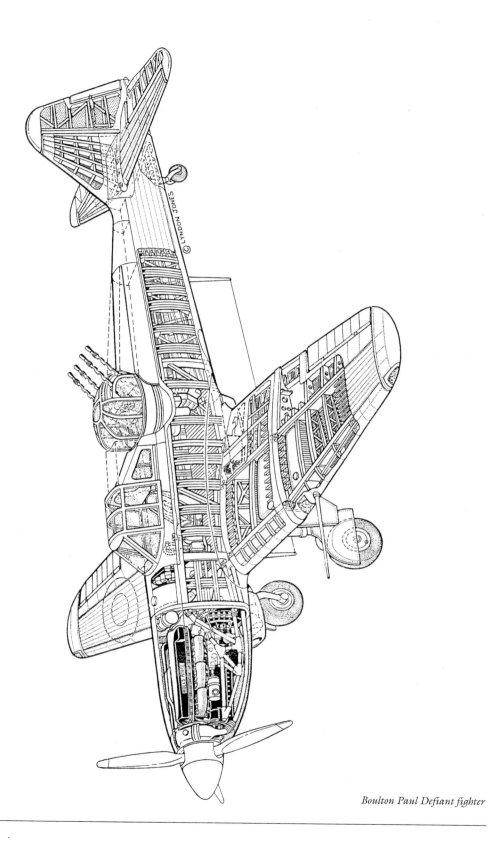

Boulton Paul Defiant fighter

7

Boulton Paul Defiant

The Boulton Paul Defiant is another British aircraft that has been at the receiving end of rough comment and criticism — all well detailed in hindsight! Some comments have stated that it was an Air Staff continuation of the Bristol F2B fighter theme, others that it was an 'anachronistic design'. It is obvious that the Bristol F2B and the Defiant have two things in common, two seats and a single engine — from there everything else deviates, for whereas the F2B's pilot was the 'hunter' with an air gunner/observer to guard his tail, the Defiant's pilot was a 'chaffeur' to the air gunner 'hunter' — and as such represented a new fighter concept. If the Defiant can be faulted in any way, then it is the failure to provide a number of guns for the pilot, and provide more power for the weight of the airframe. The Air Staff's operational concept when formulating the requirements of the specification, was that the Luftwaffe's bombers would be operating from Germany, and therefore without fighter escort; which was a fair assumption at the time, for no one could foresee the collapse of France

after a German attack, and all that this would entail. Whether the concept of a fighter with a four-gun turret, able to make attacks on enemy bomber formations from alongside or underneath, is viable or not depends on whether it is viewed in its original concept, or viewed in hindsight — and hindsight does flatter the reviewer with remarkable powers of military foresight!

J.D. North of Boulton Paul had developed a powered (pneumatic plus manual) nose gun turret for the Boulton & Paul Overstrand, and then became interested in the possibilities of a powered gun turret developed by de Boysson of the Société d'Applications des Machines Motrices (SAMM). A licence was then acquired by Boulton Paul from SAMM, and North proceeded to develop Boulton Paul turrets based on the SAMM principles.

A British power turret was also at this time being developed by Nash and Thompson (later called Frazer-Nash), and this model was installed in a Hawker Demon fighter. This particular turret carried one 0.303-in Lewis machine-gun, and protected the

Defiant prototype K8310 at the Hendon Air Display 1938. (Dunn)

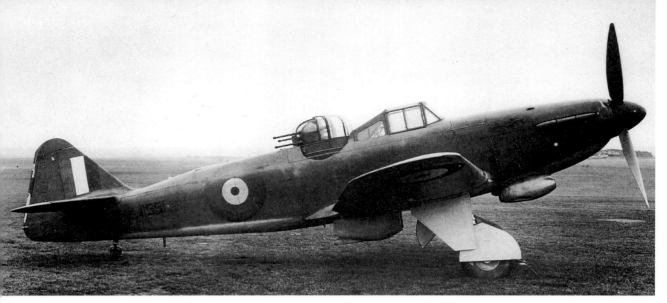

Defiant N1551 with Merlin XX engine and different oil cooler. (IWM)

gunner from the airstream by a series of curved metal cowls, that rose to protect him as he rose in the cockpit, gaining the name for the turret of 'Lobster back'.

The experience of these two turrets, plus the tactical evaluation made by the Air Staff, resulted in the issue on 20 May 1935 of specification F9/35 for a two-seat fighter to replace the Demon fighter, with a speed and manoeuvrability which would be almost comparable to a single-seat fighter, its object being to deal with unescorted enemy bomber attacks. The speed required was to be not less than 290 mph at 15,000 ft, and the four machine-guns in the fuselage were to be controlled by the air gunner.

In June 1935 tenders were invited from selected firms, and on 12 September designs were submitted by Armstrong-Whitworth, Bristol, Boulton Paul, Fairey, Gloster, Hawker and Supermarine. Selection was made by 12 December, and sanction sought from the Treasury for seven prototypes, these being duplicates from Boulton Paul, Hawker and Fairey, with a single one from Armstrong-Whitworth; which indicates the importance that the Air Ministry attached to the operational role of the aircraft. Treasury sanction was given on 6 January 1936, and contracts placed shortly afterwards, that for Boulton Paul stipulating that delivery of prototypes was to be in twelve to fifteen months time. In September 1936 the DTD supported by the DAP recommended giving a small production order to Boulton Paul, but this was rejected.

The delivery date for Boulton Paul's prototype came on 4 March 1937 and no prototype was ready, then in the same month the Armstrong-Whitworth

contract was cancelled. This was followed on 28 April by Boulton Paul being awarded an initial production order for 187 aircraft, due to the failure of Hawker to produce its prototype, the Hotspur. On 21 July 1937 the Boulton Paul prototype (K8310) was handed over to AID for inspection, and the decision made to call for no modifications resulted in the first flight of the prototype on 11 August, though without the turret and with the position faired over. With the 1,030 hp Merlin I the Defiant's speed was recorded as 302 mph.

After this came an amount of frustrating delay, for the undercarriage either malfunctioned or failed to lock 'up' over a number of months, with the result that on 7 December at a conference, Boulton Paul announced their intention of changing over from the Dowty undercarriage to a Lockheed one on production aircraft. In the same month the prototype was delivered to A&AEE for trials. By then the aircraft was nine months late.

Some of this lateness in delivery was due to the company moving its premises and construction from Norwich to Wolverhampton in January 1937, and a strike within the works around the same period, when construction work was stopped. By the end of January all components had been transferred, but the firm was short of skilled operators at the new factory, and the contract for Blackburn Rocs that the firm held was also slowing down the work.

On 11 January 1938 the Air Ministry decided to drop the Hawker Hotspur prototype from planning production, and to concentrate on the P82 Defiant as the sole two-seat turret fighter under Scheme F; so a full requirement of 389 aircraft were ordered to specification Defiant 1/P1(5/37) and a contract issued.

Flight test and armament trials continued through 1938 with the first prototype, and the decision was made to change the engine from the Merlin I to the Merlin II, which also involved modifications to the engine cowlings and exhaust system. Although this development was taking place with the first prototype, the drawings for production aircraft and progress on the second prototype was delayed, with the result that the second prototype (K8620) was not ready for contractor's trials until 18 May 1939.

When originally projected the P82 had had an estimated weight of 5,774 lb, a top speed of 323 mph at 15,000 ft, and 305 mph at 25,000 ft; but when the fully equipped P82 Defiant was tested at A&AEE the following figures were recorded:

All-up weight at take-off	7,510 lb
Power and engine	1,030 bhp Merlin III
Maximum speed at 20,000 ft	302 mph
Time to 20,000 ft	11.9 min
Rate of climb to 20,000 ft	1,680 ft/min
Service ceiling	30,000 ft

Boulton Paul's test pilot was Flight Lieutenant Feather, who had previously been employed as an armament development officer as well as a test pilot at an experimental establishment. Feather flew the first prototype and reported no aerodynamic snags, and the aircraft was only faulted at the A&AEE

during the prototype's brief handling trial as having ailerons too light for Service pilots.

Originally the Boulton Paul project was considered as having little likelihood of progressing past the experimental stage, and a production order had been placed with Hawker for the Hotspur F9/35. However, a visit paid by the DTD to the Boulton Paul factory impressed him enough to take a favourable view of Boulton Paul's construction methods. Now in 1938 the Defiant was the selected aircraft. On 15 March the A&AEE reported the successful testing of the Boulton Paul Type A turret in an Overstrand at Martlesham Heath.

During September 1938 K8310 returned from the A&AEE before the completion of its flight trials, as the engine had persistently 'cut out' during the diving trials; all the same, the report stated that the ailerons were now considered satisfactory and the controls in general well harmonised. In the same month Boulton Paul were being asked about the possible installation of the Merlin X into the Defiant airframe, but the firm considered that the modifications were so extensive that they would present a considerable delay to the present production.

The second prototype (K8620) skeleton structure was practically complete by the end of March 1938; but a redesign resulted because of various design and mock-up conferences and modifications arising from these conferences, plus the desire to make the

Defiant night-fighter N3887 at RAF Wyton 1941. (Author)

Long service Defiant night-fighter, going by the worn paint scheme. (Author)

second prototype to correspond as near as possible to a production aircraft. Consequently the contractor's trials were delayed until May 1939. The aircraft eventually reached Boscombe Down for A&AEE tests in the following September. Thus the second prototype was three years in construction and was delivered two years after the first prototype, in the same month as the first production Defiant.

In 1939 the firm completed a design study of a dual control version of the Defiant, but this was cancelled and design work on it ceased. Then the idea was resurrected in the August; but finally put to rest when DTD were informed that it would only be possible to have a dual control Defiant with extreme difficulty and complication. By 23 August the first fifteen production aircraft were proceeding normally in production. The first Defiant squadron commenced to receive their new charges in December 1939, this was 264 Squadron, which was commanded by Squadron Leader Hunter. During January 1940 the squadron was beset with engine failures and malfunctioning of the hydraulic system, which led to the grounding of the aircraft while the problems were investigated by the manufacturers concerned. The grounding ban was lifted during the first week in February and the squadron began working out tactics, both within the squadron and in conjunction with Hurricanes.

During July 1940 a sliding hood panel in the top of the pilot's hood was installed to improve the pilot's vision upwards at night, for by now

the Defiant had passed its zenith as a day fighter and was being considered for the night role. In its brief career as a day fighter the Defiant had proved its worth against the German bombers, and had even added to its score by catching out a few fighters; claiming thirty-seven shot down in one afternoon — though this was later revised to fourteen. Apparently there was originally opposition by the pilots, who had been trained as orthodox single-seat pilots, and opposed handing-over the fighting control of the aircraft to the air gunners. Squadron Leader Hunter of 264 Squadron evolved tactics that resulted in the first successes. His tactic was for the aircraft to fly in formation and maintain their position throughout the attack, engaging the enemy bomber formations in close-in beam attacks. For night flying with the Hurricanes and Defiants there was developed a multi-ejector exhaust, known as 'Blue Note', which was tested and proved satisfactory. At the end of August 1940 the Defiants were withdrawn to the north, and then in September moved south again as night fighters; with the addition of AI radar the all-up weight of the aircraft increased to 8,510 lb, so that even with the power of a Merlin XX the maximum speed was only 293 mph at 20,000 ft. It had been hoped that with the addition of the Merlin XX in the Defiant there would be an increase in performance, and this was confirmed at A&AEE in July 1941 on N1551, a Mk II, but the all-up weight was 7,975 lb and there was no AI radar.

On 15 March 1942 Sholto Douglas, in writing to

the Under-Secretary of State for Air, stated that the Defiant was operationally obsolete, and strongly recommended that the Defiant should be cancelled. During February of the same year, trials were being carried out with the redundant Defiants to check them for the air-sea rescue role; and by the end of April the decision was made to have five squadrons of ASR Defiants. This was followed by a further role, the conversion to target tug, which entailed major modifications, amongst which was the removal of the turret and the fitment of the target winch and gear. This raised the all-up weight to 8,250 lbs and reduced the maximum speed to 250 mph. The Defiant target tug saw extensive use during the war with anti-aircraft co-operation squadrons, air gunnery schools and OTUs; while some aircraft were tropicalised and served overseas, and a few saw service with the USAAF in Great Britain.

The most famous Defiant of all to the post-war enthusiast and general public would be DR944, being seen on documentary film as the vehicle for the first British ejector seat tests. This aircraft was seconded to Martin-Baker Aircraft on 11 December 1944 and in place of the turret there was fitted an ejector seat, trials commencing at Wittering on 11 May 1945. Another use for the Defiant in the experimental role was found at the RAE and the A&AEE, when some were used in engine development and armament trials. Two also served with Rotol at Staverton on propeller experiments.

The design of the Defiant was based on easy construction, with as much as possible being built on the bench jigs in small sub-assemblies. The fuselage consisted of three main sections and stressed skin was used throughout, with the exception of the forward bay adjacent to the fireproof bulkhead. The front fuselage was of stressed skin construction braced at the forward end by tubular members, with longerons on each side of the fuselage at the top and bottom, with vertical bracing by the frames. The fuselage skin was braced by 'Z' section stringers. The rear fuselage was made in three portions, a top and two sides, each having extruded angle section along the top and bottom edges braced by ribs of channel section, forming the rear fuselage frames, with alternate frames braced by tubular members, and the external stressed skin reinforced by 'Z' section stringers.

The cantilever mainplane was of light alloy stressed skin construction, tapering in chord and thickness. It was built in three separate sections with the centre plane having a two spar and auxiliary spar layout, and the skin was stiffened by 'Z' section stringers. The ribs between the spars were of the braced girder type, having 'T' section flanges and corrugated webs, with five ribs and two beams

Defiant target tug, turret removed and increased oil cooler for overseas service. (IWM)

located between the spars, with nineteen spacing ribs between the rear spar and auxiliary spar. The outer plane was also a stressed skin structure with front and rear spars, ribs and 'Z' section stringers covered by light alloy covering. The ailerons were built-up members of triangular section incorporating diaphragm stiffeners, with channel section ribs.

The tail unit was of cantilever layout and of stressed skin construction, with the tailplane built around four spars of channel section with the front and rear spars attached to the fuselage; the four spars are of lipped channel section. The elevators were based on the 'D' section spar, with flanged ribs covered by fabric. The fin was similar in construction to the tailplane, using multi-spars, ribs, stringers and stressed skin. The rudder was built around a 'D' spar with diaphragm attachment to pressed steel ribs, the whole being fabric covered.

The undercarriage consisted of two main independent units and a fixed tailwheel. The main units retracted inwards and upwards into wells in the centre section, the wheel units then being covered with fairings lying flush with the lower surface. Also retractable was the rear radio mast, which was retracted on landing.

The gun turret was of Boulton Paul design and

construction, and was designated the Type A. It mounted four Browning 0.303-in machine-guns. The turret was faired fore and aft by movable fairings, which retracted as the guns approached and rose again once the guns were past. Entrance to the turret was very difficult, being through a door on the turret or through the lower fuselage, both the exit/entrance and accommodation inside the turret was considered cramped, and certainly not suitable for a fully kitted-up overweight air gunner! The exit problem may be one of the reasons for greater casualties of the air gunners compared to the pilots. The turret transparency was altered during 1940 to provide better vision for the air gunner. This modification was the removal of the Perspex forward of the gunsight.

A certain amount of controversy over the Defiant has at odd times spilled over into the aviation magazines, and is noticeable by the amount of defence put up in its favour by aircrew who flew them. Though obviously an easy aircraft to fly, and an easy aircraft to land on rough airfields with its wide track undercarriage, its manoeuvrability did not compare to the Hurricane. With that and its lack of power it was no competitor to the Bf 109. As was explained at the start of this section on the Defiant

Defiant fighter at Church Fenton stripped down for transport to M.U. (I. Robinson)

and confirmed by a member of the Operational Requirements Department, it was never intended for fighter-fighter combat.

For the Dieppe raid twelve Defiants of 277 Squadron operated in the ASR role, and nine others escorted by Typhoons flew from Orfordness towards Ostende at 18,000 ft to decoy the German radar as a spoof bombing raid. Another role for the Defiant was in the RCM role, and in April 1942 515 Squadron was formed and fitted with 'Moonshine' equipment, and it was afterwards fitted with 'Mandrel' equipment, so as to 'take-out' German radar.

A further development of the Defiant was the P94 project, which was a single-seat version powered by a Merlin XX, which had an estimated top speed of 380 mph at 23,500 ft. To test the project, the Defiant prototype K8310 was again flown without its turret. After the test flying the estimated top speed of the P94 was reduced to 364 mph at 23,500 ft. This project was not proceeded with, but K8310 in June 1942 was fitted with, and tested, a 20mm cannon turret; and another Defiant had a Martin Maxon 0.5-in gun turret installed for tests.

As a two-seat fighter the Defiant was past its prime in 1940 in day fighter operations, and obsolescent as a night-fighter in 1942; yet its original concept cannot be disputed, unfortunately the scenario had changed — and that appears to be something that the critics ignore.

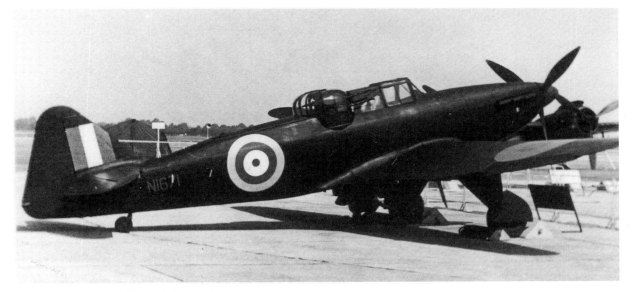

Defiant night-fighter N1671 on display at end of war. (Author)

Boulton Paul Defiant

Wingspan	39 feet 4 inch	(11.99 metres)
Wing area	250 sq.feet	(23.23 sq.metres)
Length	35 feet 4 inches	(10.77 metres)
Empty weight	6150 lb	(2892 kg)
Maximum loaded weight	8600 lb	(3901 kg)
Maximum speed at height	315 mph at 16,500 feet	(507 kph at 5030 metres)
Service ceiling	31,800 feet	(9690 metres)
Range	480 miles	(772 kilometres)
Engine	one 1260 hp Merlin XX inline	
Armament	four 0.303-inch machine-guns in turret	

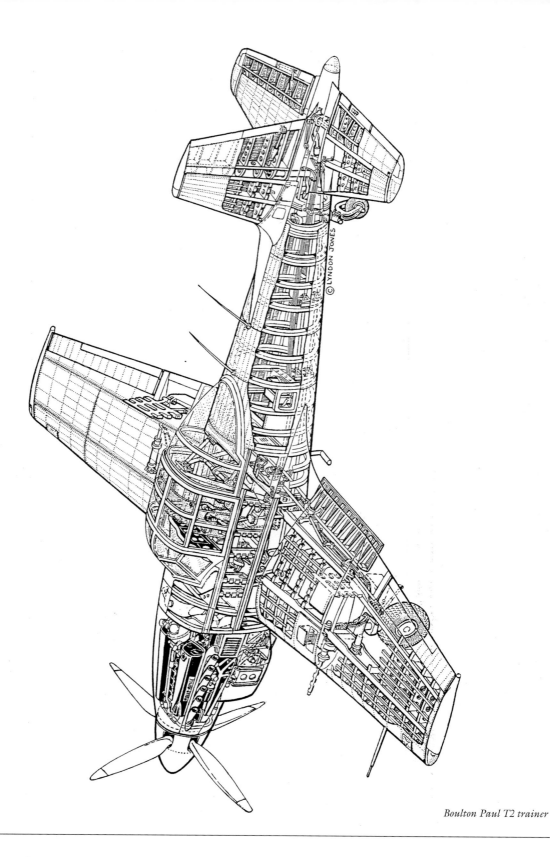

Boulton Paul T2 trainer

8

Boulton Paul Balliol T2

Aircrew training during and after World War Two varied as policies changed, and *ab initio* training and training aircraft varied just as much; but by 1945 it had been decided that this first stage of training should have an elementary training aircraft, equipped to provide the trainee pilot with an introduction to the more advanced training aircraft. The policy at that period also favoured the three-seat clover-leaf layout, in which the instructor sat on the right-hand side, with the pupil in the left-hand seat, with a further pupil sitting centrally disposed 'sitting in', and also possibly carrying out navigation work.

It had been considered that with the Percival Prentice this arrangement had been satisfactory, and

so with the issue of specification T7/45 a similar arrangement was called for, so providing a natural transition from the Prentice. Ease of maintenance was a further requirement, and in the Balliol this was achieved by Boulton Paul.

The Balliol had the distinction of being the first turbo-prop trainer to fly, when it made its first flight as a turbo-prop aircraft on 17 May 1948. Prior to this, the airframe had progressed faster than the Armstrong-Siddeley Mamba engine, which was its intended power, so was flown powered by a Bristol Mercury engine in 1947. The airframe flown in this condition appeared to be in general satisfactory, the stall was gentle and straight, and all controls were

Balliol trainer T2 prototype VW897 powered by Merlin 35. (RAF)

considered light and well harmonised.

Work on the Balliol (Type 108) commenced in early 1946, and a number of features were designed into the airframe initially not only to improve the maintenance, but also to reduce spares holdings; this was achieved by design so that the fin and tailplanes were interchangeable, the elevators were interchangeable, as were the undercarriage legs. The service and maintenance requirement was met, as in the Athena competitor, by grouping as near as possible all the various services components at accessible points.

The construction was completely conventional, with the fuselage constructed in three sections, front, rear and rear cone. The front fuselage was of all metal semi-monocoque construction, with longerons, frames, bulkheads and stringers with stressed skin covering. Built onto the rear spar bulkhead was attached the front frame of the crash pylon, with a support strut bolted to the diagonal arch. The front and rear spar bulkheads carried booms for the pick-up of the inner plane spars. The rear fuselage was of all metal monocoque construction, consisting of nine frames, to which stringers were bolted. The front fuselage longerons extended to the front attachment frame of the rear fuselage; this front frame was formed as an angle and provided the means of attaching the front to rear fuselage. At the rear of the rear fuselage was a reinforced angle to provide attachment to the rear cone. The tail cone comprised seven frames to which were attached stringers, to which the skin was attached. At the forward end of the rear cone was an angle attachment for fitting it to the rear fuselage; and stub ribs were provided for the fitment of fin and tailplane, with attachment fittings recessed into the stub ribs.

The mainplanes consisted of two inner and two outer planes, and were constructed around a front and rear spar. The spars were built up from extruded booms, plate webs and braced by interspar ribs; and the front and trailing edge sections were built up separately and attached to the spars. The interspar ribs were cut away to accommodate the fuel tanks in the inner planes, and were supported by spigots in the end ribs. In the lower surface of the inner

Balliol Trainer T2 G-ANSF, the only one on civil register. (Author)

Balliol trainer T2 VW897 illustrating wide-track undercarriage. (RAF)

plane was recessed the wheel well, which accommodated the undercarriage and wheel. The outer planes were constructed similarly to the inner planes, carried dive brakes on the upper and lower surfaces on the inboard end of the outer planes and fitted flush into the surfaces. The ailerons were attached to the outer end of the outer planes, and comprised ribs and formers attached to a spar.

The tail unit was unique in that the tailplane and fin were interchangeable: these comprised two sheet spars with doubling plates along their full length, diaphragm ribs and a two-portion skin, which joined at the leading edge. The elevators were interchangeable and comprised a spar, diaphragm ribs and stressed skin.

The main undercarriage legs were interchangeable and had a track of 15 ft, each leg fitting into an undercarriage box of a light alloy casting which forms a box structure, to which the mainplane skin

was riveted. When the main wheels retracted they were covered by a folding door. The tailwheel was non-retractable, but could be locked for take-off and set to 'steer' for taxying.

The P108 had been constructed to T7/45, but for the prototype's (VL892) first flight on 30 May 1947 it was temporarily powered by a Bristol Mercury 30 engine. Rolls-Royce had been most interested in supplying the power unit for the T7/45, but the engine chosen was the Armstrong-Siddeley Mamba. The second prototype (VL917) was Mamba powered; as was VL935, which first flew on 17 May 1948, and was the first turbo-powered trainer to fly.

The Air Staff then reversed their decision again, and decided to revert to two seats, side by side, and a conventional piston engine, the Merlin 35. Specification T14/47 was issued to cover this. Four prototypes were built to compete for the contract, the first one being VW897, which first flew on 10 July 1948. This version was designated the T2, and a batch of seventeen pre-production aircraft were ordered for extended Service trials. The first prototype T1 had meanwhile been re-engined with a Mamba.

Balliol T2 VW898 (one of the four prototype aircraft) was at A&AEE on an engineering appraisal from 18 July to 27 August 1949 when the aircraft was partially stripped and re-assembled, and several components changed. It was considered that the aircraft embodied a number of good features, such as interchangeability, and that the undercarriage would lower and lock under gravity. Difficulties were experienced in renewing some components, and it was felt that some improvement could be made with details and major items.

VR592, a pre-production T2 aircraft, was the next at A&AEE, from 3 November to 23 December 1949 on extensive flying trial of 100 hours. The aircraft was found easy to service and maintain, and during the trial only one major defect occurred. Performance figures were given as:

Maximum rate of climb	1,780 ft/min from SL to 8,000 ft
Service ceiling	22,600 ft.
Maximum level speed	252 knots (290 mph).
Maximum cruising speed	201 knots (231 mph).

During November 1950, three Balliol T2s were used for deck handling trials at A&AEE: these were VR596, VR597 and VR598. The Balliol was being considered as a deck landing trainer, and with a view to this, its characteristics were considered in this context. The trials proved the aircraft suitable for this use, but there were criticisms over the aileron and rudder power at very low speeds, and also the throttle control. It was also considered that the Balliol T1 with its Mamba engine had considerable advantages over the T2 with its Merlin engine, from the point of view of deck landings.

Balliol T1 VW892 with a Mamba engine was to be delivered to the EFTS, mainly for pilot training on handling turbo-propeller aircraft; but first it went to A&AEE during June 1952 to check its handling characteristics. These were found to be similar to the T2, but the comparative quietness and freedom from vibration of the turbo-propeller engine made the aircraft most pleasant to fly. Its speeds were listed as:

| Maximum design speed | 368 knots ias (423 mph). |

| Maximum recommended speed by contractor | 270 knots ias (311 mph). |
| Maximum speed attained by contractor | 320 knots ias (368 mph). |

With the selection of the Balliol T2 as the new advanced trainer, a large production run was envisaged and prepared for; but then a further change of policy regarding training was made in 1951, and the decision was to go for pure jet advanced training from the elementary training. This resulted in cutbacks to production, with a total production run of 162 aircraft, including thirty built by Blackburns (WN506 to 535). The Balliols initially went to No 7 FTS at Cottesmore and some went to the RAF College Cranwell; later to 228 Squadron and 238 OCU. The first production Balliol T2 WF989 had its first flight in April 1952, and between June and August of the same year this aircraft was at A&AEE on a brief handling trial. It was considered not significantly different from comparable pre-production aircraft, except that the pre-stall warning was inadequate.

The Fleet Air Arm received thirty Sea Balliols, serial numbered WL715 to WL734, and WP324 to WP333, after the prototype VR599 flew in October 1952. This prototype was at A&AEE between January and July 1953 on a partial engineering assessment, with a deck landing trial of 71 landings on HMS *Illustrious* during June, both by day and night. Serviceability was good with few defects, the main criticism being the bad view from the right-hand seat during the circuit, although the undercarriage was considered satisfactory for deck landings.

The Ceylon Air Force also acquired four Balliols from the RAF; these were WG224, WG226, WG227 and WG230. Further aircraft were obtained direct from Boulton Paul. The ones released from the RAF were replaced by XF929 to 931.

Handling of the T2, once cleared for service, indicated that the aircraft was easy to fly with no bad habits; the controls were well harmonised, light and effective. It was easy to taxy, although footloads were heavy when taxying crosswind. Normal take-offs required only +7 psi to +9 psi boost — but +12 psi boost was available if the take-off run was short — with the take-off made at about 75–85 knots. Stalling with power 'on' and the undercarriage and flaps 'up' was 65 knots. Spinning should only be carried out with the canopy closed, and the flaps, undercarriage and dive brakes retracted. During the spin the behaviour was erratic and some unpleasant yaw could be experienced. Recovery from a spin was normal and correction is made within one and a half turns, with 2,500 ft being lost within two turns.

So although the Balliol turned out to be an excellent aircraft, its use was strictly limited due to another change in training policy. Boulton Paul did civil register a T2 (construction number BP.6C) as G-ANSF for demonstration purposes, and obtained a Certificate of Airworthiness on 23 August 1954, the aircraft found no further orders with any other civil or military organisation. The only Balliol still extant, is a FAA T21 WL732, which is held in the RAF Museum collection. Meantime, the prototype Balliol VL892, after time at the manufacturers and at both the A&AEE and EFTS, was delivered on the 5 April 1954 to the RAF as an instructional airframe.

Balliol Trainer T1 VL935 powered by a Mamba prop-turbine. (Author)

Comparison of various Balliol Mks

	P108	T.Mk 1	T.Mk 2
Engine	Mercury	AS Mamba	RR Merlin 35
Engine power	840 hp	1,000 shp	1,280 bhp
Wing span	39 ft 4 in	39 ft 4 in	39 ft 4 in
Wing area	250 sq ft	250 sq ft	250 sq ft
Length	35 ft 3 in	36 ft 6 in	35 ft 1½ in
Undercarriage track	15 ft	15 ft	15 ft
Weight empty	5,939 lb	6,165 lb	6,730 lb
Weight loaded	7,595 lb	7,845 lb	8,410 lb
Maximum speed	280 mph	307 mph	288 mph
	10,000 ft	20,000 ft	9,000 ft
Maximum continuous cruise	250 mph	272 mph	231 mph
Take-off to clear 50 ft barrier	603 yards	n/k	450 yards

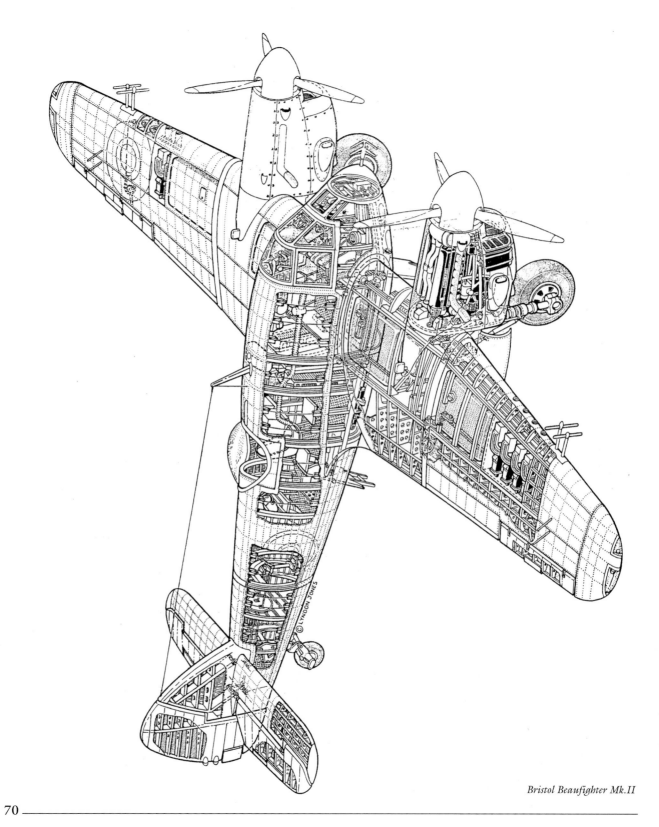

Bristol Beaufighter Mk.II

9

Bristol Beaufighter Mk II & V

With the delay in the Westland Whirlwind programme, caused by a number of factors, including lack of decision by the Air Staff, the RAF were left without a cannon fighter or escort fighter — not that they had had either previously. In casting around for an interim fighter in this category, the Air Staff were presented by Bristol with a brochure raised by Frise and Fedden, which described a cannon-armed fighter based on the Beaufort airframe and powered by two Hercules engines. The Beaufort airframe was based on unitary construction and was very strong, and appeared to offer a satisfactory unit for conversion.

On 29 November 1938 the Air Council met to consider the proposal, and on 23 December Bristols presented to Air Marshal Sir Wilfrid Freeman further details of their project, and promised that their prototype would be ready for testing within six to eight months of an order being placed. With a statement of operational requirements being made Bristols had hardened the project into a twin Hercules-powered two-seat fighter armed with four 20mm cannon, with an all-up weight of 15,500 lb and an estimated top speed of 360 mph at 15,000 ft.

Early in January 1939 it was agreed not to put the specification F17/39 out to tender so as to speed up production, and on 24 February a requisition order was placed for 300 Beaufort fighters at a cost of £11,000 each, the contract including the two prototypes using components from the 71st and 72nd Beaufort. On 31 March 1940 the preliminary mock-up conference was held and a number of alterations were called for. Meantime, the Hercules VI engines selected for the Beaufort fighter had failed to reach production status, and Bristols had reached the unpleasant decision that they would have to inform the Air Ministry that the production aircraft would have to be powered by Hercules III engines. By 19 June it was realised that the situation regarding Hercules production had reached crisis point, for the Hercules VI engines were not in production and the Hercules III would not be

Beaufighter Mk.II R2061 with low drag cowlings representing an Exe engine. (Rolls-Royce)

Beaufighter Mk.II R2402 powered by Merlin XX. (IWM)

available for the prototype aircraft or early production aircraft. These aircraft would have to accept the Hercules II engines using 87 octane fuel.

The Air Ministry accepted this change in plans as a temporary measure, and in co-operation with Bristol they were able to maintain control over the design, and the first prototype R2052 flew on 17 July 1939. During this period confusion in various departments had got out of hand, for the words 'conversion of Beaufort' had given the impression that it was a straight conversion of the Beaufort, as opposed to the use of Beaufort components matched to a new fuselage and powered by Hercules engines. This was rectified on 17 May 1939 when it was suggested that the name Beaufighter should be used, and further correspondence afterwards referred to the aircraft under this name.

When the first Beaufighter flew it was powered by Hercules HE1SM engines driving DH two-pitch propellers of 13 ft diameter, and oil coolers were slung under the engines. Handling trials indicated the need to alter the fin area slightly and also the elevator circuit, and also a change to the main undercarriage oleo struts. Though it achieved a speed of 335 mph at 16,800 ft, its reduced manoeuvrability mitigated against its use in the escort role. When the third prototype R2054 in full operational trim and powered by two Hercules II

engines was tested at A&AEE, the top speed was only 309 mph at 15,000 ft. So a programme of development was initiated to reduce the drag and improve handling, which would be incorporated in production aircraft. The nacelle drag for instance was lessened by lengthening the engine nacelle over the top of the wing and reducing the cross-section below the wing; undercarriage doors were produced that completely enclosed the main wheels; the jettison pipes (ex Beaufort) were relocated in the tail of the nacelle and the oil coolers repositioned in the leading edge of the wings.

With the end of the Battle of Britain and the commencement of the night-time Blitz, there was need for a night-fighter capable of accommodating AI radar; for this role the Beaufighter had adequate performance and ample space; but it was not until 26 July 1940 that the Beaufighter 1 was cleared for RAF use, and the time came to start equipping it for the night-fighter role. The first fifty Mk Is were only armed with four 20mm cannon with 60 round drums, but the following aircraft were fitted with an additional six Browning 0.303-in machine-guns in the wings, which became the standard armament.

Production of the Hercules engine began to lag behind the programme. Consequently MAP made the decision to provide a further source of engines, and so a crash programme was initiated to re-engine the Beaufighter with Merlin XXs, the aircraft then being designated the Mk II. It could not be claimed that this model was a 100 per cent success, for the swing on take-off of the Mk I was accentuated on the Mk II. This combined with the longer take-off run with the Merlins were not features appreciated in a night-fighter. Its powerplant was designed at Hucknall as a self-contained unit, and incorporated a wedge shaped intermediate bay to pick up with the Beaufighter nacelle, manufacture being carried out at Morris Motors, Cowley. The advantage that the Mk II had over the Mk I was its slightly higher ceiling, but its maximum speed was less.

The first Beaufighter Mk Is began to reach the squadrons in September 1940, the first squadron being No 25, but these Beaufighters lacked AI radar and other equipment, and were still equipped with the drum-fed 20mm cannon; a situation which would continue for quite a few months.

Two aircraft (R2058 and R2061) were the first Merlin-powered prototypes, with R2058 being fitted with Merlin X engines at first, due to a shortage of the Merlin XX engines. This aircraft flew Merlin-powered at Hucknall in July, but it was not delivered to Bristol at Filton until 30 December 1940. Bristols then began trials to reduce the tendency to swing, including a high aspect-ratio fin and rudder, then a dorsal fin, but these modifications appear to have

had little effect. One Mk I aircraft (R2268) was fitted with a widened tailplane with end plate fins and rudders, but this was not made standard.

The idea of fighters carrying four-gun turrets took quite a long time to die, and against specification F18/40 secondary requirements, a Beaufighter Mk II (R2274) was submitted. This had been modified with AI radar, the two centre 20mm cannon removed and a Boulton Paul Type 'A' turret installed on top of the fuselage just behind the pilot; this was designated a Beaufighter Mk V. A second prototype Mk V (R2306) was similarly equipped and loaned to the squadrons for field trials. However, pilot's opinions were unfavourable, due to the turret restricting the pilot's emergency exit and because of the lower maximum speed. When R2274 was tested at the A&AEE it achieved a maximum top speed of 302 mph at 19,300 ft and 294 mph at 22,000 ft. The only means of entry or exit from the pilot's seat was through the roof hatch onto the mainplane, and obviously in an emergency this would have been extremely difficult.

The first production Mk II R2270 flew first on 22 March 1941 and was the first of 447, all built at Filton, with the first ones going to 604 and 600 Squadrons. Four USAAF Squadrons trained and flew Beaufighters before departing to the Middle East as night-fighters, and some were supplied to Fleet Air

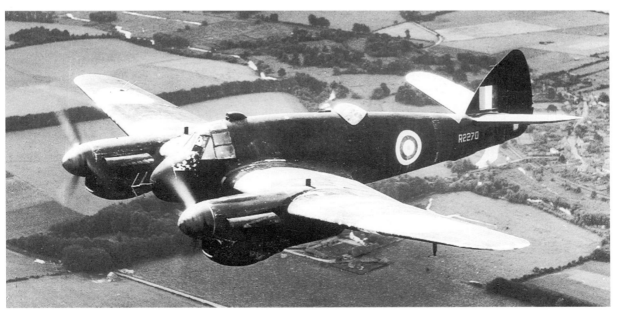

Beaufighter Mk.II R2270 with original fin. Fitted with early AI radar. (IWM)

Top: Beaufighter Mk.II with extended fin and rudder on trials at A&AEE. (RAF)
Above: Beaufighter Mk.II with extended dorsal fin on test at A&AEE. (RAE)

Arm Requirement Units.

The performance of a standard Mk II aircraft was tested at A&AEE on R2270, over a height range from 2,000 to 25,000 ft; at 8,000 ft the maximum speed was 295 mph; at 15,000 ft it was 316 mph; at 20,000 ft it was 328 mph, and at 24,000 ft the maximum speed was 320 mph.

Its construction was very similar to the Beaufort, with the fuselage of all metal semi-monocoque and built in three sections, front fuselage, rear or main fuselage and stern frame. The whole of it was of light alloy sheet riveted to formers and beaded angle stringers. Most of the formers are of lipped 'Z' section, which were notched to clear the stringers. The longerons were fitted port and starboard and two substantial keel members extended forward from the rear fuselage to the front fuselage. Armour plate was fitted forward and downwards from the windscreen, which was of armoured glass. Armour plate was also fitted in the rear fuselage aft of the

rear spar with an armoured bulkhead aft of the observer. The sternframe was of similar construction and carried the bridge piece that supported the rudder and elevator countershafts. Structure was built in for tailplane attachments, tailwheel unit and rudder attachments.

The mainplane was cantilever and built around two spars, with the centre plane spars continuous through the fuselage and butted to it. The spars were of extruded light alloy booms and Alclad web; the construction of the whole mainplane was of Alclad ribs, spanwise stiffeners of extruded beaded angle section covered by an Alclad skin.

The tail unit was of a cantilever tailplane, fin, rudder and elevators; some later aircraft had a dihedral tailplane. The tailplane was built in one piece with two Alclad channel section spars, flanged Alclad sheet ribs, covered by Alclad skin. The elevators were built in separate halves with a tubular spar, Alclad ribs and fabric covering. The fin was built around a front and rear fin post with a rear member of channel section with Alclad ribs and a covering of the same material. The rudder was of the same construction as the elevators and also fabric covered.

The undercarriage consisted of two independent units with a tailwheel unit. All were raised simultaneously by hydraulic power, with the main units retracting to the rear into the engine nacelles, while the tailwheel retracted forward and upwards into an underside of the stern-frame. The engine nacelles accommodated the Hercules engines, which were mounted on a welded steel tubular mounting, and similarly in regard to the Merlin engine.

The four 20mm Hispano Suiza cannon were mounted in the lower part of the fuselage, and were loaded from inside the fuselage. The original installation had drum fed magazines, but later models had beltfeed; the removal and installation of the guns being from outside the fuselage by means

of a long cowling each side.

Beaufighter Mk IIs were delivered in Special Night finish, but squadrons began to try out other schemes as the black finish tended to give an even darker silhouette on a clear night. Farnborough were also involved in this change of colours, and specific tests were carried out in March 1942 on squadron aircraft, with also changes in the size of the national markings.

No further orders for Merlin-powered Beaufighters were issued, for Hercules production was now established at Filton and shadow factories. Though R2061 was allotted to Rolls-Royce for trials with 'Exe' engine nacelles, and T3177 as a Griffon engine test bed, these were the last of the Rolls-Royce powered Beaufighters. The Beaufighter would continue in production powered by Hercules engines, built Bristol fashion, powered Bristol fashion. Known Servicewise as the 'Mighty Beau', she was an outstanding and strong aircraft.

Beaufighter Mk.V R2274 with Boulton-Paul 'A' turret. (RAF)

Bristol Beaufighter Mk. II.

Wingspan	57 feet 10 inches	(17.63 metres)
Wing area	503 sq.feet	(46.73 sq.metres)
Length	42 feet 6 inches	(12.95 metres)
Empty weight	13,800 lb	(6,272 kg)
Maximum loaded weight	21,000 lb	(9,545 kg)
Maximum speed at height	337 mph at 21,000 feet	(547 kph at 6,400 metres)
Service ceiling	30,000 feet	(9,144 metres)
Engine	two 1280 hp Merlin Mk.XXs inline	
Armament	four 20mm cannon and six 0.303-inch machine-guns	

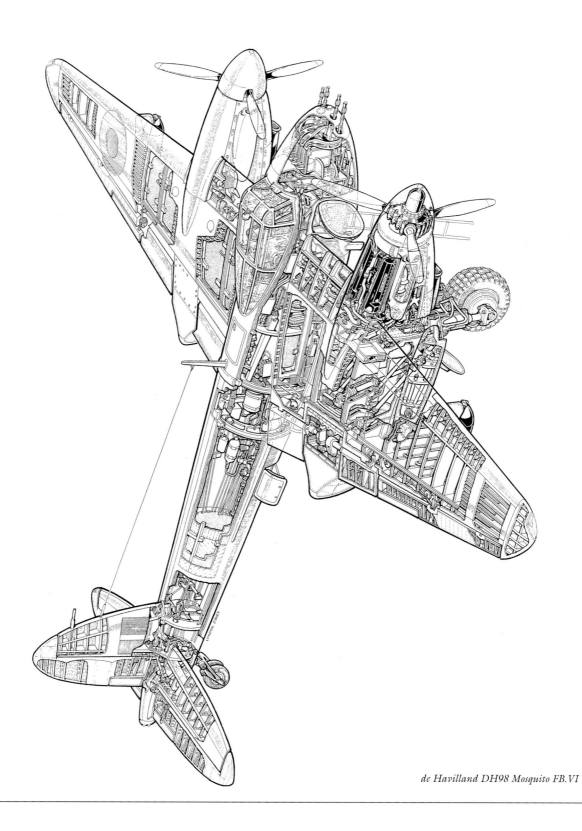

de Havilland DH98 Mosquito FB.VI

10

de Havilland Mosquito

The DH98 Mosquito has, since its design and development, established itself as the focus of admiration, the basis of many books, interested many enthusiasts (including the author) and pleased many pilots. It has also been the centre of a few myths; authors have embellished their books on the Mosquito with such sentences as 'Air Staff had blinkered outlook', 'de Havillands were unable to make headway against official policy' and 'Unarmed bomber concept viewed with distaste etc.' — all good hardhitting stuff! Yet the facts are that over 12 months prior to DH's approach to the Air Ministry, G.R. Volkert of Handley Page had in May 1937 submitted to the Ministry a 20 page memorandum on bombing policy and the unarmed bomber — a high speed unarmed bomber comparable in size to those envisaged in the P13/36 specification (Halifax and Manchester). This memo compared the saving in weight or the increase in bomb-load with the armed P13/36 bomber. The memorandum did the rounds of the various departments, and the

correspondence it raised, was in general, hardly that of disinterested, hidebound officials. Not only were discussions on the subject stimulated, (the Air Staff named the unarmed bomber for recognition purposes the 'Volkert') but also a paper was raised within the Air Staff called 'Consideration of the need for a light bomber for use in the RAF' — a high speed unarmed light bomber to replace the Blenheim, which had as its basic features many of these raised by Volkert's memorandum (Public Record Office file AIR2/2059).

De Havilland's approach to the Ministry on the unarmed bomber was made in October 1938, over 12 months after Volkert. This was followed by a further meeting between Air Staff and DH members on 23 November 1939, when Farren (DD/RDA) suggested that the aircraft be based on a long range reconnaissance type with provision for accommodating 1,000 lb of bombs. Within a few days a provisional draft operational requirement was sent to DH, in which the following points were made:

Mosquito Mk B.II ML914 'Nigeria' with slipper fuel tanks. (P.W. Porter)

(a) The aeroplane is primarily to be suitable for the duties of long distance high and low altitude reconnaissance, but it should be capable of easy conversion to operate as a bomber.

(b) The all-up weight of the aircraft is to be kept as low as possible, and a type not greatly in excess of 20,000 lb flying weight when operating as a bomber is visualised.

(c) Wooden or composite construction, employing materials and classes of labour which are not used to any great extent at present on standard aircraft for the Royal Air Force.

In September 1939 de Havillands had been studying a number of projects on the unarmed bomber theme powered by two engines, some powered by Napier Sabre and Dagger, with wingspans varying from 48 feet to 51 feet, but the final project submitted was based on two Merlin engines, which at an all-up weight of 15,075 lb gave a performance:

Maximum speed	419 mph at 20,000 feet.
Cruising speed	332 mph at 15,000 feet.

Ignoring various embellished stories in the past, it must be obvious to even the layman, that with a number of aircraft already in production, plus a restricted budget, that the Air Staff could not rush headlong into any project without discussions and evaluations, and so it turned out. This resulted with a positive decision being made and on 12 December 1939 a prototype was ordered against provisions of specification B1/40, the aircraft to be powered by two Merlin RM3SM engines. A mock-up conference was held on the 29th of the month, and after further conferences a contract (69990) was placed on 1 March 1940 for 50 aircraft.

Unfortunately, after Dunkirk, Beaverbrook as the Minister for Aircraft Production ordered work stopped on the DH98 (Mosquito), as priority on materials was restricted to the production of five basic types of aircraft, Hurricane, Spitfire, Blenheim, Wellington and Whitley — all the same, work continued in a subdued manner on the prototype, until on 12 July 1940 Beaverbrook was convinced by de Havilland of the small demands on the metal industry that the DH98 would make, and so it was officially reinstated as a priority.

The prototype (W4050) was completed in November 1940 at Hatfield, with taxying trials commencing on the 24th — the aircraft carrying at that time the marking EO234, being altered later to W4050. On 25 November Geoffrey de Havilland Jnr began the day with the usual taxying and braking tests, followed by a short 'hop'. On the same afternoon the aircraft loaded to a weight of 14,150 lb made its first take-off.

Back in July de Havilland was ordered to

DH.98 Mosquito prototype on first flight. (Author)

Coastal Command Mosquito FB being re-armed with rocket projectiles for North Sea strike. (RAF Museum)

complete one of the batch of fifty production aircraft as a fighter prototype, this was W4052; it was to mount four 20mm cannon and four 0.303-in machine-guns. Then on 16 November a separate contract was placed for fighter aircraft, based on specification F21/40. Eventually the first contract for fifty aircraft materialised as ten PRIs, thirty NF IIs and ten B IVs.

The prototype W4050 had, when first tested, short engine nacelles which terminated at the wing trailing edge. This was found after further testing, to be the cause of tailplane buffeting, and was rectified — after trials with various shapes and sizes of fairings — by a lengthened nacelle trailing edge aft of the wing. Tests at A&AEE were in general complimentary, and W4050 was in the course of its career modified with many stores, all manner of equipment including a mock-up of a four-gun turret, and was re-engined with a number of Marks of Merlin, including the Mks 61 and 77. With Merlin 61 power in November 1941 it achieved a speed of 432 mph at 17,000 ft in level flight. Fortunately, W4050 can now be seen retired at Salisbury Hall museum.

The intruder role had first been exploited in World War Two by the Germans in 1940–41, and British experience in this role commenced with the Blenheim, then expanded by the Beaufighter. With the introduction of the Mosquito further expansion was obvious, for its longer range would allow even deeper penetration; and so the NF II (Special) carrying two short-vane 500 lb bombs in the bay behind the cannons became the FB VI, and this Mark became the version of greatest production, 2,289 in all. The first FB VIs were the Series I, carrying two 250 lb bombs in the shortened bomb-bay and two more 250 lb bombs slung under the wings, and the Series II followed, in which two 500 lb bombs were slung internally and two 500 lb bombs slung under the strengthened wings . . . introduced first on the B Mk V.

The FII prototype W4052 was fitted experimentally with a mock-up of a four-gun turret of Bristol manufacture — apparently, someone still had a desire to fit four-gun turrets on fighters — and it was estimated that such an installation would lower the maximum speed by 10 mph, ignoring the extra weight. In any case, the project was dropped and the FII went into production with the normal armament, although one further project that was considered was the fitting of upward-firing fixed guns. The night-fighter versions were originally finished in a standard 'lamp black' tone, then a smooth black tone was tried, but both tended to emphasise the silhouette effect on a clear night, so was changed to a Sea Grey

Mosquito B.II MW335 in Middle East, fitted with slipper fuel tanks. (L. Jones)

finish with Dark Green camouflage on top. Various night-fighter versions were introduced later, such as the NFXII, NFXIII, NFXVII and NFXIX, all fitted with British or USA built AI radar.

With the shortage of PRIs, due initially to the changes in the original contract, a number of FIIs were converted to the PR role, some being converted locally. A number of BIVs were also converted to PRIVs to overcome the shortage, as photo recce of targets at long range was in some cases beyond the range of the PR Spitfires; the first two BIVs converted were DZ411 and DZ419.

In the anti-shipping role, the most potent striker must have been the Mosquito FBXVIII, which was a FBVI modified to carry a 57mm cannon in the nose instead of the 20mm cannon. The 57mm cannon was an adaptation of a standard anti-tank gun and fired 25 shells in 20 seconds. Only one prototype and twenty-six FBXVIIIs were produced.

High altitude development of the Mosquito commenced with the development of the Merlin 61 range of engines, and the flight of W4050 with Merlin 61s at a height of 40,000 ft, which surpassed even DH's original estimates of the Mosquito. The first high altitude version was the production BIX, which commenced coming off production in March 1943 and featured Merlin 61 engines and a pressure cabin. The first was MP469, and was modified by the removal of its transparent nose and grafting on a

NFII nose and armament, a certain amount of lightening was carried out and the wingtips extended to give a span of 59 feet.

PR development was also improved with the introduction of the Merlin 61, with the PRVIII making its first flight on 20 October 1942, then the PRIX coming off the production line in April 1943, the latter being a development of the BIX version.

Originally in 1942, day bomber Mosquito casualties were in the order of 16 per cent, due mainly to the way, or manner of operation; this forced a revision of operating procedure, with flights at high level on clear days and at lower levels as cloud cover permitted; so that by the end of 1942 the casualties had dropped to 8 per cent. This improved further during the war, so that by the war's end the Mosquito had the lowest casualties in Bomber Command of 0.63 per cent. But the initial casualty rate must be considered against the aircraft's success rate of sorties and bombs on target, and the type of target that they were attacking.

In regard to structural failures, the Accident Investigation reports stated that the Mosquito was relatively high, and there were periods when several breakups occurred in the UK every month. In the majority of cases extensive disintegration of the airframe occurred, with the majority occurring during recovery from dives, some from violent manoeuvres, with others due to a variety of causes, including elevator failures, undercarriage doors breaking away from the nacelle and stalling.

With the intention by the Air Staff to re-equip some of the Far East squadrons with Mosquito aircraft in the near future (the distances in the Far East being ideal for the 'long legs' of the Mosquito), four F2s were sent to India for weathering tests. Then on 4 December 1943 'A' Flight of 27 Squadron began to equip with Mosquitos; it is obvious from the squadron records that the Mosquito did not measure up to the Beaufighter in the aircrew and groundcrew's opinions, and their preference for their Beaufighters against the Mosquito appeared to be due to the latter's unglueing wooden joints and the engines, which were stated as fractious. A similar experience was borne out by 47 Squadron when they moved to the Far East from the Middle East and converted to Mosquitos. Yet the Mosquito was to prove its worth in the long distance PR role, and would become the Air Ministry's standard bomber/strike aircraft in the Far East after the war's end.

While in Europe the Mosquito received, probably initially from the Press, the name 'Wooden Wonder', in the Far East it gained the name 'Termites Delight' — some say jealousy by operators of other aircraft. There is no doubt however that it never achieved in the Far East the reputation of the Beaufighter regarding serviceability, and was withdrawn at one

period for examination of the glued structure, after a number of structural failures.

This in no way detracts from its fine achievements in Europe, where it operated in many roles, and one of the most satisfying from Bomber Command's point of view must have been with 100 Group in the intruder role. With Pathfinder Force it commenced a new technique in the manner of marking, and Air Vice-Marshal D. Bennett was unstinting in his praise of it.

Its main construction was of wood, with a one-piece two-spar mainplane, having a Piercy modified section RAF 34 aerofoil, with the spars having laminated spruce booms and plywood webs. The spars were joined by spruce and plywood ribs in compression and nose ribs and front leading edge built into a D nose. The ailerons and flaps were of similar construction. All the wood structure was covered with Madapolam fabric, doped over and painted.

The fuselage was of oval section and was built in two halves, split vertically for ease of assembly of equipment and electrical looms. The outer skin was a balsa sandwich of outer and inner plywood skins, and supported by seven bulkheads. The tail unit had an all-plywood covered tailplane and fin with the rudder and elevators being of wood construction fabric covered — though metal skinning of these components was introduced in 1943 to improve handling at high speed in dives and evasive manoeuvres. The plywood covered fuselage and tail

Mosquito Mk.33 of Israeli Air Force during transit. (Author)

Mosquito Mk.39 target tug after conversion at Gal Hanworth, with modified nose and drogue winch in bomb-bay. (Author)

unit were, like the mainplanes, covered with Madapolam fabric, doped and painted. The construction is best shown in the sectioned drawings, which more adequately explain it.

The undercarriage was unusual for an aircraft of that period and design, in that it utilised rubber blocks in compression instead of the normal oleo-pneumatic type strut, yet the undercarriage would appear from reports to have given little trouble.

The first Mosquito in which the two-speed two-stage Merlin was matched with the Mk XIX airframe was MM686, becoming the prototype NF30 in 1944. The production NF30 models were powered with the Merlin 70 series engines. Due to problems with the exhaust shrouding of the engines, causing hot air to be deflected into the radiator, and resulting in overheating, the NF30 did not see operational service until late 1944. This overheating problem was only peculiar to the Merlin 60/70 series engines.

By mid-June 1943 the Mosquito, modified to carry the 4,000 lb bomb, was being readied for flight; this was DZ594. The first flight of this modified Mk IV took place in early July; it was despatched to A&AEE for acceptance trials, returning from there to Hatfield for further modification. But it was not until October 1943 that the final decision was made for the

production and conversion of bomber airframes to this configuration. The 4,000 lb bomb-carrying version was finalised with the introduction of the B.Mk XVI aircraft, powered with 72 to 76 series Merlins, having a pressure cabin and an all-up weight at take-off of 25,200 lb. The first flight of the first production B Mk XVI was on 1 January 1944. The B Mk IV modified versions suffered initially from longitudinal instability with a bomb-load of four 500 lb bombs, and in this condition were test flown by A&AEE pilots, who reported their dissatisfaction. Modifications to the tail surfaces were tried and an improvement effected by fitting larger horn balances to the elevators.

In July 1943 the FB Mk XVIII powered with Merlin 25s for anti-shipping activities first flew. This model with rocket projectile installations was first flown in September 1943, and it had an all-up weight at take-off of 22,255 lb. At the conclusion of the trials with this model so equipped, the decision was made for the incorporation of this type of installation points on Coastal Command FB aircraft.

Also in July 1943 in the photo-reconnaissance field the PRXVI with a fuel capacity of 860 gallons first flew; followed later on by the PR 34 as a very long range reconnaissance aircraft with a fuel capacity of 1,269 gallons, no armour or protection, powered by Merlin 114 engines and an all-up weight of 25,500 lb. The range of this model was in excess of any other PR aircraft, and it could cruise at 325 mph at a height of 31,500 ft.

The Mosquito was produced both in Australia and Canada as well as in the United Kingdom. In Canada the decision was made to build the bomber version, though this was later amended to include the fighter-bomber version as well as trainers; Canadian built aircraft being used in the European theatre of operations. Australian production centred on PR, FB and trainer aircraft.

For over two years in Europe the Mosquito was almost unstoppable, day or night, by any enemy aircraft in level flight, and the following table explains why.

With the introduction of the OBOE radar bombing aid the Mosquito was the only aircraft ideally suited for its operation, for the system range was limited by the altitude to which it could be carried. So in July 1942 equipping of the Mosquito with this radar aid began. In February 1944 H2S was installed in the Mk XVI aircraft, and began a career as a marker aircraft for Mosquito spoof night raids; in this state the Mosquito all-up weight was 24,064 lb.

So the Mosquito, armed with 20mm cannon, bombs, rockets, or a 57mm cannon was a formidable weapon. With a 4,000 lb bomb it could strike at Berlin without a fighter escort — an outstanding aircraft by any standard.

Mosquito T.3 RR299 (G-ASKH) at Hawarden 1976. (Author)

Performance comparisons of some Mosquito marks

	FII	BIV	NF30	BXVI	PR 34
Wingspan	41 ft 2 in	54 ft 2 in	54 ft 2 in	54 ft 2 in	54 ft 2 in
Wing area	436.3 sq ft	454 sq ft	454 sq ft	454 sq ft	454 sq ft
Length	41 ft 2 in	41 ft 2 in	41 ft 2 in	41 ft 2 in	41 ft 2 in
Aspect-ratio	6.7	6.7	6.7	6.7	6.7
Tare weight	13,355 lb	13,400 lb	15,240 lb	14,901 lb	15,631 lb
Loaded weight	18,649 lb	22,380 lb	23,275 lb	25,200 lb	25,500 lb
Maximum speed	370 mph	385 mph	424 mph	408 mph	425 mph
Cruising speed	265 mph	280 mph	380 mph	300 mph	315 mph
Operational ceiling	36,000 ft	27,000 ft	35,000 ft	29,500 ft	36,000 ft

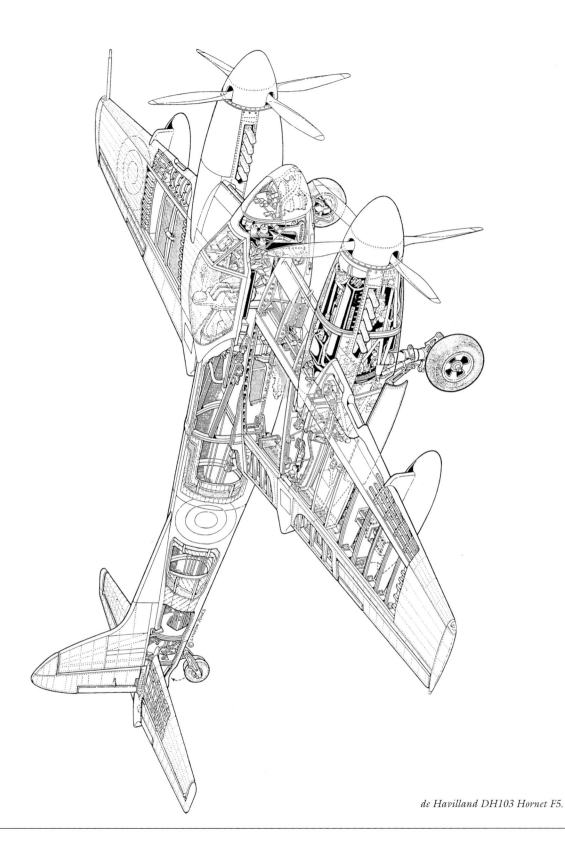

de Havilland DH103 Hornet F5.

11

de Havilland Hornet

As aviation enthusiasts know, aviation does at times have a peculiar habit of standing on its head, and this is certainly illustrated in the history of the Westland Whirlwind and the de Havilland Hornet. The Hornet when introduced had 'handed' engines, and radiators concealed in the leading edge of the wing centre section — all acceptable to the Air Staff. Yet when the Whirlwind fighter to specification F37/35 was introduced in 1938, and with those same features, it was not only criticised, but handed engines considered not necessary by the powers that be!

Whereas the Whirlwind was denigrated by the single-seat biplane fighter barons of the time, the Hornet was accepted in 1945 whole heartedly as a further faster fighter design — so the twin-engined (piston engine) single-seat fighter theme that began with the Whirlwind, finished with the Hornet — the fastest one of all.

Design commenced in late 1942, with the project envisaged as a fast single-seater fighter for long range use, with the possibility at its eventual use in the Far East as a Beaufighter replacement. By January 1943 the mock-up was completed, and though inspected by MAP it was not until June that permission was granted for work to proceed; then specification F12/43 was issued, so giving official back-up to a private venture project. By the beginning of 1944 the fuselage shell was completed, followed shortly by the mainplane, and the first prototype (RR915) had its first flight on 28 July 1944. On its contractor's trials flown by Geoffrey de Havilland Jnr it reached a maximum speed of 485 mph. The second prototype (RR919) flew shortly afterwards. A production order was now under consideration, but due to the war nearing its end its entry into service was dragged out. The two prototypes were at this time fitted with Merlin 130 engines in both nacelles — same direction of rotation.

A&AEE tests on the Hornet F1 determined that the view over the nose was good, brakes powerful,

Hornet F1 RR919 illustrates its neatness, sleakness, wide undercarriage and slipper fuel tanks. (IWM)

Sea Hornet F1 VZ664 in Far East. (P.W. Porter)

easy to taxy and no take-off problem. Against this it was deficient in longitudinal stability, had rudder overbalance under sideslip conditions, and on engine failure the aircraft quickly entered a dive. A certain amount of re-design took place and a second production F1 went to the A&AEE for trials in September 1945, the production aircraft having Merlin 130 (port) and Merlin 131 (starboard) engines. Although not completely satisfactory, rudder overbalance still being a feature, a total delivery of sixty F1s began in April 1945, serial numbered PX210 to PX288.

The first unit to receive the Hornet F1 was 64 Squadron, but not until the early part of 1946; even then only three more squadrons received them, Nos 19, 41 and 65. In 1951 the Hornets were withdrawn from these squadrons and transferred to the Far East, where they were used to re-equip 33, 45 and 80 Squadrons, which were engaged in the Malayan campaign.

A small number of PR2 aircraft were built, but not issued to any squadron. The design was then revised into the F3, which featured a dorsal fin and increased fuel capacity. This was followed by the FR4, which mounted a F52 camera in a vertical position and retained its fighter capability.

The total production run of the Hornet was 204, which included F3 models from PX289 to WF967. The first F3 aircraft to be selected for trials at A&AEE was PX312. The F3s handling was

described as easy to taxi, good view over the nose; powerful brakes; easy take-off, keeping straight with the rudder, providing that the throttles were opened up evenly (the throttle levers had short travel for the power obtained); the tail came up easily and the aircraft could be flown off at 110 knots (127 mph). The aircraft was easy to fly under all loads and conditions, with ailerons light and responsive at all speeds except at the lower end of the scale. The elevators were moderately light except when trimmed in the dive, when the pull force for recovery was high. The rudder was light, but at high speeds had to be used with care, as it was possible to induce yaw and impose excessive strain on the airframe structure. When flying on asymmetric power at or near the critical speed with full rudder and trim, rudder tramping could be experienced. On the F1 under similar conditions or in a sideslip, rudder overbalance could be experienced — on some Hornet F1s retrospective modification action fitted a dorsal fin. The stall on the Hornet was quite straightforward, for warning of the stall was usually given by slight buffeting, and at the stall the nose dropped gently. The stall at maximum landing weight with power 'off' and with the undercarriage and flaps down was 95 knots; and with power 'on' under similar conditions the stall was 85 knots.

It was quickly realised that with its opposed rotating propellers and performance the Hornet had distinct possibilities as a potent fleet fighter. So three early F1 airframes were selected for conversion, and Heston Aircraft Ltd were chosen as the sub-contractor to carry out the conversions, which included hydraulically-powered folding wings, high drag flaps and an arrester hook. At the end of 1944 specification N5/44 was issued calling for a carrier-borne fighter, to which de Havilland tendered their Hornet Mk 20. The first prototype (PX212) Sea Hornet had its first flight on 19 April 1945, and was delivered to the A&AEE on 10 May 1945, too late for the European or Asian war. Trials determined a magnificent view all round, no weathercocking on landing, and no taxying or take-off problem, but the ailerons were not acceptable for deck landings. On 10 August 1945 it commenced its first deck landings on HMS *Ocean* at an all-up weight of 14,545 lb. The second prototype was PX214: this aircraft and the first prototype did not have folding wings, so as to speed up the development programme. The third prototype (PX219) was the first one to be fully navalised.

The first production Sea Hornet F20 (TT186) had its maiden flight on 13 August 1946. The first squadron with them was formed on 1 June 1947 but only 801 Squadron was completely equipped, though other units had them on their strength. Only seventy-eight were built and the first unit of them

was embarked in HMS *Implacable* in 1949.

The fuselage, like its predecessor the Mosquito, was constructed of a sandwich of balsa wood between plywood skins, forming a monocoque with seven bulkheads. The fuselage was built in halves to allow assembly of equipment, looms etc., before being joined at the top and bottom centre lines, where it was reinforced with spruce and plywood members. Cutaways in the fuselage accommodated the cockpit canopy and wings. The fuselage was covered by madopolam and doped over. The cockpit canopy was composed of a windscreen of bulletproof laminated glass and a moulded Perspex sliding cover.

The mainplane was built around two 'I' section spars of composite metal and wood construction, with a covering of stressed plywood top skin reinforced by spanwise spruce stringers, and a light alloy bottom skin reinforced by extruded dural stringers. The leading edges, outboard of the engines, were made up and assembled to the mainplanes as units, and comprised a metal skin and ribs reinforced by spanwise stringers. Flaps extended from the fuselage side to the inboard end of the ailerons, being of all metal construction and hydraulically operated. The ailerons were of all metal construction with single spars to which were riveted ribs and nose formers.

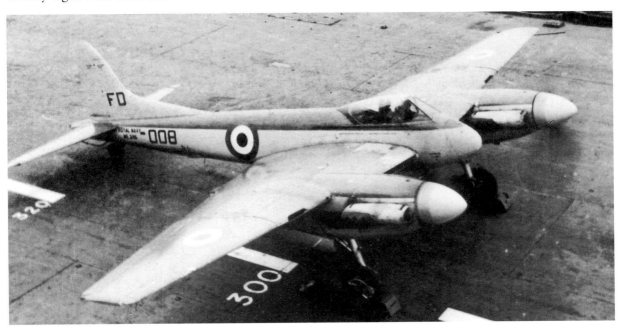

Sea Hornet landing on HMS Indomitable *1946. (K. Glover)*

The tail unit was of conventional cantilever design, with a one-piece tail plane of symmetrical aerofoil, having two 'U' section spars, light alloy ribs and spanwise stringers; the whole was covered by stressed light alloy skin. The elevators were interchangeable of all metal construction, comprising a spar, pressed light alloy ribs and stiffeners with a stressed skin covering. The single fin was a symmetrical section metal structure having two 'U' section spars, pressed light alloy ribs and stringers covered with a light alloy skin; on the F3 a dorsal fairing was added on forward of the fin, being bolted to ferrules in the fuselage and riveted to the fin structure. The rudder again was of light metal construction and covering, being based on a metal spar and trailing edge with ribs and stiffeners riveted on.

The fuel system consisted of eight self-sealing tanks which were housed in the wings, with two on each side of each engine bay, all being accessible from underneath the wing by detachable panels. The total capacity of the fuel system was 432 gallons on the Mk F1 and 540 gallons on the Mk F3, with a long-range capacity of 832 gallons (two 200-gallon drop tanks) and 740 gallons (two 100-gallon drop tanks) on the F1 and F3 respectively.

The alighting gear consisted of two interchangeable single wheel units of a single shock absorber mounted upon a triangulated structure that was secured to the mainplane at the front spar and engine mounting. Each unit was provided with a single joint radius rod, stabiliser and hydraulic jack. The shock absorbers were similar to the Mosquito type — rubber in compression. The tailwheel unit was also of the rubber compression shock absorber type, fully castoring and retracting into the rear fuselage, being mounted on the rear fuselage bulkhead 7. The Sea Hornet undercarriage differed in that Lockheed airdraulic legs replaced the

Hornet F Mk.IIIs of 33/45 Squadrons at Butterworth, Malaya, prior to being scrapped 1955. (P.W. Porter)

compression rubber type.

A night-fighter version was next needed by the end of the war to cover fleet operations, so specification N21/45 was issued for a FAA two-seat night-fighter which would be radar equipped. The Sea Hornet being already an accepted fleet fighter it was a natural progression to modify a Hornet airframe to fulfil this role. The first prototype was a conversion of a Mk 1F PX230, and again the Heston Aircraft Co were called upon to carry out the conversion. This again was hydraulically-powered folding wings, and external Vee frame with forged steel arrester hook (penalty approximately 500 lb increase). The radar set was positioned in an extended nose in front of the pilot, and the radar operator in a separate cockpit well behind the pilot. Entry to this cockpit was from below the fuselage. The engine exhausts were shrouded in a manner similar to that used on the earlier Halifaxes. The folding wings were introduced on the second prototype PX239.

Prolonged testing was carried out at the Naval AFDU and at the Service Trials Unit, with the first deck landing being made on HMS *Illustrious* on 25 October 1948, followed immediately by night flying trials. During testing at A&AEE of the first prototype (PX230) NF21, during a high 'g' test on 16 May 1947 an engine detached itself, followed by the whole aircraft starting to disintegrate; fortunately the cockpit area stayed complete long enough for the pilot to bale out successfully — but a little low.

There is no doubt that the Hornet was a pilot's aeroplane, and the fastest piston-engined fighter aircraft to serve with the RAF, and with its excess of power and good all-round view it was superb for aerobatics. Pilots exulted in its superb performance and handling, the feel of an outstanding and first-class fighter aircraft, often illustrated by looping with one engine feathered — beautiful to look at and a wonderful flying machine — the last and fastest twin piston-engined fighter in the RAF.

Hornet F1 PX210 in Far East colour scheme. (IWM)

Comparison over four marks of Hornet

	F1	F3	F20	NF21
Wingspan	45 ft	45 ft	45 ft	45 ft
Wing area	361 sq ft	361 sq ft	361 sq ft	361 sq ft
Length	36 ft 8 in	36 ft 8 in	36 ft 8 in	37 ft
Engine (two) Mark.	130/131	130/131	133/134	133/134
Power (each)	2,030 bhp	2,030 bhp	2,030 bhp	2,030 bhp
All-up weight	17,600 lb	20,900 lb	18,250 lb	19,530 lb
Maximum speed	470 mph	472 mph	431 mph	426 mph
Service ceiling	37,500 ft	35,000 ft	35,000 ft	36,500 ft

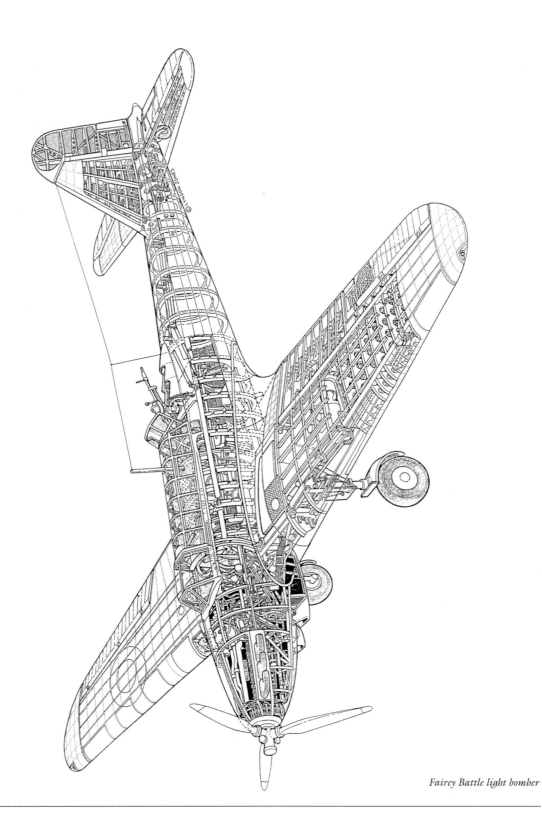

Fairey Battle light bomber

12

Fairey Battle

The Fairey Battle must be *the* aircraft that critics of the Air Staff, and historians, love to criticise, yet have either not the knowledge or interest to explain fully the reasons for its failure in combat. It has even been suggested that the Air Staff should have bought the Henley instead (the Henley was not designed to the same specification). Whether they had had Henleys or even Junkers Ju 87s, they could not have survived the German onslaught on France without a heavy fighter escort, and the Battle did not have these fighter escorts, operating in a scenario where the enemy held air superiority.

In 1932 the Air Ministry were considering the need for replacement of the Hawker Hart and Hind day bombers, and so in August of that year asked a number of aircraft manufacturers to consider outline studies for a fast day bomber. Fairey Aviation visualised it as a fast, compact two-seat monoplane powered by their Fairey P12 Prince V12 liquid-cooled engine.

In April 1933 the Air Staff issued specification P27/32, which was more definitive, and to Fairey's

surprise dictated a rather larger airframe than was envisaged under the outline studies. The Head of Design at Faireys was M.J.O. Lobelle, who was a Belgian by birth and like R. Fairey prepared to utilise any idea or design improvement, irrespective of its country of origin. With regard to the Prince engine, the Chief Engine Designer was Capt. G. Forsyth, and independent engine design had begun under him in 1930, and developed into the Prince engine. This engine in 1934 was in direct competition with Rolls-Royce, and further advanced in development and satisfactory engine running than the PV12.

Lobelle, having viewed the P27/32 specification, came to the conclusion that such an increased equipment load would require a larger airframe with a larger span, so sent a number of design memos to the Air Ministry to stress the need to change the specification, or the need to use two engines if the performance of the specification was to be met — otherwise an inferior performance would ensue. The Air Ministry refused to budge away from the requirements, and so Fairey began a number of

Fairey Battle prototype K4303 in flight over Fairey's airfield. Note the original canopy shape. (Fairey)

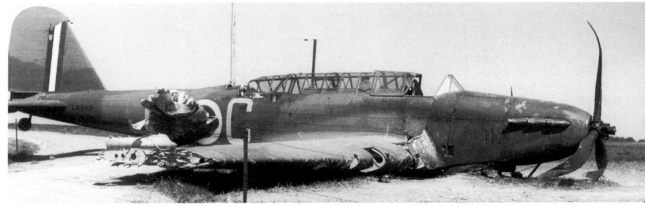

Top: Battles of Belgium Air Force. Note air gunner's 0.5-in FN machine-gun and extended air intake. (J. De Vos)
Above: Battle L5540 of 150 Squadron shot down on 10 May 1940 attacking German columns. (Bundesarchiv)

design studies. Eight in all were eventually considered, and these were paralleled by projects based on twin engines, with various wing positions and shapes.

On 24 October 1933 an alteration was made to the requirements by the Air Staff, which increased 'normal' and 'long-range' requirements to bring it in line with the specification B9/32 twin-engined bomber. The object of this project being to make a comparison between the P27/32 and B9/32 bombers!

Invitation to tender was sent out to twelve manufacturers, but only seven submitted designs; these were Armstrong-Whitworth, Bristol, Fairey, Gloster, Hawker, Vickers and Westland. The Fairey tender design was near to the specifications, but they also submitted a number of other proposals, and

with their design claimed a maximum speed of 223 mph at 15,000 feet against the specification's requirement of 195 mph at 15,000 feet. Though the specification had been written with the R-R. Griffon engine in mind, Fairey was anxious that its Prince engine should be installed in its design.

The design of the Battle was such that, whether it was a single or twin-engined design, all main structural components would be suitable for all Fairey's P27/32 projects, for instance, the single leg retracting undercarriage was chosen for the reason that it could be almost fully retracted into the mainplane chosen or into an engine nacelle if it was necessary. The Ministry accepted the single-engined proposal from Fairey, and on 11 June 1934 placed a contract for one prototype each from Fairey and Armstrong-Whitworth, with the delivery to be within fifteen months (September 1935). Fairey was under the impression that its prototype would be powered with the Prince 12 engine, but no contract covered this.

On 18 October 1934 Richard Fairey wrote to the Ministry asking for a postponement of the delivery date until December 1935, as having toured the USA he wished to carry out a re-design based on knowledge acquired; this was followed on the next day with performance calculations and general arrangement drawings of the re-design; this indicated a change from a semi-cantilever mainplane to a pure cantilever design; bombs enclosed inside the wings; improved airflow over the cockpits (one long enclosed canopy), structure weight heavier and performance slightly down. On 19 January 1935 the Air Ministry notified Fairey of their acceptance, followed by the issue of specification 23/35 covering further development; this updated the aircraft and added a further crew member, who would be a wireless operator air gunner. Fairey opposed this as further increasing the load and degrading the performance; but the Ministry insisted that the third crew member was necessary to man the rear gun, when the aircraft was on the bombing run and the observer engaged in bomb dropping. Fairey disputed the whole concept of the light bomber specification, but the Ministry remained adamant.

In 1935 when Scheme C was being discussed, the sub-Committee on Air Parity recommended that an immediate order for 150 Battles should be placed; this was not acted on at the time, and it was not until 23 May 1936 that the first production order was placed. The Air Staff by that time had realised that the specification was not going to produce a high performance day bomber, but rather than cancel because of the bad impression this would create, allowed the contract to continue.

When the prototype was first flown on 10 March 1936 it was as advanced in design as any similar light bomber anywhere. The flying was carried out by Flight Lieutenant Chris Staniland, and the aircraft was powered by a Merlin Mk I driving a fixed pitch Fairey Reed propeller. Martlesham Heath trials indicated that the Battle prototype was easy, simple and normal for take-off and landing; easy to 'motor in' on full load; ailerons light and responsive at slow speeds and remaining so up to maximum speed; the rudder was sluggish at take-off and slow speeds, and as speed was increased became heavier but had quicker response; the elevators were light and responsive at all speeds except take-off.

On 28 July 1936 a conference was held at the Air Ministry on the A&AEE report, followed on 1 August with a report on the amount of extra work required on the Battle to satisfy the Air Staff. DTD writing to Fairey on the 9 October instructing him on what flight trials to carry out before sending the Battle to A&AEE for full tests; then the specification 14/36 was issued for the production Battle Mk I.

Official trials indicated that all-up weight of the aircraft was now placed at 10,770 lb, and at this weight the aircraft met the requirements for a 1,000

Battle K9264 of 103 Squadron on recce over France 1940. Note incorrect position of roundel. (RAF)

Battle K7558 on trials at A&AEE 1939. (RAE)

mile range carrying 1,000 lb bombs at 200 mph at 15,000 ft. The increase in all-up weight was not helped by the fact that the Merlin I was down on power — the Merlin I engines being diverted from the Hurricane production.

The Battle was easy to fly, although the pilot's cockpit on a Summer's day did get a little warm and smelly from the engine fumes. It was easy to maintain, even by personnel used to aircraft of an earlier period, such as the Hart. Its construction was robust, having the thickest wing skin of any British aircraft of that period. The fuselage basic construction was an oval monocoque, comprised of light alloy hoop frames, which were pressings with notches to accept the four special longerons and the preformed skins. The skin was an example of ingenuity, being rolled and cut in strips with the upper edge rolled to form an integral stringer, so no separate stringers were required.

The mainplanes were of two-spar construction throughout, being of girder form changing to flanged beam in the outer section of the outer wings, the mainplane being built in five sections, with the centre section integral with the fuselage. The ailerons were of metal construction fabric covered. The flaps were of the split trailing edge type, metal constructed and skinned. The bomb-load was 1,000 lb, and was carried on four 250 lb carriers, which were hydraulically retracted into the wings and covered by the bomb-doors during retraction.

The tail unit was conventional comprising tailplane, elevator, fin and rudder, all of metal construction with the fin and tailplane having three

spars and being dural covered. The elevator and rudder were fabric covered.

The alighting gear consisted of two independent retractable units and a non-retracting tailwheel. The mainwheel units were retracted to the rear and upwards hydraulically, leaving a small portion of the wheels exposed.

The defensive armament consisted of a fixed forward-firing Browning 0.303-in machine-gun mounted in the starboard mainplane between ribs 2 and 3; a Vickers 'K' or Lewis 0.303-in machine-gun on a Fairey free-mounting for the air gunner. During discussions at the Air Ministry early on in the design, consideration had been given to deleting the forward

Radio operator air-gunner of Battle wielding his 0.303-inch 'K' gun. (R. Pearce)

gun, but it was left for 'crew morale' reasons! During the 1939–40 French campaign it was found necessary to install a further Vickers 'K' gun on a rather crude mounting in the bomb-aimer's position firing to the rear — what with no self-sealing fuel tanks and the aircraft's slow speed, such extra armament was totally ineffective.

The Battle was one of the key types of the RAF expansion scheme, being the only light bomber developed to an Air Ministry specification ready to go into production. While the prototype was built at Fairey's factory at Hayes, a new production line was set up at Heaton Chapel (Cheshire), and by 1938, one at Austin's shadow factory. By December 1940 over 3,100 Battles had been produced, which was two and a half times the number originally intended to be ordered under Scheme F of 1936.

At Fairey's request the Stockport factory carried out a number of design studies in 1937, based on the use of large quantities of Battle assemblies; these studies centred around a twin-engined fighter-bomber powered by either Merlin engines or Fairey's own P24 engine, but achieved no response from the Air Ministry, (the P24 being the first project to appear from Forsyth's contra-rotating twin-engine theme of 1935). It was estimated that if the P24 had been developed to its maximum rating, the Battle with one P24 would have had a maximum level speed of approximately 365 mph.

The Battle was the first service aircraft to carry the 'shadow shading' camouflage of green and brown, known in the RAF as 'sand and spinach'; and during the Munich crisis of 1938 the national markings were replaced with concentric rings of red and blue only.

Regarding production of the Battle already mentioned, in April 1939 it was found necessary to issue stop-gap orders for Battles in order to maintain industrial capacity and labour force, whilst tooling and jigging up for replacement aircraft types. Some of these orders were for trainers and target tug aircraft. A number of aircraft were also diverted for use as engine test beds, as their strong construction made them capable of accepting engines of far higher output than the Merlin of that period. For instance, there was K9222 at Rolls-Royce with the 'Exe' engine; K9270 at Napiers with the Sabre engine; N2042 and N2184 at Bristol on Hercules development; as well as K2234 at Rolls-Royce with a Merlin XII engine and chin radiator.

Also by then, Fairey had its own K9370 with the P24 engine installed, which, although flown at A&AEE and RAE Farnborough, has had no performance figures released. It had completed its 50-hour test in the early Autumn of 1939 and logged approximately eighty-seven hours flying in the UK, before being despatched to Wright Air Force Base USA on 5 December 1941. Approximately 250 hours flying had been completed before it was returned to RAE.

The day before war commenced, 2 September 1939, twelve Battle squadrons of the RAF AASF arrived in France at airfields in the Reims area, with two Hurricane squadrons to give defence! (the Luftwaffe had only 1,000 Bf 109s for the attack in

Battle P2177 of VX Squadron at Vraux, France in 1939. Bomb load on ground under wings. (Author)

the West.) The Air Staff as well as Bomber Command were fully aware of the restricted operations that the Battle could accomplish in the face of fighter opposition. When operations did commence, the Battles were usually without fighter escort, the normal procedure being that the fighters patrolled the target area; this resulted in the Battles being picked off en route or falling victims to the flak — even Junkers Ju 87 aircraft did not have that problem, there were always enough Bf 109 fighter escorts, and the German flak was far more effective than the British.

After the Battle's evacuation from France, some of the squadrons were converted to other types of aircraft, but some Polish squadrons were formed with the Battles as their initial equipment, and proceeded to use them to attack the barge concentrations in the French Channel ports, which were part of the German 'Sea Lion' invasion fleet.

After their withdrawal from operational flying, numbers of them were used for training and target towing, some being sent to Canada and Australia for the training schemes in those countries. A small number in Canada were also fitted with Bristol mid-upper turrets for gunnery training. No 98 Squadron took their Battles to Iceland to join Coastal Command in the defence of that large island; while at RAE Farnborough a number were used for various experiments throughout the war, including the dropping of aerial mines and flying into suspended balloon barrage cables. This latter duty the Battle shared with its younger brother, the P4/34; severe damage being done to the airframe by the collision of the cables with the mainplane, sometimes cutting through to the main spar!

By 1939 the Fairey Battle was obsolete, yet was called upon to operate in an environment where the enemy held total air superiority. After its baptism of fire it continued earning its keep in other roles — maybe it kept going because it was an 'old gentleman's' aeroplane — it was well built but too heavy for one Merlin engine of early mark.

Merlin Mk.III powerplant of Battle. (Author)

Battle trainer, two cockpit canopies as on original bomber design. (IWM)

Comparison between specification and aircraft

	Specification	*Prototype*	*Production*
	P27/32	*K4303*	*K7558*
Bare weight	6,300 lb	6,647 lb	6,700 lb
All-up weight	Not stated	10,770 lb	10,898 lb
Max speed at 15,000 ft	Not less than 195 mph	252 mph	252 mph
Cruising speed	Not stated	220 mph	219 mph
Maximum speed	Not stated	257 mph	252 mph
Service ceiling	Not less than 22,000 ft	25,200 ft	26,500 ft
Take-off distance over 50 ft barrier	500 yds	445 yds	690 yds
Landing distance over 50 ft barrier	200 yds	250 yds	350 yds
Range at 15,000 ft	720 mile	904 miles @ 200 mph	1,050 miles @ 200 mph

Comparison between the Battle and Ju 87B in 1940

	Battle	*Junkers Ju 87B*
Wingspan	54 ft	45 ft 3⅓ in
Wing area	422 sq ft	343 sq ft
All-up weight	10,898 lb	9,560 lb
Bomb-load	1,000 lb	1,102 lb
Crew	Three	Two
Maximum speed	243 mph @ 16,200 ft	238 mph @ 13,410 ft
Service ceiling	23,500 ft	26,248ft
Maximum range with full load	1,050 miles	621 miles
Armament (machine-guns)	Two 0.303 in	Three 7.9 mm

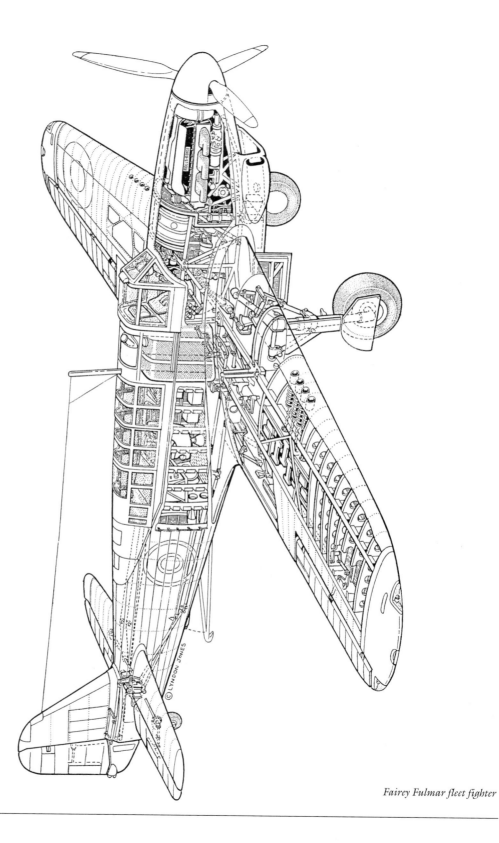

Fairey Fulmar fleet fighter

13

Fairey Fulmar

When Fairey Aviation in 1932, along with other aircraft manufacturers, was acquainted with the Air Staff's need for a fast day bomber to replace the Hawker Hart and Hind, they had in mind a compact two-seat fast bomber to compete for the specification. Their concept was completely negated when specification P27/32 was issued. Fairey's light bomber design philosophy was to take positive form only with the issue of specification P4/34, which called for a two-seat day bomber with dive-bomber capability for tactical operations, and a bomb-load of at least 500 lb. Although two prototypes were contracted for and built in 1937, it was the other competitor to the specification — Hawker Henley — which was selected.

The P4/34 was a beautifully sleek looking aircraft, the ultimate for a two-seat light bomber — even for

a two-seat fighter given a more powerful engine. It was basically a smaller and lighter version of the Battle, and was strongly constructed to fulfil the dive-bombing role. From the Merlin in the nose to the end of its rear fuselage there was a sleekness of look, yet a look that spelt strength.

In early December 1937 a conference was set up to discuss the provision of a two-seat fleet fighter for the FAA; it was considered an extremely urgent matter at the time as it was thought that the Skua and Roc would be complete failures. On 20 January 1938 Admiralty Staff draft requirements were raised, but it was not until 2 April that draft specification O.8/38 was issued. O.8/38 called for a two-seat, front-gun fighter, constructed as a ship-plane but convertible to a float-plane; it was not to exceed 8,750 lb as a ship-plane; capable of shallow dive

Fulmar Mk.II N1854 registered by Fairey as G-AIBE. Now at FAA Museum, Yeovilton. (Author)

bombing with bomb-load up to 500 lb, but this was not to interfere with its main function as a fighter. There were of course the specific problems facing any design to Fleet Air Arm requirements; namely, wing folding, limitations on the size of the aircraft and a good take-off performance — one could also add, a sturdy and serviceable undercarriage. It was also to be capable of operating from base for hours, which of course dictated the need for an observer (who also doubled up as a radio operator); the Royal Navy's insistence on an observer obviously did not extend to the fighters that they purchased from the USA!

Performancewise, the specification called for a maximum speed not less than 230 knots (264 mph) at an operational height of 10,000 ft; with a stalling speed not to exceed 56 knots (65 mph). A mock-up was to be ready for inspection within three months of the issue of an order. On 10 March 1938 a requisition for the purchase of 127 fleet fighter aircraft was raised; this after a discussion with DTD proposing to correlate the draft requirements and Fairey's proposals. Fairey proposed a modification of the P4/34, which would meet all performance requirements except that the take-off figure of 225 ft would be more like 240 ft. Fairey also wished to use its own eight-gun installation, whereas it was considered that the Hawker Henley installation was the best submitted.

The draft specification O.8/38 was amended to have an all-up weight of 9,000 lb and also an increase in the amount of ammunition carried. Copies of these draft specifications were sent to the RTO at Fairey for the information of the firm, and on 2 April 1938 the specification was approved by DTD. On 5 April the first production order was placed and it was agreed that no separate prototype contract would be issued, the P4/34 in a modified state being accepted in lieu. Two hundred and fifty Fulmars to O.8/38 were ordered on 30 September, but it was not expected that delivery would be made until March 1940.

The second P4/34, K7555, was the airframe chosen for conversion to a fleet fighter prototype. Eight inches were removed from each wingtip, the tailplane was raised 8 in, a 1,060 hp Merlin RM3M was fitted, and the fuselage strengthened to accept deck arrester hook and catapult points. In this condition K7555 was despatched to A&AEE for testing, and though their report was generally satisfactory, they did fault the following:

Stalling characteristics,
fore and aft pitching,
unstable laterally,
rudder considered heavy.

Rectifications were put in hand and the contract stipulated the 1,080 hp Merlin VIII engine.

By 1 September 1939 the fleet fighter situation

Fairey P4/34 light bomber at Hendon Air Display 1938. (W. Goldsmith)

Fairey Fulmar naval night-fighter fitted with AI radar aerials landing on HMS Nairana *1943. (G. Appleby)*

was now considered serious, and the Admiralty was not in agreement with the production order going to Fairey alone. The Naval staff felt that if the company knew that there were no other competitor there would be no incentive for Fairey to hurry the job along. All the same the company did press on and the first production aircraft, Fulmar N1854, first flew at Ringway on 4 January 1940. N1854 is sometimes referred to as the first prototype, but there was no actual Fulmar prototype, P4/34 K7555 being accepted in lieu. The contractor's trials were carried out and the company test pilot considered the Fulmar aircraft satisfactory, so N1854 went to the A&AEE for trials on 23 May 1940. There it was joined by the second production aircraft, which had flown on 6 April. A&AEE pilots found the Fulmar had good stability and handling, controls light and responsive, steady in the dive and difficult to stall. During diving tests it reached 4 'g' on pullout, in the process losing the cover over the ammunition boxes and having a cracked engine cowling. It was reported that a large amount of height was lost in the recovery from a spin — the spin tests on the second aircraft were completed by 12 May 1940.

On 3 June N1856 carried out landing trials on HMS *Illustrious*, four landings being carried out successfully. The take-off was straightforward except for a tendency to crab to the left. It was found easy to land on the deck, the control and view being very satisfactory, but not as stable laterally as most deck landing aircraft. On 9 November 1940 performance and handling trials were being conducted at Boscombe Down on N1854, N1855 and N1858. Unfortunately, although the aircraft was easy and pleasant to fly, in comparison with land-plane fighters of the period it had too low a top speed, and the rate of climb and ceiling were too low for a fighter. Although the Fulmar was easily manoeuvrable at its top speed, its manoeuvrability did not compare with the Hurricane, partly because of the heaviness of the ailerons in a dive.

The structure of the Fulmar resembled the Battle, not only in that it was strong, but the forward fuselage was strengthened by tubular steel members, with the remainder of the fuselage being monocoque with transverse dural frames and covered by riveted Alclad sheet, which ended at Frame 20. The rear frames carried transverse and vertical tubes, which provided attachment points for the tailplane and fin.

The mainplane tapered in thickness and chord from its root to its tip, and consisted of a stub plane attached to two spars which passed through, and were part of, the lower centre fuselage. This stub plane provided both attachment points and housing for the undercarriage, and had a front and diagonal spar, whose construction was of high tensile steel booms riveted to web plates of duralumin. The stressed Alclad skin was riveted to nine ribs and duralumin stringers.

The outer planes were built around two spars having Hiduminium 'T' section booms reinforced with laminations of steel, which decreased in number from root to rib 20 on the front spar, and rib 15 on the rear spar. The stressed Alclad skin was attached by riveting to the ribs and stringers. Ailerons were fitted between ribs 15 and 25, and consisted of a steel tubular spar, dural ribs and fabric covering.

The flaps were hydraulically operated, and were fitted to the aft part of the trailing edge. They were formed around a box spar of Alclad sheet, aft of which were 20 diaphragms riveted in pairs in 'V' formation to the Alclad skin, while the ribs forward of the spar were set fore and aft. The trailing edge of the flaps was reinforced with a special drawn section.

Naturally, with an aircraft for shipborne operation, the undercarriage had to be robust and preferably of wide track; this was true of the Fulmar. Its alighting gear comprised two independent, retractable main undercarriage units with a non retractable tailwheel unit; with the main wheel units swinging upwards and inwards into wheel wells in the stub planes. The main units were hinged at two diaphragms between ribs number 6 and 9, and were retracted and lowered by hydraulic pressure from an engine-driven pump. Oleo-pneumatic shock absorbers were fitted to all three legs. The tail wheel was carried in a forked leg, which could slide and rotate in an oleo cylinder, which was attached at the top to a fitting in the upper decking plate of the rear bay, and at the lower end to a saddle plate on the underside of the fuselage.

Failure of the engine-driven pump did not prevent lowering or raising of the undercarriage, as in the pilot's position there was a handle, which when rotated drove a differential gear through a chain drive, the gearbox shaft then moving the undercarriage through a quadrant.

Fairey continued a process of development of the Fulmar, and the first Mk II (N4021) was a converted Mk I, which first flew on 20 January 1941, being powered with a Merlin 30, which became standard for this mark. Changes were also made to the propeller, fuel system, rudder, radiator and oil cooler. Three hundred and fifty Fulmar Mk IIs were built. In the Mk II airframe, weight reductions were made in the structure by changes in material and design to obtain lighter weight yet retain the strength, and these improvements were made after the 155th machine. Some of the early Mk IIs were converted Mk I airframes.

During August 1940 Fairey's Stockport factory began to fulfil its promise of twenty-five aircraft per month as contracted, two and a half years after receiving the specification details. By the end of 1940 one hundred and fifty-nine Fulmars had been delivered. With the submission by Fairey for the Merlin 30, an order was placed in the Autumn of 1940 for the Mk II, the production aircraft commencing with X8525. About one hundred aircraft were converted to night-fighter duties with AI radar.

The first FAA squadron to receive the Fulmar was No 808, which started receiving them in June 1940; then in 1941 five more squadrons received Fulmars. The Fulmar eventually equipped fourteen squadrons as well as individual aircraft being based on CAM ships (Catapult Armed Merchantman). Crew reaction to their new aircraft was favourable, as it was well armed, strong, competitive and had a wide track undercarriage. On landing the aircraft on a carrier it was the procedure for the pilot to keep power 'on' to maintain slipstream over the rudder and elevator to retain control effectiveness.

The first major action for the Fulmar took place during the attacks against the Malta convoys, and although its debut was satisfactory, the weight of the extra crew member plus his equipment made its speed and climb inferior to the enemy single-seat land based fighters; so if the Fulmar's first chance of a 'kill' was lost there was rarely chance for another. Against this it lost nothing as regards manoeuvrability and firepower, and it had a good range of 800 miles — the latter varying with power used. Fulmars operated with the Russian convoys, with the Far East Fleet and in the Middle East, operating from Malta on night intrusion operations.

Although obviously not comparable in performance with the Hellcats and Corsairs, it was more capable of accurate navigational sorties. It filled a necessary niche in Royal Navy operations, and was considered by its crews as a fine aircraft.

The first production Fulmar aircraft was later converted to a Mk II standard and subsequently registered by Fairey Aviation as G-AIBE: it now resides at the Fleet Air Arm Museum at Yeovilton in its true colours and carrying its serial number of N1854.

Fairey Fulmar Mk.II naval fighter at Boscombe Down. (IWM)

Fairey Fulmar

Wingspan	46 feet 4½ inches	(14.13 metres)
Wing area	342 sq.feet	(31.77 sq metres)
Length	40 feet 2 inches	(12.24 metres)
Empty weight	7384 lb	(3349 kg)
Maximum loaded weight	10200 lb	(4627 kg)
Maximum speed at height	272 mph at	(438 kph at
	16,500 feet	5030 metres)
Service ceiling	27,200 feet	(8290 metres)
Range	780 miles	(1255 kilometres)
Engine	one 1260 hp Merlin Mk.30 inline	
Standard armament	eight 0.303-inch machine-guns	

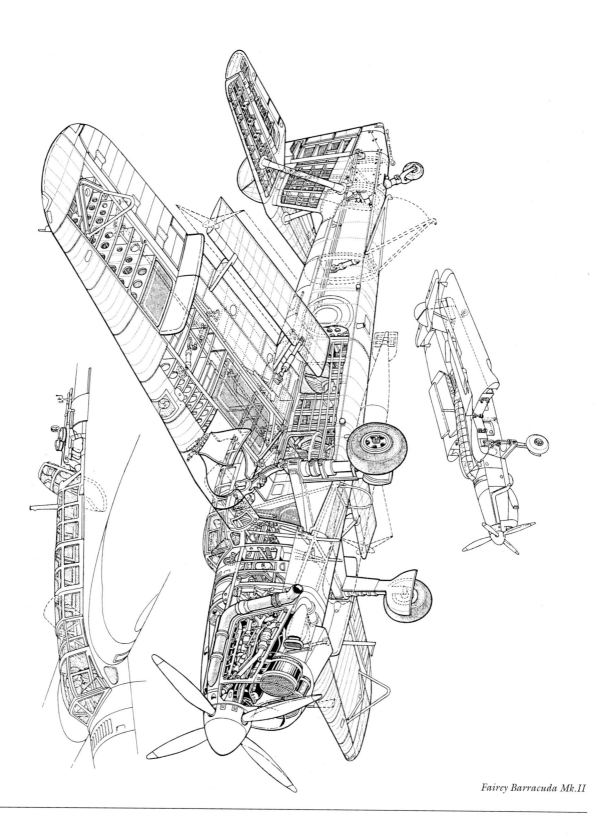

Fairey Barracuda Mk.II

14

Fairey Barracuda

When one first took a look at a Barracuda the first thought was 'Here is an aircraft designed by a committee' — without being rude, it just did not appear correct, with its high gawky undercarriage, strut-braced high-set tailplane and its shoulder-wing. Yet, when one is appraised of all the requirements and roles that this aircraft was supposed to comply with, and all the equipment and weapons in its arsenal, one starts to wonder if Their Lords at the Admiralty knew what they wanted. Accepting that the specifications were drawn up by the Air Staff, these are not initiated without the Navy putting their seabootsworth in as to what they required.

Specification S24/37 was issued on 9 November 1937 and called for a torpedo/dive-bomber/reconnaissance aircraft, and on 4 February 1938 an invitation to tender was sent out. On 7 March tenders had been received from Blackburn, Fairey, Hawker, Supermarine and Westland. At the tender design conference RAE stated that the Fairey design was best, and so a decision was made to order prototypes from Fairey and Supermarine. Fairey's design had a delivery time of fourteen months for the first prototype and seventeen months for the second. On 29 April 1938 a production order for the Fairey design was being considered, but a recommendation against this was made, as it was felt that if this were done then the other companies would not be prepared to produce prototypes. On 15 August the Air Ministry made the point that they wanted to order four prototypes from Fairey, but it was not until 30 January 1939 before a prototype contract was placed with Fairey — a ten month gap since the tenders had been received.

Specification S24/37 called for an all-up weight not to exceed 10,500 lb as a ship-plane and 11,500 lb for a float-plane; stalling speed not to exceed 58 knots (67 mph); cruising speed to be not less than 185 knots (213 mph) at maximum continuous economical power; take-off run as a reconnaissance aircraft not to exceed 225 ft against a 20 knot wind; and the power to be supplied by a Rolls-Royce Boreas engine.

In December 1938 the mock-up of the Type 100 (Barracuda) was inspected and approved and a

Barracuda prototype P1767. Note the low-set original tailplane. (RAF)

Rather tired looking Barracuda carrying training torpedo. (RAF)

contract considered for two prototypes. This was followed by a contract and the drawing office commenced detail design on 2 February 1939, followed by a requisition for the purchase of 250 aircraft on 23 March. On 5 May the Admiralty confirmed to the Air Ministry their agreement to the order for 250 aircraft, requesting that if possible these were to be manufactured at Stockport. A production specification was approved on 21 June and the first production order placed on 10 August. Hardly had this been placed, than Hives of Rolls-Royce in a letter to Air Vice-Marshal Sir Wilfrid Freeman recommended the dropping of the 1,300 hp Boreas sleeve-valve engine. After consultation with Fairey it was agreed that the substitution of a Merlin would make no difference in performance; this was reluctantly agreed to by Freeman.

In a letter to Freeman on 16 September 1939 Fairey gave its estimate for the Barracuda powered with three different engines:-

Boreas (EXE) engine	243 mph at 5,000 ft
Taurus II engine	260 mph at 5,000 ft
Merlin engine	288 mph at 9,500 ft

This information was passed to the Admiralty for agreement, along with the information that the prototype would be powered by the Merlin VIII engine. The Admiralty naturally wanted to know how the use of the Merlin would affect the Fulmar production. The Air Ministry not only confirmed that this would have no effect on the Fulmar production, but without the complication of parallel production there should be a steady flow of Merlins.

The delivery date for the first Barracuda prototype according to the contract was July 1939, and delivery to the A&AEE was October of the same year; but by the time the delivery date had arrived

the first prototype was nowhere near ready, for a certain amount of delay was imposed by the re-design of the airframe to accept the Merlin engine and its liquid-cooling installation in place of the aircooled Boreas engine.

The Barracuda's construction revolved around the requirements for a TSR aircraft, for a good downward view is required for the observer; all-round vision for the TAG; with a good view forward and downward for the pilot for torpedo dropping, approach and landing. In view of this a high shoulder wing position was chosen, which affected the wing-folding arrangement. This in turn brought its own share of problems with the dive brakes and undercarriage. The undercarriage retraction geometry led to an unorthodox layout, which must be admitted was very satisfactory. The wing flap arrangement was likewise complicated by the desire of the designer to provide a good lift when desired and a high drag component to enable dive-bombing to be carried out at a reduced diving speed, which would remain constant. These requirements, after a lot of consideration, resulted in the end, due to the wing folding arrangement, to the choice of an external flap.

Wind tunnel tests indicated that during diving conditions the high drag position of the flaps would give an appreciable change in longitudinal trim, and the drag wake would cause interference at the tail. During the flight trials both of these faults were confirmed under diving conditions. This resulted in the decision being made to raise the tail plane and elevators out of the drag wake and reposition them up the fin, but the longitudinal trim problem was only solved later on by the interconnection of the flap movement to the elevator trim.

The undercarriage was hinged to the side of the

fuselage, but due to the geometry provided a wider track than normal with fuselage mounted undercarriages. The main leg was an inverted 'L' which was hinged at the top end of the 'L' to the fuselage, so that as it retracted upwards one leg of it retracted into the fuselage, the remainder with the wheel fitting into the wheel-well in the wing. Someone in an unkind moment stated that the Barracuda with everything folded for 'striking down' gave a good impression of an accident!

On 15 December 1940, after much discussion in Parliament and requests within the services, Elliott (ADAP) reported that the reason for the delay with the Barracuda prototype was that it was not an easy aircraft to manufacture; that the completion of the production drawings was due to lateness of the prototype; so forgings were not ordered. Further to this there were difficulties with finding a sub-contractor to do the machining because most were involved with war work already. The Barracuda was not only the topic of discussion over its production, it was the point of discussion about the Fleet Air Arm in the House for a period of time.

The first prototype (P1767) was first flown from the Great West Aerodrome (Heathrow) on 7 December 1940, two years after the contract had first been placed. This plus the ten month gap in the official timetable between receipt of the tender design and the prototype order, delayed the Barracuda's entry to service by over three years. This first prototype aircraft had a low-set tailplane, and test flying soon determined that this position was causing problems; for it was found that the aerodynamic effect of the flaps was tending to blanket the tailplane, and when set at a negative angle for dive-bombing, created buffeting and vibration of the tailplane, as well as loss of elevator effectiveness. The flaps on the Barracuda were a little different from most others; these were designed by Youngman of Fairey and was a separate aerofoil surface mounted underneath and separate from the trailing edge of the mainplane. They were set at a maximum of 20° for take-off, fully lowered on landing and at a negative angle of 30° for dive-bombing.

In October 1941 the prototype was delivered to the A&AEE for trials, followed by its initial deck landing trials on HMS *Victorious*. It was then returned to the manufacturer for fitment of operational equipment and the new tail surfaces. The A&AEE reported a maximum level speed with reconnaissance load of 250 knots (278 mph) and as a torpedo-bomber a speed of 236 knots (272 mph); both speeds at a height of 10,000 ft.

Deliveries of the Barracuda Mk I began in September 1942, only twenty-five being produced. On 3 December 1942 the Minister at the Aircraft Supply Council was concerned over the production of the Barracuda, and enquired at the meeting over the

Barracuda Mk.II P9795 fitted with a paratroop container under each wing. (IWM)

possibility of obtaining the services of a good designer and production engineer, so as to modify the aircraft for easier production! This first batch of Barracudas after the prototypes P1767 and P1770, were serial numbered P9642 to P9666 and were powered by the 1,260 bhp Merlin 30 engine driving a three-blade propeller. Prototype P1767 had its undercarriage accidentally retracted on the ground whilst at Boscombe Down, which resulted in approximately three months being lost whilst it was being repaired, while P1770 had its first flight on 19 June 1942. This second prototype and the production aircraft all had the high-set tailplane as standard.

The Barracuda from the Mk I onwards had twin Vickers 'K' guns on a flexible mounting in the rear position for the TAG, but in 1940 a turret installation was projected for this position, similar to the Grumman Avenger; this did not progress past the project stage and no approval was given. Originally it was intended to provide the observer with a free-mounted Vickers 'K' gun, but this likewise did not materialise. Its offensive load could be either a 1,610 lb torpedo or a 1,500 lb mine carried under the fuselage, or four 500 lb or six 250 lb bombs slung under the wings; this load varied slightly with the Mks II and III, though the Mk III was mainly intended as an anti-submarine/reconnaissance aircraft, and so had an ASV radome under the rear fuselage.

The fuselage was constructed in three main sections, with the forward portion around the pilot cockpit area and rear fuselage bay braced by tubular members covered with Alclad panels. The centre and rear fuselage were of monocoque construction of frames and longitudinal stringers covered by a light alloy skin. The centre section fuselage was built integral with the centre section wing, and the frames in the area of the cockpits were 'U' shaped, with the cockpit area covered by a framed continuous transparent hooding.

The mainplane consisted of the centre section and port and starboard outer planes. The centre plane was built around two main girder spars while the outer planes had front and rear spars built up of Hiduminium booms of extruded 'T' section re-inforced with steel laminations; the laminations decreased in number from root to rib 17 on the front spar and rib 13 on the rear spar. The front spar was further reinforced at the top and bottom booms with sections of steel and light alloy extrusions. The inter-spar portion housed the fuel tanks and bomb

carrying structure. The outer spar web was of light alloy sheet reinforced with vertical angle stiffeners. A separate hinged trailing edge could be folded over the top of the outer plane on wing folding. Ailerons were built upon a steel tubular spar to which hinge fittings were attached at three points, with ribs and trailing edge covered by fabric. Flaps had a main spar with two auxiliary spars, diaphragm ribs and Alclad sheet covering.

The tail unit comprised a tailplane bolted to the top of the upper portion of the fin, which was rigidly attached to the fuselage and braced with streamlined struts. Both the fin and tailplane were similar in construction, and based on two spars, flanged edge ribs, 'J' section stringers and Alclad skinning. The rudder was based on a tubular spar and nine light alloy ribs attached to the spar and trailing edge member, with the leading edge metal covered and the rest fabric covered. Both the port and starboard elevator were similar to each other, and similar in construction to the rudder, but having ten light alloy ribs. The ribs were riveted to the spar and attached to a trailing edge member, with the leading edge metal covered, the remainder fabric covered.

The main differences between the Mks I to III as regards performance and data really centred around the change of Merlin mark, which allowed an increase in all-up weight from 13,500 to 14,100 lb, but with little difference in maximum speed. The service ceiling increased from 18,400 to 20,000 ft and range from 525 to 684 miles.

The Barracuda first entered service in January 1943 when Mk IIs became the equipment of 827 Squadron, and eventually formed the equipment of twelve front line squadrons. During the training period with the first Barracudas a larger than normal rate of accidents occurred — which hardly added to the type's reputation. These accidents were initially thought to be due to the aircraft being so much faster and complicated than the Swordfish. An investigation into the accidents was constituted and its deliberations determined a number of points; for instance, in a dive with the dive brakes in the dive position the Barracuda pulled to port, and it was necessary to trim out the nose-lifting tendency. Then when the dive brakes were retracted at the bottom of the dive, the aircraft assumed a nose-down tendency. So the cause was considered as due to this combination, and that in recovery from a dive it was necessary to trim out with the retraction of the dive brakes, or there was a good chance of the aircraft

Barracuda DP855/G production aircraft on test at A&AEE. (IWM)

diving straight into the sea. It was also noted that in a dive with the dive brakes out in the dive position, the brake drag was so high that the airspeed remained almost constant. Flutter was another problem that was experienced occasionally, and was considered to be possibly due to the nose-lifting tendency.

Both the Mk II and III were produced with Merlin 32 engines of 1,640 bhp and driving four-bladed propellers. The total production was 2,572 aircraft of all marks, the Mk II being produced by Blackburn, Boulton Paul, Fairey and Westland. The Mk V version was Griffon powered, and the first production version did not fly until 22 November 1945, and saw no operational service. The Barracuda's first action was with 810 Squadron at Salerno at the time of the Allies amphibious landing; but will probably be best remembered for the attack on the *Tirpitz*, when a strike force of Barracudas from Nos. 827, 829, 830 and 831 Squadrons scored

15 direct hits. Soon after VJ Day most of the squadrons that were still operating Barracudas were disbanded; though in 1947 one squadron was re-equipped with the Mk III version and were only superseded by Grumman Avengers in 1953.

The Barracuda could not be classed as an outstanding aircraft, nor could it be said to have been an aircraft that won a battle, but it did a job of work that was arduous and was hung with all manner of weaponry. It carried bombs, torpedoes, mines, depth charges, even an air-sea rescue lifeboat. One Mk II (P9795) was experimentally fitted with special containers slung under the wings, one each side, to carry two paratroopers per container; but as far as is known it was never used operationally. It was an aircraft that received a bad reputation, which it was never to completely wipe out, mainly because it did a job of work away from publicity — as was the lot of the Fleet Air Arm.

Fairey Barracuda Mk. II.

Wingspan	49 feet 2 inches	(14.99 metres)
Wing area	367 sq.feet	(34.09 sq.metres)
Length	39 feet 9 inches	(12.11 metres)
Empty weight	9350 lb	(4241 kg)
Maximum loaded weight	14100 lb	(6396 kg)
Maximum bombload	1800 lb or one 1620 lb torpedo	
Maximum speed at height	228 mph at	(367 kph at
	1,750 feet	535 metres)
Service ceiling	16,600 feet	(5060 metres)
Range	1150 miles	(1850 kilometres)
Engine	one 1640 hp Merlin 32 inline	
Standard armament	two 0.303-inch machine-guns	

Hawker Hurricane Mk.IIA

15

Hawker Hurricane

In 1931 the Air Staff issued specification F7/30 to the British aircraft industry, calling for a single-seat day and night fighter. This specification stated requirements that were well advanced over the design features of contemporary fighters, and included the following:

Higher performance
Exceptional manoeuvrability
Long endurance
Steep climb out on take-off
Low landing speed
Four machine-guns.

the aircraft to be powered by the Air Staff's preference, the Rolls-Royce Goshawk, which was an evaporative-cooled development of the Kestrel.

Six companies tendered to this specification, amongst whom were Hawker with the PV3 and Supermarine with the Type 224. Delays and testing continued through the years, until in 1935 the contract was awarded to Gloster's SS37 (Gladiator), which was a private venture in the contest and was powered by an aircooled radial engine! The contributary factor in this was possibly because the monoplanes entered had not achieved an advance in performance sufficient to convince the biplane protagonists, for instance, the SS37 was faster than the Supermarine 224 by 4 mph and could climb to 15,000 ft in 6½ minutes — 1½ minutes faster than the 224.

Camm at Hawker meanwhile had already commenced to scheme out a Fury Monoplane, but still based on the Goshawk engine, and in many ways based in general on the features of the F7/30 specification. Its armament was four Vickers 0.303-in machine-guns, two in the sides of the forward fu-

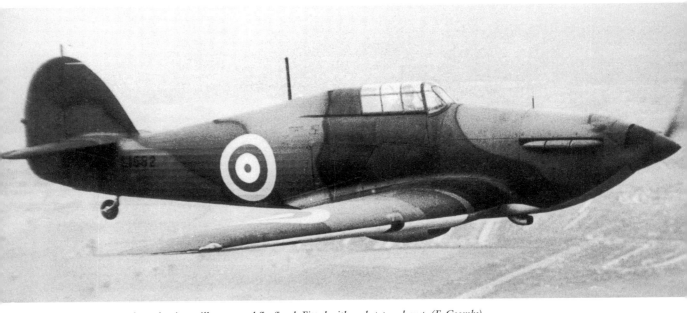

Hurricane Mk.I early production, still no ventral fin fitted. Fitted with early type exhaust. (F. Coombs)

selage and two more in the wingroots. Its construction followed the well known Hawker construction methods of patent metal tube, Warren girder fuselage with a multi-spar metal constructed wing, fabric covered.

Then came the promise of Rolls-Royce's new engine, the PV.12 — later to be named the Merlin — this was sufficient for Camm to go ahead on a private venture path of re-designing the Fury Monoplane into the High Speed Monoplane. Stressing commenced in March 1934, with details beginning to be drawn in May 1934; so that by September of the same year Hawker was able to submit to the Air Ministry its detailed design and estimated performance — some of the details with an eye on the F5/34 specification, which called for six or eight machine-guns, enclosed cockpit, oxygen for the pilot and a retractable undercarriage.

On 21 February 1935 Hawker received a contract for a 'High Speed Monoplane' K5083 against specification F36/34, and with armament of four machine-guns. Then the Air Staff decided, on the basis of investigation by Squadron Leaders Sorley and Spreckley, to update their armament requirements, and on 25 March 1935 the Operational Requirements Committee called a conference to discuss two heavily armed types of fighter projects, one of these being the F10/35,

Hurricane IIC fresh from the production line on test. (Hawkers)

Hurricane Mk.I of 73 Squadron in France being refuelled and re-armed 1940. (K. Campbell)

Top: Hurricane Mk.II KZ706 fitted with long rocket rails. (Hawkers)
Above: Hurricane Mk.IIB of 486 Squadron at Wittering 1942. (Author)

where the first mention of cannon appears. So no longer were the Air Staff interested in four 0.303-in machine-guns; it was now either cannon, or at the minimum at least eight machine-guns. This became hard fact, when on September 27 an amendment was made to the F36/34 specification calling for an armament of eight 0.303-in machine-guns. Fortunately, Camm, with his eye on the F5/34 specification had already been investigating the possible levering in of eight machine-guns to his

monoplane wing, as well as the designing of an all-metal stressed skin mainplane, so with a little re-designing of the original wing layout, accommodation was provided for eight Browning 0.303-in machine-guns and their ammunition boxes. Meanwhile, in 1935 Camm began the investigation and design of a stressed skin all-metal wing, but decided — some say fortunately — to treat this as a long term project, so the Hurricane in its production form was produced with a fabric-covered wing, more

Hurricane Mk.I of 501 Squadron 1940 in France being serviced in the field. (RAF)

than 490 Hurricanes being delivered by the commencement of war on 3 September 1939.

The stressed skin all-metal wing was constructed around two main spars and two intermediate spars, and did not fly until April 1939, when it was accepted and went into production — so one can only guess how many Hurricanes would have been available for war, if the Hurricane had been delayed while the all-metal wing was developed.

With the issue of the F10/35 specification calling for heavier armament, — yet with the F36/34 and F37/34 designs still being required to carry four 0.303-in machine-guns — a review was undertaken within the Air Staff, as the conflicting requirements were causing considerable internal correspondence. This review resulted eventually in the withdrawal of the F10/35 specification and the aforementioned amendment to the F36/34 (Hurricane) and F37/34 (Spitfire) specifications. Meanwhile, at the end of May 1935 the DCAS, Air Vice-Marshal Courtney in a letter to Dowding wrote:

'. . . In the first place I quite agree that nothing should be allowed to delay the construction and flying tests of these aeroplanes (meaning the Hurricane and Spitfire). But I think we could possibly bring these aircraft into line with the F10/35 specification without necessarily imposing delays.'

The first flight of the prototype Hurricane was made on 6 November 1935 by P. Bulman, and as no Browning 0.303-in machine-guns (now the accepted gun for the RAF) were available, the flight was made without them, ballast being placed in the wings in lieu. The engine was the Merlin C, but this version was still causing problems and required further development. On 3 June 1936 Hawker received Air Ministry contract for 100 Hurricanes to production specification 16/36 and to be powered by the Merlin F (Merlin I). The Merlin 1 turned out to be down on power and still with problems, so these were allocated to the Fairey Battle programme and the Merlin G (Merlin 2) substituted.

Typical of all estimated power and weight figures against a specification, the Hurricane's estimated design gross weight was 4,800 lb initially, but with the amended F36/34 the estimated gross weight rose to 5,200 lb. When the Hurricane prototype was weighed it hit 5,416 lb, and the production Mk 1 was even heavier at 6,500 lb, but by then a number of modifications and equipment changes had taken place.

In August 1936 the Browning machine-guns had been received and fitted, and K5083 went on armament trials. These trials were successful up to a point, for at high altitude the low temperatures were found to cause gun stoppages, which led in late 1937 to a further re-design and channeling of hot air to the gun bays. Even then, gun stoppages due to low temperatures were still occurring in the early years of the war.

On the prototype the tailplane was strut braced, and amongst the first modifications embarked on was the removal of these struts, also the removal of the hinged wheel doors at the bottom of the leg fairings. A small ventral fin would also eventually be fitted and the radiator enlarged. The addition of the small ventral fin was to improve directional stability and spinning characteristics, and to fair-in the fixed tailwheel.

During 1938 an investigation was embarked on into the use of a slotted wing, also into the fitment of a Merlin VIII, but these projects were eventually stopped, possibly because of the design and development of the all-metal wing and the need for greater production — the Munich crisis had occurred.

Between September 1938 and January 1939 the first production Hurricane 1 L1547 and L1696 had been at the A&AEE Martlesham Heath on trials. A&AEE report M/689A reporting after these tests stated that the trials had established the maximum speed as 315 mph (the F36/34 specification had expected a maximum speed of 320 mph at 15,000 feet) at 16,200 feet. In regard to the controls and flying characteristics, the ailerons changed from light to heavy as speed increased, though aileron response

was rapid. The rudder became heavy in the dive and as speed increased. As much as 5,800 ft was lost in an eight-turn spin, but recovery posed no problem. At the same time the cockpit hood was criticised for being difficult to open at above 380 mph in a dive. The major failure point was the collapse of a bottom fuselage fairing during a series of dives, when a number of formers and stringers had failed.

The difference between the Hurricane and Spitfire in their method of construction was in the approach of their designers, for whereas Mitchell with the Spitfire was breaking new ground for his company and using monocoque construction, the Hurricane was a continuation in development of the pattern set by previous Hawker aircraft, such as the Fury etc. Its fuselage was based on four longerons and braced in the Warren-truss method, with the whole construction consisting of steel and duralumin tubing braced with frames and steel-swaged wires. On this basic construction was mounted a decking of plywood formers and stringers to give a more streamlined form. Mounted at the front end of the longerons was the firewall, and forward of that was the detachable engine mounting. While the forward end of the fuselage was metal skinned and panelled, the remainder was fabric covered.

The tail unit was completely conventional of metal construction with a metal D nose and fabric covered,

White-sprayed Sea Hurricane with a broken back after landing on HMS Nariana *1943. (G. Appleby)*

Top: Hurricane Mk.IIC PZ868 on engine run at RAF Coningsby 1975. (P.W. Porter)
Above: Hurricane visiting 17 SFTS RCAF Souris, Canada. Note DH Hamilton propeller. (P.W. Porter)

and the elevator and rudder were constructed around a tubular steel spar and fabric covered.

The undercarriage consisted of two inward retracting oleo-pneumatic shock absorber struts, with the main wheels mounted on stub axles and fitted with pneumatic brakes, the whole retracting into the mainplane centre plane. Originally the tailwheel was retractable, but in 1938 modification action was taken which replaced this with a fixed tailwheel on production aircraft, faired in by the aforementioned ventral fin.

The wing of the Hurricane 1 production aircraft comprised two widely spaced main spars, built up on the Hawker patented construction, and the spars crossed braced by Warren girder bracing. The nose of each mainplane was in the form of a D and was metal covered, with the remainder of the mainplane fabric covered. So as to maintain the aerofoil section and to secure the fabric, a patented method of attachment was used, metal strip channels being fixed by fasteners to secure the fabric to the ribs.

In adopting this totally conventional approach in design of construction, Camm ensured that the manufacture of the airframe would be of a method which his work force were conversant with, production would be quick, and repair of the airframe would be easy.

When the Hurricane was first issued to the squadrons it was fitted with a ring and bead gunsight, and even after the introduction of the reflector type gunsights, the ring and bead were kept as a 'back-up'. Gun harmonisation was set at a point at 400 yds in accordance with Fighter Command instructions, but during the Battle of France and later in the Battle of Britain a number of squadrons revised this to 250 yds; followed later by a Fighter Command instruction in which gun grouping was introduced as a harmonisation pattern.

The Watts two-blade, fixed-pitch wooden propeller was initially fitted on the Hurricane when equipping the squadrons; but then during the Battle of France a panic measure introduced the fitment of de Havilland three-blade two-position bracket type propellers, so as to counter the performance of the Bf 109E. The fitting of this type of propeller was not universal until about June 1940, and then this was followed by the introduction of the Rotol constant speed type propeller, which improved the take-off and climb performance, but at the expense of a maximum speed reduction of about 4 mph — the aircraft all-up weight had now increased to 6,750 lb.

The Hurricane entered squadron service approximately eight months before the Spitfire, and with its wide undercarriage was a more acceptable aircraft for the average grass or dirt airfield at home or overseas than the Spitfire. It was easier to service and repair than the Spitfire. For instance, in regard to the armament, the thick Hurricane wing offered more space for stowage, and the grouping of the guns and ammunition boxes allowed all to be exposed by the removal of one cover per wing. In the field as well as at Maintenance Units the repair of monocoque structures was far harder than the Warren-truss type of tubular construction. Against this of course this latter type of construction limited performance improvements, so that Hawker would eventually introduce monocoque construction — but not with the Hurricane. The strength of the Hurricane wing is illustrated by the fact that it was the only single-engined aircraft to mount 40 mm cannon armament.

The Hurricane 1 performance has been variously quoted — or misquoted — one for instance being 325 mph at 17,500 ft and a ceiling of 36,000 ft, and a climb to 20,000 ft in 9 minutes — but the ones quoted in this text are the figures from the A&AEE reports. One wonderful way of confusing friend and foe alike occurred during 1938, when the CO of 111 Squadron (the first to receive the Hurricane) Squadron Leader Gillan, flew a Hurricane from Edinburgh to Northolt at an average speed of 408 mph — there happened to be a stiff tailwind.

During development testing at the High Altitude Flight of A&AEE, it was found that the Hurricane at high altitude became uncontrollable during certain manoeuvres, but this was improved by rectification action. Then further testing, this time on Z2416, showed that at 30,000 feet when changing direction, the aileron response was so bad that the aircraft

824 Squadron FAA Sea Hurricane coming into land on HMS Unicorn May 1943. (P.W. Porter)

rolled on its back, and at 33,000 feet the aileron locked solid and control was not regained until at 18,000 feet — but the trouble in this case was traced to grease on the controls freezing.

When the F37/35 specification was issued for tender, Camm tendered a Hurricane derivative armed with four 20mm cannon, but this was rejected on the grounds of weight to power, and the contract went to Westland and the Whirlwind. In 1939, with the emphasis, as regards armament, being on heavier calibre weapons, Hurricane L1750 was fitted with a pair of 20mm Hispano cannon, one slung beneath each wing. This went for trials at A&AEE for comparative trials against a standard Hurricane eight-gun fighter, where it recorded a maximum speed of 302 mph at 16,800 feet. Then during 1940, Hawker managed to get approval to use two battle damaged wings, into which four 20mm Hispano cannon were mounted; these were flown on V7360, and on 15 August 1940 this aircraft departed to A&AEE for firing trials. The maximum speed of the aircraft in this condition proved the wisdom of the Air Ministry's rejection of Hawker's proposal to the F37/35. Nevertheless, the installation was satisfactory, and Service evaluation reports were sufficient to give Hawker encouragement to persevere; and with the delivery of the Merlin XX engine and its 1,280 hp at 3,000 rpm at 11,750 feet, sufficient power was available for the four-cannon installation.

With the introduction of the Merlin XX engine three versions of the Mk 2 Hurricane became available, these were:-

Mk 2A.	carrying eight Browning 0.303-in
Mk 2B.	carrying twelve Browning 0.303-in
Mk 2C.	carrying four 20mm Hispano cannon.

and these aircraft entered service use in 1941.

Apart from being used as a day-fighter, a certain number were also used as night-fighters, depending on 'eyeball' identification after being vectored onto their target by ground radar; but the use of the Hurricane was far from a total success in this role, as conditions of weather affected the pilot's visibility.

A further extension of the Hurricane was the conversion of it to the fighter-bomber role, an experimental bomb carrying version being flown at A&AEE in 1941, but it was only with the introduction of the Mk 2 Hurricane that the fighter-bomber became a standard model. The Hurricane was capable of carrying two 500 lb bombs, but in general two 250 lb bombs was the normal standard, with the aircraft's radius of action being 150 miles.

By 1942 the Hurricane was hardly comparable in performance with the German fighters operating in the West, and a further role opened up for the Hurricane as a ground attack aircraft. However, although the Hispano 20mm cannon was very effective against soft-skinned vehicles, its effectiveness against AFVs had decreased as the Germans had increased their armour. To combat this a Hurricane 2 had two 40mm Vickers guns slung under the wings, trials were carried out at A&AEE on Z2326, and the designation Mk 2D was allocated. The 2D was armed with the two aforementioned weapons, plus two Browning 0.303-in machine-guns for sighting purposes. In this form the Hurricane had a maximum speed of 286 mph, and of course with a speed like this and being used for ground attack it required a fighter escort. With the firing of each 40mm shell, the nose pulled down a matter of 5°, though the correction for this would be a natural instinct for the pilot.

A development of this Mark was the Mk 4, which carried the same armament as the 2D, but which had a new universal wing capable of carrying various stores or armament, and was powered by the Merlin XX, 24 or 27, with the pilot protected with a little more armour.

With insufficient aircraft carriers and shortage of long-range fighters and long-range maritime recce aircraft, British convoys were not only suffering from U-boats but Fw Condors as well; so to overcome this problem, a number of Mk 1 Hurricanes were modified with catapult spools and sufficiently strengthened for catapulting. These were then housed on merchant ships, known as CAM ships (Catapult Armed Merchantmen), on which was mounted a catapult. Once airborne the pilot could only ditch when his fuel ran out or head for the nearest land — yet there was no shortage of volunteers, and it was satisfactory as an interim measure until the escort carriers came along.

With the addition of a deck arrester hook and the necessary strengthening of the airframe, Hurricanes were operated from escort, auxiliary and main aircraft carriers; continuing in this role until 1944, by which time it was well past its peak.

With the commencement of war the Hurricane went to France with the AASF and Air Component, and inspite of it being outnumbered in its involvement with the enemy, it acquitted itself well.

Hurricane IIC G-AMAU (PZ865) 'Last of the Many'. Retained by Hawkers. (Author)

During the Battle of Britain it far exceeded the Spitfire in numbers, and though it has been stated that during that battle the Hurricanes could not have lived without the Spitfires, likewise, the smaller number of Spitfires could not have lived without the Hurricanes. Furthermore, it may not have been noticed, but the majority of British 'aces' achieved that honour flying the Hurricane.

Comparison between Bf 109E and Hurricane

	Bf 109E.	Hurricane 1.	Hurricane 2A.
Wingspan	32 ft 5 in	40 ft	40 ft
Height	8 ft 5½ in	8 ft 9 in	8 ft 9 in
Length, tail down	28 ft 10½ in	31 ft 4 in	31 ft 4 in
Wing area	172.84 sq ft	258 sq ft	258 sq ft
Aspect-ratio	6.0	6.2	6.2
Weight empty	4472/4526 lb	4982/5034 lb	5467/5594 lb
Weight gross	5667/5747 lb	6040/6750 lb	7233/8050 lb
Armament	four 7.9mm mgs or two 7.9mm plus two 20mm cannon	eight 0.303-in mgs	eight 0.303-in** mgs
Maximum speed at SL	283 mph	246 mph	268 mph
at 5,000 ft	302 mph	264 mph	285 mph
at 15,000 ft	338 mph	303 mph	314 mph
at 20,000 ft	343 mph	305 mph	319 mph
at 25,000 ft	328 mph	290 mph	313 mph
Maximum speed at FTH	348 mph at 17,500 ft	311 mph at 17,500 ft	323 mph at 21,000 ft
Service ceiling	35,200 ft	32,800 ft	36,600 ft
Time to operational hgt	20 min 23 sec	21 min 15 sec	19 min 57 sec
25,000 ft	11 min 39 sec	13 min 12 sec	9 min 48 sec
30,000 ft	17 min 12 sec	17 min 30 sec	13 min 20 sec
Rate of climb at 25,000 ft	1,340 ft/min	1,260 ft/min	1,840 ft/min
30,000 ft	740 ft/min	660 ft/min	1,160 ft/min
Engine type	Daimler DB601	Merlin III.	Merlin XX
Propeller type	VDM constant speed	Watts two-blade fixed pitch	Rotol constant speed
Bhp at take off	1,100	1,030	1,300
Bhp at full throttle hgt	950	965	1.075

** On the Hurricane Mk 2 different armament equipment was installed. ie: Mk 2B had twelve 0.303-in machine-guns and Mk 2C had four 20mm cannon.

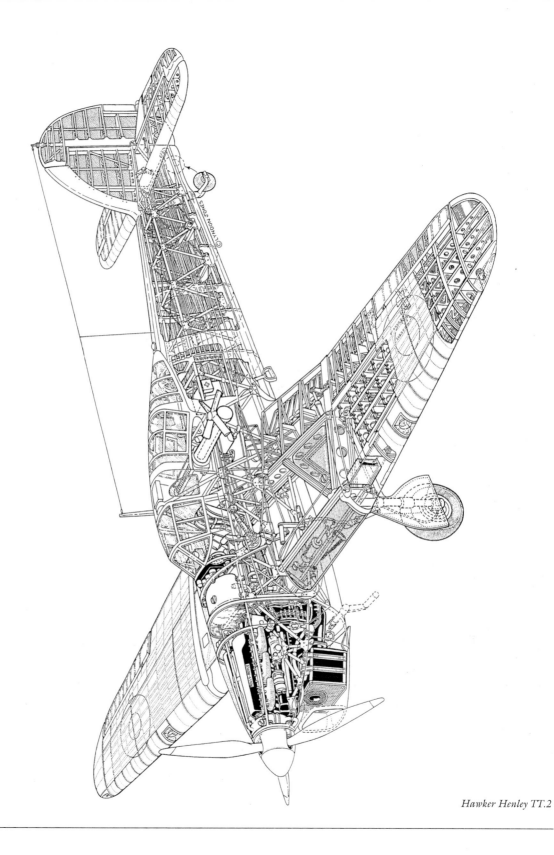

© LYNDON JONES

Hawker Henley TT.2

16

Hawker Henley

The specification P27/32 was issued calling for a light bomber, then in October 1933 the requirements were revised to bring the 'normal' and 'long-range' items in line with the B9/32 specification for a twin-engined bomber. By then the Air Staff was of the opinion that the light bomber formula was not a viable one for the RAF, yet still issued specification P4/34, which called for a light bomber with dive-bombing capability! It has been said that this was a Battle replacement; how could it

have been when orders for the Battle were not placed until 23 May 1936.

Both Hawker and Fairey competed for the contract, but this went to Hawker Aircraft Ltd, who, using Hurricane components to produce prototype K5115 had the aircraft in the air for its first flight on 10 March 1937. This aircraft was then powered by a Merlin F driving a DH hydraulic-operated metal propeller. The engine was replaced with a Merlin II, and flew again on 5 June 1937. The basis of the

Hawker Henley prototype K5115 light bomber with fabric-covered wings. (Hawkers)

Hawker proposal was the use of Hurricane components, and true to Camm's design philosophy the airframe was a mixture of established practice and new technology, use still being made of the Warrentruss system, multi-spars and a mixture of stressed skin and fabric covering, as described under construction and illustrated in the sectioned drawing of the Henley.

The prototype had Hurricane fabric-covered outer mainplane and tailplane, the wing being mid-mounted. Provision was made for a 500 lb bomb carried internally, external fittings for bomb racks, internally wing mounted Vickers V machine-gun for the pilot and a flexibly mounted Lewis 0.303-in machine-gun for the gunner. The aircraft was completed in 1936 and had its first flight at Brooklands in 1937. An order for 350 Henley light bombers was then placed, but due to a change in policy at the Air Ministry over the light bomber the order was rescinded, to be replaced by an order for 200 Henley target towing aircraft. The second prototype (K7554) was re-engineered as a target tug, re-engined with a Merlin II, and so did not have its first flight until 26 May 1938.

The first prototype K5115, still with fabric-covered wing outer panels and tailplane, was despatched to the A&AEE for trials. Faults found at the establishment were the pilot's seat; no trim indicator to the rudder and elevator trims; incorrect positioning of the undercarriage and flap levers, being on the opposite side of the cockpit to the throttle and rpm levers; failure to provide any handhold along the fuselage side for the pilot. The handling was listed as follows: taxying was easy; tail came up easily and there was a tendency to swing to port; climb-out made at 90–95 mph; elevators were light throughout speed range but became heavier at higher speeds; ailerons effective throughout speed range but became heavier as speed increased; rudder heavy at all speeds except when approaching the stall, when it became light and ineffective below 140 mph; stability was good at all speeds, though it deteriorated as speed fell off, and unstable at aft C of G position; flaps gave a sufficiently steep glide at 80–85 mph with small use of engine, but if the engine was not used the handling became difficult due to ineffectiveness of the elevator, and there was a tendency for a wing to drop if flattening out was carried out too early.

Powered by the Merlin I the prototype achieved 292 mph at 17,100 ft at the all-up weight of 8,495 lb, the propeller then being a DH bracket type two-position pitch propeller. The two prototypes were manufactured at Hawker's Kingston works, but the production order for the Henley target tug was sub-contracted to Gloster's Hucclecote works.

The first Henley target tug aircraft for testing at A&AEE was L3243, which was powered by a Merlin II of 1,030 bhp. The report on its handling was very similar to the prototype's, in that it had unsatisfactory longitudinal stability and control at low speeds. It was emphasised that care was necessary in getting the tail up as soon as possible to prevent the aircraft bouncing into the air on the take-off run, and because of the aircraft's nose heaviness a low landing weight was needed. Nevertheless, the aircraft dived to a speed of 420 mph and the recovery from the dive gave 6.4g without anything falling off!

The first prototype (K5115) had its fabric-covered outer wings replaced by metal ones later, but the second prototype (K7554) which was listed as the Henley II and all subsequent aircraft were produced with metal wings and powered by the Merlin II or III. The second prototype was first flown at Brooklands by P.G. Lucas, and retained by Hawker as the model for the target towing version.

Acceptance trials at Martlesham Heath took place between 10 January and 12 March 1938, the aircraft being flown by three pilots, with the aircraft all-up weight at 9,400 lb. This was the only Henley I and was powered by a Merlin I engine. During 1942 a Henley II L3276 powered by a Merlin V completed an assessment as a target tug at A&AEE Boscombe Down. It was also during the trials in March that it was flown with a bomb load of 1,000 lb. The A&AEE report appeared to be less critical in its conclusion, yet in the results appeared to be similar in handling as previously; it was recommended to get the tail up as soon as possible to stop the aircraft bouncing on take-off, and nose heaviness on landing still applied. It was recommended that when carrying a bomb-load and attempting to land on a rough airfield, the bombs should be dropped 'safe' before landing. The flap/undercarriage selector was as on the Hurricane, with one lever operating the two selectors, and was criticised for its position, not its operation.

As a target tug the aircraft went into production against specification 42/36, and production aircraft served with various training schools and anti-aircraft co-operation units. Whether it would have been as successful as a light bomber is hypothetical; for none

Hawker Henley target tug in service at Wyton 1940. (Author)

of the light bombers in Europe were successful unless operated under a massive fighter umbrella, and the dive-bomber myth was soon exploded when there was strong fighter opposition — this role being taken over by the fighter-bomber and rocket armament. The Henley was a far from viceless aircraft, and needed to be treated with a firm hand and a watchful eye.

The construction of the Henley was typical of Hawker construction of the period, basically a mixture of the biplane era leading into the stressed skin era. The mainplane consisted of a two-spar construction with a metal-covered centre section and a stressed skin outer section, the whole mainplane tapering from root to tip in plan and thickness. The centre section was based on two spars braced by a Warren-truss system and attached to the fuselage by spool fittings and tubular bracings. The front spar was continuous and at right angles to the aircraft's plane of symmetry, with the rear spar in two parts joined at the centre so that the two halves slope

forward from the centre. The spars had the Hawker polygonal booms with duralumin sheet webs, with the Warren-truss system consisting of two girders and a tubular strut and diagonals with the whole structure covered by duralumin sheeting.

The outer planes had a stressed skin covering which is riveted to a series of spars, stringers and sheet duralumin rubs. There were four spars, with the front and rear one having plug end fittings for attachment to the centre section, the distance between the spars decreasing from root to tip with the ribs parallel with the fore and aft line.

The fuselage was of the metal type tubular construction typical of the Hawker Hart etc., using steel and duralumin tubes connected by bolted or riveted joints. No welding was employed. The engine mounting was of similar construction and completely detachable from the fuselage, being bolted on at the front. The centre of the fuselage contains the two cockpits and most of the equipment, the whole being covered by a single glazed coupe top. Aft of the pilot's seat was a steel pylon to give protection to the crew in case of a turnover, and aft of the pylon was the target operator's cockpit with winch and equipment. On the basic tubular airframe was mounted a decking and fairing of wood formers to give a more streamlined shape, the whole fabric-covered except towards the front, where metal or plywood panels were used. The cockpits were separated, with the pilot's section of the coupe top having an opening top as well as side flaps. The aft portion of the coupe top over the target operator consisted of a one-piece duralumin frame carrying the port and starboard side panels and roof. Aft of the target operator was a cone shaped cabin fairing, that when rotated retracted to give the operator a better view aft.

The tail unit was totally conventional with cantilever tailplane and fin, elevator and rudder. The construction of the tailplane was similar to the mainplane outer section, only with three spars, transverse stringers and sheet metal ribs of light alloy; covered by a light alloy sheet riveted to the framework by mushroom-headed rivets. The elevator halves were built on a simple tubular spar which were bolted together to form one continuous spar, the front of which was covered above and below by a duralumin nosing. The remaining structure was tail ribs, apart from the horn balance area which had nose ribs as well, the whole covered with fabric attached by a patented method. The fin was based on front and rear finposts of high tensile steel girder section with a nosing of duralumin, a number of ribs and the whole covered with fabric attached by a patented method. The rudder was also fabric covered, and consisted of a tubular steel spar with ribs attached and completed by a duralumin trailing edge; the whole was bolted on the rear finpost by four hinges.

The flap was the only movable surface that was metal covered on the Henley, and was of the split trailing edge type. They consisted of rib stiffened duralin sheets mounted on tubular spars with each

Henley target tug L3243, first production aircraft. (RAF)

supported on four bearings and operated by hydraulic power.

The main undercarriage consisted of two units, each one comprising a shock absorber strut, radius arm and sidestay. At the base of the oleo was a stub axle on which was mounted the main wheel. These units retracted inwards and upwards, with a small amount of rearward movement, so that the undercarriage retracted into the underside of the centre section between the spars. The tailwheel, which was self-centring retracted into the fuselage fairing simultaneously with the main units, and was also hydraulically operated.

The fuel system had a total capacity of 200 gallons, which were in four separate tanks, two inter-spar tanks of 47 gallons each and two leading-edge tanks of 53 gallons each.

The continuation of Battle production and the use of the Henley as a target tug have been the source of speculative stories, yet what must be realised is that the Battle's bomb-load was 1,000 lb as against the Henley's 500 lb; the Battle was just a step in re-equipping the light bomber squadrons, which would under normal circumstances have been completed by 1941; and that the Henley would have faired no better in France than the Battle without a fighter escort. The Henley's dive-bombing capability could have been no more exploited than was the Battle's at Maastricht, with the German flak and Bf 109s holding air superiority.

Three Henleys were employed by Rolls-Royce as flying test-beds, with K5115 and L3302 being powered by Vulture engines and L3414 powered by a Griffon 2 engine, all based at Hucknall for flight test development. The Henley as a target tug suffered the indignity of short engine lives, for the slow flying speeds involved in target tug duties were conducive to engine overheating.

Comparison between two Mks of Henley

	Henley P4/34.	Henley TT.
Wingspan	47 ft 10½ in	47 ft 10½ in
Wing area	342 sq ft	342 sq ft
Aerofoil section (centre)	Clark YH	Clark YH
Tailplane span	14 ft 9 in	14 ft 9 in
Tailplane & elevator area	56.25 sq ft	56.25 sq ft
Engine	Merlin 1.	Merlin II & III.
Propeller	DH bracket	DH bracket
Track	12 ft 3 in	12 ft 3 in
Fuselage length	36 ft 5 in	36 ft 5 in
All-up weight	9,795 lb	8,840 lb
Maximum speed	292 mph	270 mph (with target)
Service ceiling	27,200 ft	27,200 ft

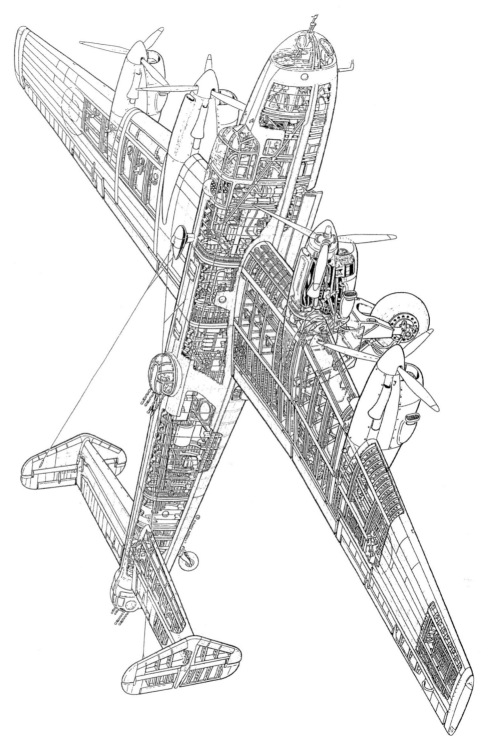

Handley Page Halifax II Srs 1A

17

Handley Page Halifax Mks I, II & V

With the issue of the P13/36 specification for a medium bomber having a cruising speed of 275 mph at 15,000 ft at two-thirds maximum power, Handley Page along with others tendered a design. Having already tendered to the B1/35 specification, Handley Page observed that the two specifications would require an almost similar aircraft, so 'HP' raised this with the Air Staff, and proposed that the HP56 fulfil both — in other words there was no need for two specifications. Eventually the tender to the B1/35 specification was withdrawn and the tender to the P13/36 specification accepted, as was Avro's 679 (Manchester). Amongst some of the requirements of the specification were, maximum load at catapult launch to be not less than 4,000 lb; maximum range to be not less than 3,000 miles; maximum possible bomb-load of 8,000 lb and a service ceiling of not less than 28,000 ft at normal loading. Also required were a method of carrying and dropping two 18-in torpedoes; message pick-up

hook (!) and 70 degree dive-bombing.

In May 1937 Volkert had also submitted to the Ministry a 20-page memorandum covering the unarmed bomber concept against the specification P13/36

After the design had begun and model testing been initiated, the Air Staff then requested Handley Page to change the HP56 design to four engines, as by then it had become obvious that there would not be sufficient Vulture engines for both the Avro 679 and the HP56. This was next followed by the realisation that there would not be sufficient Frazer-Nash turrets available for both aircraft! By now Handley Page was trying to get through to the Ministry that putting four engines into a twin-engined design was completely wrong; for there was the need for four engine nacelles on the mainplane, separate fuel systems and controls for four engines; and if this was accomplished then the resulting aircraft would be far larger than originally envisaged.

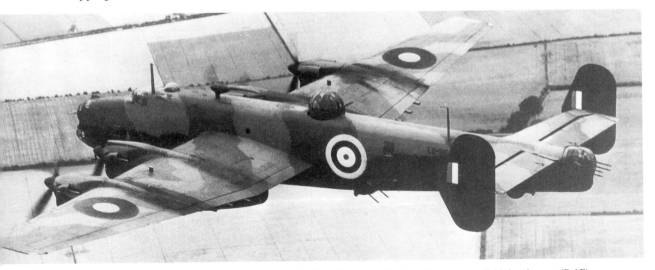

Halifax Mk.I. L7245. As well as front and rear turrets, fitted with mid-upper and mid-under turret and side hatch guns. (RAF)

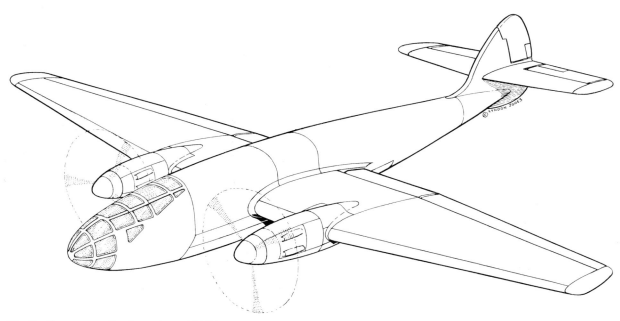

Handley Page unarmed bomber project to P13/36

Nevertheless Handley Page was forced to develop along these lines, and the aircraft that emerged, as the HP57, was considerably larger and heavier than the HP56, with an empty weight of 23,000 lb and an all-up weight of 50,000 lb. G.R. Volkert of Handley Page had revised the design to accept the four Merlin engines, and in the process the mainplanes had changed from having a large sweepback on the leading edge only, to a mainplane where the outer and intermediate wings had leading and trailing edge taper. He was also interested in the Messier hydraulic system because of its higher operating pressure, and also because the total system was lighter in weight than an equivalent British system. The fully stressed skin wing was also of new construction with integral fuel tank layout and housed three bomb-rack positions each side as well as the fuselage bomb-bay.

By 15 June 1937 the 70 degree dive-bombing requirement had been altered to 25 degrees, because of the extra strength required in the structure for the requirement, which would reduce the load the aircraft could carry. Then further relief was given to the design team by the Air Ministry's decision to drop the requirement for carrying torpedoes. This was followed later by deletion of the catapulting requirement, as an investigation by Handley Page's Aerodynamics Section had proved that with four Merlin engines the take-off run to clear a 50 ft screen would be 710 yds, making the catapulting requirement unnecessary. The DTD then made the decision to delete the dive-bombing requirement, although at the same time requesting from Handley Page that as large a diving angle as possible be provided.

During the period of design of the HP56/57 the NPL had circulated information on 18, 21 and 25 per cent thick wings, and in reviewing this Handley Page decided for structural reasons to opt for the 21 per cent thick wing. It was later found that the NPL information was incorrect, as turbulence in their new wind tunnel had given misleading figures. This in conjunction with the mid-mounted engine nacelles, the Merlin nacelle cross-sectional area and the small wing area would restrict the aircraft's performance in the future. The thick wing and mid-slung nacelles created extra drag in cruise, even though the thick wing offered space for offensive stores. The original design had made provision for integral fuel tanks, but these were not used on production aircraft, for by then operational experience had dictated the need for self-sealing fuel tanks; this however reduced the fuel capacity from 1,980 gallons to 1,552 gallons. With changes in the fuel system over the next twelve months the capacity would be increased again to 1,882 gallons.

With the priority of the Frazer-Nash turrets assigned to the Avro 679, Handley Page became interested in the Boulton Paul turrets of Samm Design. A conference was held at Boulton Paul works on 28 September 1937, followed by a visit on 4 October by Haynes of Handley Page. This was followed up later by the Air Ministry confirming installation of this type of turret in the HP57. The engine nacelle length was also to prove a problem. The nacelles were originally terminated underneath at the trailing edge of the wing, but during prototype testing were found to create unnecessary drag, so modifications were introduced to extend the nacelles to the trailing edge of the flaps, the rear portion deflecting with the flaps. The Air Ministry at this late stage was now asking Handley Page to consider alternative engine installations! Napier Dagger, Bristol Taurus and Hercules were some of those mentioned. Nevertheless Handley Page persisted with the Merlin installation, though at the same time far from satisfied with Rolls-Royce performance in producing a satisfactory installation. In October 1939 Farren of DTD suggested that Handley Page should investigate American engines of similar power to the Merlin; fortunately the design team had already seen the possibility of the Hercules engine, and commenced a programme regarding its installation.

The first prototype (L7244) was taken to 13 OTU Bicester, where it was erected by a picked team from Radlett, and on 25 October 1939 made its first

Above: Halifax Mk.II (Special) banks towards photographing aircraft.
Below: Halifax Mk.II being prepared at LPG Leavesden for delivery.

flight piloted by Major Cordes. This and subsequent flights were totally without incident and generally satisfactory, although rear fuselage oscillation was experienced, eventually being traced to vortices breaking away from the relatively blunt rear fuselage, and was rectified by the resetting of the turret deflectors to 7°. The performance estimates that had been made were found to be too optimistic — the science of drag estimation, nacelle design etc. still being not very advanced. The estimated cruising speed for instance being 265 mph at 15,000 ft, whereas the actual was 204 mph at 18,000 ft. It must be emphasised however, that Handley Page was disappointed with the performance and immediately began investigations into ways of improving it. When the Halifax went to the A&AEE for trials these began at 50,000 lb and were very satisfactory; very little swing when opening up on take-off and the aircraft flew itself off the ground. Regarding controls, the elevator was reasonably light and effective down to the stall, rudders heavy but satisfactory, ailerons too heavy at all speeds. Stability was overall quite satisfactory, and when flown during the stall tests then the control column had to be pulled back about three quarters of its travel from the mid-position to stall the aircraft. The stall was straightforward with no wing dropping.

On the early Mk 1 aircraft the tailwheel unit was retractable, and during the A&AEE tests and initial service, a number of the retraction jack-rods were found to get bent, which in some cases caused shimmy and in the worst cases damage. This was rectified by the tailwheel being fixed in a down position.

Landings were considered straightforward and brakes could be applied at any time during the landing run, without any tendency to swing. During these initial tests rudder overbalance was found to occur at speeds below 150 mph, but it was felt that this could be investigated during further testing. Unfortunately, the Halifax was required for a number of Commands and roles, so fittings for various roles were built in, basic weight increased, and the all-up weight increased to 60,000 lb. This was the point where the aircraft for its power loading and wing loading was incapable of high altitude cruising, and its handling had deteriorated so that the rudder overbalance problem was critical, especially when sideslipping or flying at a low airspeed. The rudder overbalance was basically due to the fins of the Halifax being too small and the rudders too powerful. These problems became prominent in 1942, and A&AEE and Handley Page initiated a programme to rectify this, the final solution being the increase of the fin area by approximately 40 per cent, which introduced the 'D' shaped fins.

In 1941 the Technical Department at Handley Page was engaged on the introduction of the Hercules engine to the Halifax airframe; the Mk II was entering production powered by the Merlin XX.

Halifax Mk.V of 38 Group towing off a fully loaded Hamilcar, the only aircraft type capable of this task. (IWM)

The Halifax all-up weight was then 60,000 lb, the fuel capacity was 1,882 gallons, but performance was no better, as the beam guns installed in the Mk I had been replaced by the 'C' type (Hudson) mid-upper turret, which created a lot of drag. The tare weight was now 34,980 lb against the Mk I Srs I's 33,860 lb.

For SOE operation Handley Page produced the Mk 2 Srs I (Special), which had the nose and mid-upper turrets removed, fuel jettison pipes deleted, and the airframe generally 'cleaned up'. This improved the performance to the point that No 4 Group squadrons asked for these modifications to be introduced. Meanwhile, in line with this, Handley Page had been carrying on a development programme with the 31st production Mk I (L9515), the airframe first having been given a streamlined metal nose, inner nacelles extended aft of the flap trailing edge, Merlin XX engines substituted for the Merlin Xs, and Morris single block radiators in improved cowlings fitted. The improvement

Boulton Paul 'D' turret of Halifax Mk.II. (Author)

in performance was sufficient for the incorporation of a number of these features, and the aircraft so improved designated the Mk II Srs IA. With this Mk the metal nose was translated into perspex of the same shape, a Type A mid-upper turret was installed and various protuberances removed — this mark was found to be faster than even the Mk II Srs I (Special).

Due to a shortage of Messier undercarriages, MAP took the decision to ask Dowty to proceed with an alternative design –– Dowty having spare work capacity — adapting the Manchester undercarriage to suit the Halifax pick-up points. Though this design work did not have any immediate use, as Messier production picked up; but eventually the Dowty undercarriage plus Dowty hydraulic system was incorporated into a Halifax model, the Mk V aircraft. Unfortunately, for Handley Page, Halifax production, and the RAF, to speed production a number of the Dowty undercarriage parts were produced as castings instead of forgings; in a relatively short space of time stress cracking occurred in these parts, causing the landing weights to be restricted to 40,000 lb to ease this. With this, Halifax V production in Canada was cancelled and production of the Mk V in the UK restricted.

The Halifax was later fitted with Bristol Hercules engines, and capable of operating up to an all-up weight of 68,000 lb. These were designated Mks III to AIX, depending on equipment and roles. The Halifax was used in many roles and most theatres of war; for its strong construction and commodious fuselage made it an ideal aircraft for various duties, and although it could not carry the bigger bombs like the 12,000 lb, it was capable of towing an operationally loaded Hamilcar glider — being the only British bomber capable of this, and cleared for this role. It was also the first four-engined British-built bomber to serve in Coastal Command; first to carry the 4,000 and 8,000 lb bombs; the first to be fitted with H2S, and the only British-built four-engined bomber to serve in the Middle East and Far East during the 1939–45 war. In fact, of all the four-engined British-built bombers it was the most versatile.

Construction of the fuselage was totally conventional, being built on the Handley Page process of four sections, which were completely equipped prior to final assembly, and were constructed of hoop formers and frames, longitudinal stringers and aluminium alloy stressed skin. There were two longerons which ran either side of the fuselage and carried the loads imposed on the fuselage by the bomb and equipment load. The centre section wing was built integral with the centre fuselage around two main spars. The front spar consisted of parallel extruded channel booms joined and braced by vertical and diagonal members. The rear spar used 'T' section booms joined by a sheet metal web.

The intermediate wing and outer wings were based on a two-spar construction, the whole wing being covered by an Alclad metal stressed skin over the ribs and spars. The outer wings on early aircraft were equipped with leading edge slots, but these were later locked in. The trailing edge flaps were hinged at the wing trailing edge and constructed around a 'D' nose spar, the flaps being of metal construction fabric covered.

The tail unit comprised a straight tailplane with twin end plates, all of metal construction and stressed skin covered. The elevators were of metal construction fabric covered and were hinged to the tailplane by six hinges. The rudders were of similar construction to the elevators and consisted of upper and lower sections, metal constructed but fabric covered.

The Messier undercarriage and hydraulic system of the Marks I and II was not only strong and effective, but once having been got used to, offered many advantages, not least being the number of methods available to lower the undercarriage in an emergency. Its only disadvantage was the size of the undercarriage arch, which induced more drag than the normal type of undercarriage. Messier carried out some improvements over a period of time and reduced the retraction time of the undercarriage and thus reduced the time that the undercarriage was down after take-off. The basis of the hydraulic system was that as the undercarriage, flaps etc. were retracted the transfer of oil compressed air in accumulators for each circuit; these circuits were isolated at each accumulator until the system was required.

A further improvement introduced when the aircraft was in service was the addition of undercarriage uplocks of the mechanical variety, which were inserted with the undercarriage in the 'up' position and ensured that the undercarriage did not fall down if the hydraulic system was hit by enemy fire.

Merlin engines Mk XX and 22 were the normal power units of the Mk II and V aircraft, and although one trial installation was made with a Merlin 24, this never went into production. A further trial installation and modifications to satisfy a request from the DTD were the alterations to HR756. The airframe was modified with underslung

Experimental Merlin exhaust on Halifax. (RAF)

Halifax prototype L7244 on test, less turrets. Initially fitted with leading-edge slats. (IWM)

engine nacelles — as per Lancaster — and the outer nacelles projected a foot further forward and the inner nacelles extended aft of the trailing edge by about three feet; Merlin 65 engines were supposed to be fitted, but as none were available Merlin 22 engines were installed. The aircraft was designated the Mk II Srs II, and was never put into production, but was loaned to Rolls-Royce as a trials aircraft for engine development. The improvement in performance with Merlin 22 engines was not considered enough over the Mk II Srs IA to put it into production — especially as the Hercules-engined airframe was already under development.

Like the Lancaster, no alteration to the calibre of the guns in the turrets was made until late in the war, and it was not until the German night-fighter *Schrage Musik* became known that an under-defence position was reconsidered — Halifaxes with trial installation under-gun turrets had been test flying early on in the war — so under-gun positions with 0.5-in Browning guns were installed on a number of Halifax, Lancaster and Stirling aircraft.

The Mk II Srs IA along with the Mk V Srs IA were the first to be retrospectively fitted with the D type fin and rudder and to include the Morris single block radiators as standard fitment. These were to be followed by the Mk III with Hercules engines, but would remain one of the most versatile heavy aircraft, its characteristics were typical of the period, its equipment dependent on the operator, and it operated in most theatres of the war — to its crews it was one of the best aircraft of the Second World War, an aircraft second to none.

Handley Page Halifax Mk. II Srs 1A

Wingspan	98 feet 8 inches	(30.09 metres)
Wing area	1250 sq.feet	(1161 sq.metres)
Length	71 feet 7 inches	(21.82 metres)
Empty weight	33,700 lb	(15,318 kg)
Maximum loaded weight	60,000 lb	(27,272 kg)
Maximum bombload	13,000 lb	(5,897 kgs)
Maximum speed at height	264 mph at 18,000 feet	(428 kph at 5,486 metres)
Service ceiling	21,000 feet	(6,400 metres)
Engines	four 1280 hp Merlin X inline	
Standard armament	ten 0.303-inch machine-guns	

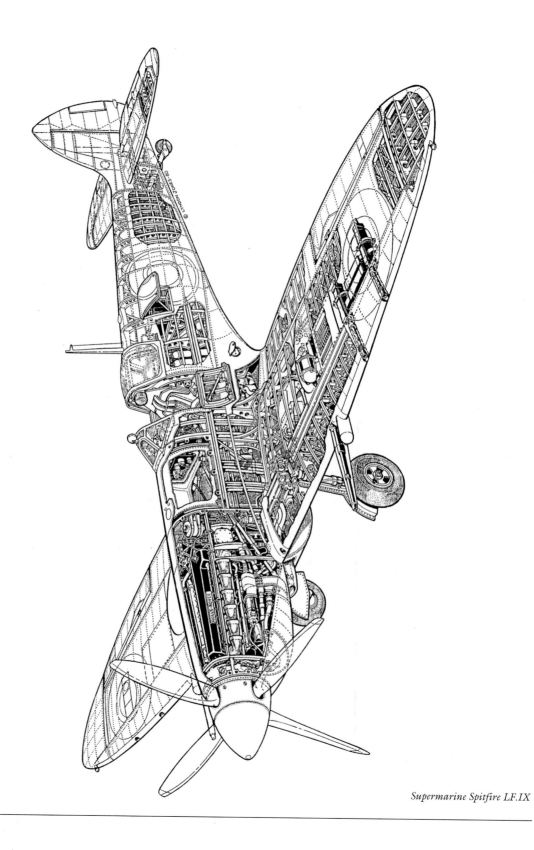

Supermarine Spitfire LF.IX

18

Supermarine Spitfire

To the British public the Spitfire is synonymous with Fighter Command, and its defiant name was embellished during wartime by the media and Ministry of Information; so that from articles and books the general public can be forgiven for thinking that this was the all-dancing, all-thinking fighter machine. Yet to older members of the RAF the Spitfire will stand *alongside* the Hurricane, for we remember that they were companion fighters against the Luftwaffe in 1940, and that in the Battle of Britain there were 459 Hurricanes and 292 Spitfires. This is not to detract from its beauty of line, its handling characteristics, as well as the roles that it undertook, but to put the Spitfire in its proper perspective, and to state facts and not myths.

As stated under the Hawker Hurricane heading, Supermarine as well as Hawker tendered to the F7/30 specification, yet for R.J. Mitchell, who was Supermarine's designer, fighter design had not been his forte, in fact one could broadly state that he had concentrated until then on flying boats and seaplanes, being best remembered for his Schneider Trophy winners. The design submitted to the F7/30 specification was Supermarine Type 224, which was a low-cranked-wing monoplane, and powered by the Air Ministry's choice of engine, the Rolls-Royce Goshawk. The Type 224 was in no way outstanding in any feature, in fact, it has even been described as a

Spitfire Mk 9 MJ730 powered by a Merlin Mk.66 flown by W/Cmdr A. Forbes-Wilson. (P.W. Porter)

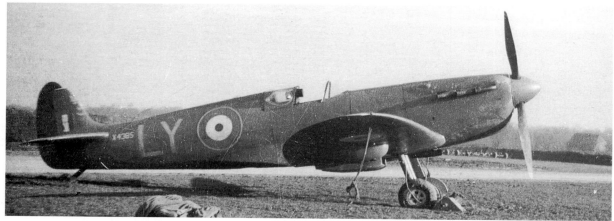

Top: Supermarine F7/30 aircraft with RR Goshawk engine, ancestor of the Spitfire. (Author)
Above: Spitfire PR Type IC X4385 at Alconbury during 1940. (Author)

'pedestrian design', for its undercarriage was fixed and covered with fairings that extended to the wings, there was an open cockpit, and the four machine-guns that were fitted were located as follows:

Two Vickers 0.303-in in the fuselage synchronised to fire through the propeller.
Two Vickers 0.303-in, one on the inside of the undercarriage fairing each side.

During the period that the Type 224 was under construction Mitchell was toying with improvements to the design, and having built an aircraft (which he was not satisfied with) to the specification, he began to commit to paper a further design. This was basically a further development of the Type 224 and still incorporated the Goshawk engine, but the mainplanes were of smaller span and tapered to the tip on both the leading and trailing edges, with both flaps and retractable undercarriage envisaged as part of the final design.

Supermarine's own specification No. 425 covered this development, which was still basically a

development of the Type 224, and this proposal was accepted by the Air Ministry in early 1934.

Supermarine's 224 in the F7/30 competition justly proved how right Mitchell was in launching forth on further development, for the Gloster SS37 (which became the Gladiator) which was awarded the contract, was — even though a biplane — 4 mph faster than the Type 224, and took 1½ minutes less in climbing to 15,000 feet.

The new design to the Supermarine specification 425 was given the Type 300 designation, and was originally listed as a cleaned-up version of the Type 224, but by November 1934 Mitchell was further refining the design. By then Rolls-Royce had unveiled news of their PV12 engine with promises of 1,000 bhp in the future, though at that time it was far short of that figure, and had not passed its type test.

Specification F5/34 had at this period of time been issued for tender, calling for an armament of at least six, preferably eight machine-guns, and though Supermarine did not tender to the specification, the armament requirement was obviously one that

Top: Spitfire Mk V AB910 powered by Merlin Mk.55. Flown by Jeffrey Quill, Vickers Aviation at Wisley. (Author)
Middle: Spitfire Mk XI minus propeller and reduction gear after 0.86 Mach TV dive at RAE Farnborough by S/Ldr Martindale. (RAE)
Bottom: Spitfire Mk.9 crashlanded at Hawkinge after combat. Armourers unloading cannon. (Author)

would be repeated in other specifications and contracts in the future — and maybe even heavier calibre weapons.

As the Type 300 design became more positive, and no Government contract was apparently forthcoming, the Board of Vickers-Supermarine decided to go ahead as a private venture, but almost immediately specification F37/34 was issued by the Air Staff, as it was realised that apart from armament, the Type 300 was almost similar to their specification F10/35. So with the Hurricane and Spitfire prototypes approaching hardware status, the specification F10/35 was withdrawn, and shortly afterwards re-issued as F37/35 calling for a cannon-armed fighter. This specification was tendered to by

Hawker and Supermarine as well as other manufacturers, but was won eventually by Westlands with their Whirlwind design.

Even with the issue of the F37/34 specification the use of the Goshawk engine had not been deleted, yet the evaporative cooling system was obviously more vulnerable to enemy action than even the normal liquid-cooled system, and meant that condensers had to be positioned on the exterior of the airframe, and would occupy a large area. The Goshawk was a development of the Kestrel, but with problems. The emergence of the PV12 engine gave to both Camm and Mitchell that extra bhp without the complication of evaporative cooling, but now came the problem of how to dissipate the heat

Top: Spitfire Mk.I of 66 Squadron at Duxford with F/O Frank Rimmer. Winter 1939/40. (P.W. Porter)
Above: Spitfire of P/O Leon Collingbridge, 66 Squadron at Duxford 1940. (P.W. Porter)

generated by a 1,000 bhp engine, without using a large drag-creating radiator.

This was solved at RAE. A scientist there named F. Meredith had, over a period of time, been very thoroughly developing a ducted radiator; in which the radiator cooling air was expelled giving a small amount of thrust, whilst at the same time the radiator design reduced drag. This was a development that was to make not only the Spitfire design more viable, but others also.

Returning to the period after the rejection of the Type 224, but remaining on the engine situation, amongst a number of proposals was a suggestion from the Air Ministry that the Type 224 should be repowered with a Napier Dagger engine. This proposal did not find favour with the Supermarine Board of Directors and so no further decision was made in that direction.

With the advent of the Rolls-Royce PV12 engine (later to be named Merlin) Supermarine was able to take further steps in the design of the Type 300, and based around the specification was able to satisfy the Air Ministry with the design, which resulted with a contract for one prototype (K5054) being given in January 1935. This contract (361140/30/C4(a)) and specification mentioned the following requirements (amongst others):

Fitted with RR. P.V.12 engine.
Airscrew of wooden construction.
Service load as specified in F7/30.
All four guns may be installed outside propeller diameter.
Tailwheel to be fitted if practicable.

The first flight of the prototype K5054 took place on 5 March 1936 with 'Mutt' Summers at the controls. The prototype was a slim metal-stressed skin monocoque design with a neat single-strut main undercarriage which folded outwards, and the engine drove a wooden propeller having a special fine pitch. Although Summers pronounced the flight as satisfactory, when an accurately flown course was measured the maximum speed was recorded as 335 mph at 17,000 ft. This was very disappointing to Supermarine and Mitchell, for a figure of 350 mph had been expected; so a bit by bit investigation of the airframe was carried out, with small reductions in drag being achieved by the cleaning up of various excrescences. But the main drag and loss in maximum speed was identified as the particular fixed pitch propeller that had been fitted. A new fixed

pitch propeller was designed and fitted, and a further performance check recorded a level flight speed of 350 mph.

Testing also revealed that the Spitfire was sensitive to rearward movements of the C of G, which caused a certain amount of instability. On 26 May 1936 K5054 was despatched to A&AEE for initial trials and a quick assessment was made in which the Spitfire was considered suitable for Service use. Further testing followed at a loaded weight of 5,332 lb, when the ground handling was considered satisfactory; the following comments were made:

(a) Elevator too light and too powerful — recommended that the elevator control could be improved by reducing the gear ratio in the control circuit.
(b) Unstable in the glide with undercarriage and flaps down.
(c) The moulded Perspex windscreen distorts the vision.
(d) Diving speed is limited to 380 mph.
(e) Guns refused to fire at altitude due to low temperatures.

The performance figures pleased Mitchell, for it recorded a maximum speed of 349 mph, a service ceiling of 35,000 ft, and the take-off distance over a 50 ft barrier of 235 yards.

The Air Ministry had budgeted £10,000 against the F37/34 specification aircraft, but the prototype had cost Supermarine £15,776. Nevertheless it was apparent to the A&AEE and the Ministry that the Spitfire was *the* fighter to join Fighter Command, and on 3 June 1936 a production contract (527113/36) was given against production specification F16/36 for 310 Spitfire Mk Is. The contract called for the delivery of the aircraft to commence in May 1937 with the contract to be completed by March 1939. Unfortunately, Supermarine was a small firm, and problems and production difficulties delayed the first flight of the first production aircraft (K9787) until 15 May 1938.

During this time, production got underway and construction of the aircraft itself was improved for easier production and structure modification allowed the diving speed to be increased to 450 mph.

In July 1938 K9787 went to the A&AEE for its type trials and the second production aircraft (K9788) flew on 12 July. The first squadron to begin re-equipping with the Spitfire was No 19, which received its first Spitfire (K9789) on 4 August 1938.

Top: Spitfire Mk.16 SL542 powered by a Packard Merlin 266, preparing to start up – if the female will move! (J. Keene)
Above: Spitfire Mk. 16 TE 392 powered by a Packard Merlin 266. Shown post-war, minus its cannon. (R. Deacon)

In 1937 consideration was given to using the Spitfire to raise the World's Speed record, so a Spitfire I airframe (K9834) was prepared that was powered by a specially modified Merlin 2 engine using 'doped' fuel and high boost pressures. The record however was raised by an Me 109R in April 1939 to a figure beyond K9834's capability, whose maximum speed was 408 mph.

At Rolls-Royce the Merlin had reached the XX series by 1939, and was developing this to power the Hurricane and Spitfire to higher speeds, but in production the Spitfire was only fitted with the Mk III.

With the introduction of the Spitfire II powered by the Merlin 12 operating on 100 octane fuel, driving a Rotol RX5/1CS constant speed propeller, an increase in altitude of 2,000 feet was achieved, the engine delivering 1,150 hp at 14,500 feet. This entered service in 1940, and was followed by the PRIV and the Mk V. The Spitfire V was a combination of a Mk II airframe and the Merlin 45 engine, and went into production just before the end of 1940. This occurred after a Mk I airframe had been fitted with a special Merlin X (which incorporated a special supercharger), the special Mk X becoming the Merlin 45. During the production of the Mk V aircraft a shortage of 20mm cannon occurred, so a number of Mk V aircraft had eight

RAF Memorial Flight Spitfire on ground-run at Coningsby. (P.W. Porter)

0.303-in machine-guns installed instead, and were designated as Mk VA's.

The Spitfire over its operational period was built or modified into a number of roles, low-level fighter, photo-reconnaissance, and high altitude fighter, the first high altitude development was the long span (40 ft. 2 in) Mk VI, which was pressurised; this was followed by the Mk VII, which incorporated amongst other features an extensively redesigned fuselage and a Merlin 60.

Other versions were the Mk VIII which were produced as both high and low level versions; the Mk IX aircraft produced by combining the Merlin 60 with a Mk VC airframe; and the Spitfire XVI which was similar to the Spitfire IX but powered with the Packard Merlin.

In 1942 the Fw 190 was getting the better of the Spitfire VB. The advent of the Mk IX HF took care of this problem and the VB was restricted to lower level operations, but even so it was no match for the Fw 190. To overcome this problem, two modifications were introduced. These were: to clip the wing tips to improve manoeuvrability at low level; and to crop the impeller tips of the supercharger on the Merlin 45, which then became the 45M. These engines were fitted to the Mk VC. As most of the aircraft so modified were reputed to have flown about 1,000 hours each, it was said that the 'C' in the Mk VC stood for 'clapped, clipped, cropped'. Apparently, these two modifications were first carried out in the Middle East on the North African Front, without official approval from the 'head office' — and made

the Mk VC more competitive, so were eventually sanctioned in the UK.

To reduce the Spitfire Marks to a reasonable point it may be of interest to read the following tables:

Wing Designation

Wing 'A'   (original) had eight machine-guns of 0.303-in calibre fitted.

Wing 'B'   had two 20mm cannon and four 0.303-in machine-guns fitted.

Wing 'C'   termed the 'universal wing' — could accommodate either four 20mm cannon or two 20mm cannon and four 0.303-in machine-guns.

Wing 'E'   carried two 20mm cannon and two 0.50-in machine-guns.

Airframe Designation

'A'   (original) Accommodated the Merlin II. III and XII.
Formed basis of Mk 1A. 1B. IIA. IIB. PRIV.VA. VB. VI. PR VII and XIII

'B'   (designed for Mk III) Basis of IC. VC. PRXI and XII.

'C'   Mks VII, VIII and XIV.

'D'   Mk 21.

The Mk IX Spitfire was produced in 3 different versions, an LF with a Merlin 66 engine, an HF with a Merlin 61 or 63, and a special HF powered by the Merlin 70. By the end of 1943 with the Allies already committed to attacking in the West, the IXF was in great demand for low level action, whilst at the same time the HF was capable of combatting the Fw 190A in most manoeuvres, although at 15,000 to 22,000 feet the Fw 190A was superior. Orders for the Spitfire by the end of 1943 were mainly for the Spitfire VIII and IX.

With the success of the Spitfire the Admiralty, in late 1941, requested the supply of Spitfires suitably modified for the Fleet Air Arm. This was actioned in December just before Christmas with a Spitfire VB, BL676 being fitted with an arrester hook and slinging points. This aircraft then commenced deck landing trials on HMS *Illustrious*, after which an order was placed for two variants; there was the Seafire IB based on the Spitfire VB with 'B' wings, and then the Seafire IIc based on the Spitfire Vc with 'C' type wings. The name Sea Spitfire had originally been used, but was compressed into Seafire, and officially recognised.

The Seafire's weight was approximately five per cent greater than the Spitfire, and the drag caused by the slinging points and arrester hook reduced the maximum level speed by approximately 5 mph. Neither the Seafire IB or IIc had folding wings, and the contract work of conversion was carried out by AST Ltd Hamble and Cunliffe-Owen of Eastleigh. The IIc was the first major production Seafire, and on this model catapult points were also installed and the areas strengthened; an external fish-plate in the fuselage aft of the pilot's bulkhead was also installed to beef up this area, where the arrester hook stresses were felt. As the same Merlin Mk was used on both Seafire marks, the IIc's maximum speed was about 15 mph slower than the IB, as the IIc's all-up weight was greater than the Mk IB by about six per cent and the drag was greater from the added modifications. A

number of IIc aircraft were converted to LIIc by the installation of a Merlin 32 and a strengthened undercarriage. The IB aircraft were first embarked in HMS *Furious* in October 1942, as on this carrier the lift size was larger than normal and could accommodate the non-folding wings.

Folding wings were first introduced on the Seafire FIII, which was powered by the Merlin 55 driving a four-blade propeller. This model had a gain in performance over the IIc, being 20 mph faster at all heights, and an initial rate of climb of 4,600 ft/min. Its folding wings were jointed in two places in each wing, the major joint being inboard of the inboard cannon mounting, and the second joint at the wing to wingtip joint. As Supermarine decided on manual unfolding and locking of the wings, the weight penalty was only 125 lb. This model commenced in March 1943.

The Seafire was at that time one of the fastest carrier aircraft, but due to its landplane background and narrow track undercarriage, was far from an ideal carrier aircraft. Far more were damaged or lost in service due to its weaknesses than to enemy action, but it served as a stopgap while specifically designed naval aircraft were acquired from the USA. Against this, the Seafire FR 47 was still on sale by Vickers-Armstrong as a development of the Spitfire 24 in 1948! In service the Seafire's main weakness was its narrow track undercarriage, which also sheared off at the pivot points on heavy landings, and the rear fuselage wrinkled — sometimes a sign of service!

The Spitfire will be, and is, remembered by many for the wartime fighting, remembered also for its sleek fuselage and beautifully shaped wings, it appeared an aircraft of character, defiant, a spitfire.

Seafires wrecked on HMS Attacker *after one missed the barrier. (P.W. Porter)*

Spitfire Mk.16 SL721 (G-BAUP) restored. Owned by Warbirds of Gt Britain 1978. (Author)

Basic differences of Spitfire Marks

Mk I.	Merlin II or III. External bulletproof windscreen. Fabric-covered control surfaces. Watts fixed pitch prop or DH two position or DH constant speed.
Mk II.	Merlin XII. External bulletproof windscreen. Fabric-covered control surfaces. Rotol constant speed propeller.
Mk III.	Merlin XX. Internal bulletproof windscreen. Fabric-covered control surfaces. Clipped wing. Rotol constant speed prop.
PR IV.	Merlin 45, 46, 50, 55, and 60. Plain windscreen. Metal-covered ailerons. DH constant speed prop.
Mk V.	Merlin 45. Internal bulletproof windscreen. Metal-covered ailerons. Wingspan 30 ft 6 in or 36 ft 10 in. Rotol constant speed or DH Hydromatic prop.
Mk VI.	Merlin 47. Special non-sliding hood. Metal-covered ailerons. 4-blade Rotol prop. Wingspan 40 ft 2 in.
Mk VII.	Merlin 61. Different control surfaces. Double glazed sliding hood. Wingspan 40 ft 2 in. 4-blade Rotol prop.
PR VII.	Merlin 45 or 46. Internal bulletproof windscreen. Metal-covered ailerons. DH constant speed prop. Wingspan 36 ft 10 in.
Mk VIII.	Merlin 61. Reduced span ailerons. Internal bulletproof windscreen. 4-blade Rotol prop.
Mk IX.	Merlin 61. Frise ailerons metal covered. Internal bulletproof windscreen. 4-blade Rotol prop. Wingspan 36 ft 10 in.
PR X.	Merlin 64. Double glazed sliding hood. Metal-covered ailerons. Wingspan 36 ft 10 in. 4-blade Rotol prop.
PR XI.	Merlin 61, 63, 63A, and 70 Plain Perspex windscreen. Metal-covered ailerons. 4-blade Rotol prop. Wingspan 36 ft 10 in.
PR XIII.	Merlin 32. Internal bulletproof windscreen. Metal-covered ailerons. Changed tail unit. 3-blade DH prop.
Mk XVI.	Merlin 266. Internal bulletproof windscreen. Frise metal ailerons. Changed tail unit. 4-blade Rotol prop.

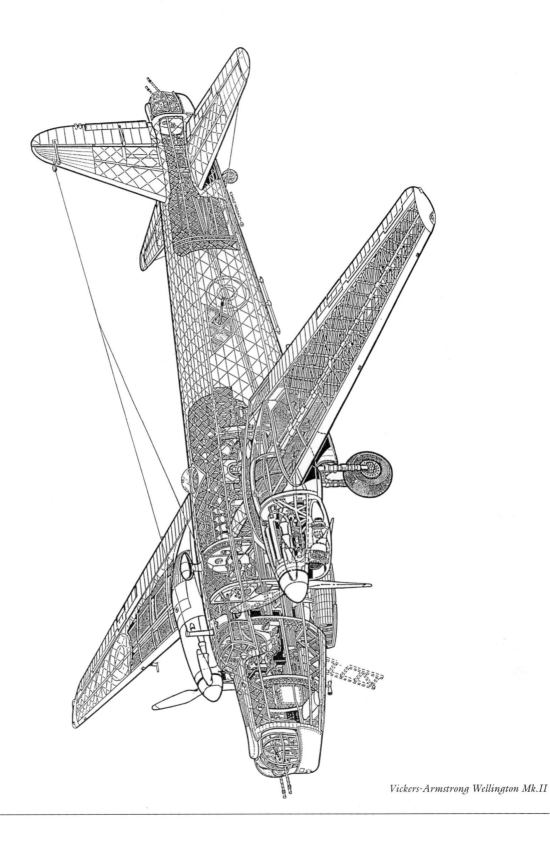

Vickers-Armstrong Wellington Mk.II

19

Vickers-Armstrong Wellington
II & VI

The Wellington in one Mark or other saw service throughout the 1939–1945 war in one role or another, while serving in a variety of operational areas. It was designed to Specification B9/32, which was issued to provide a replacement for the Sidestrand/Overstrand heavy bombers. Tenders were received by the Ministry from Bristol, Gloster, Handley Page and Vickers to the specification, two of the requirements of which were:

Bombload of 1,000 lb for 720 miles.
Range of 1,500 miles at the aircraft's maximum weight.

The Vickers-Armstrong tender by R.K. Pierson was made in March 1933 and covered a high-wing monoplane with a fixed undercarriage, and was to be powered by either the Bristol Mercury or Rolls-Royce Goshawk. Further design studies and an evaluation of the Wellesley project were made, which resulted in a revision to the tender in October of the same year. The aircraft was now presented as a mid-wing monoplane with retractable undercarriage, the power being at this stage by the same engines as proposed earlier.

The Vickers and Handley Page tenders were accepted, and a contract placed with Vickers-Armstrong in December 1933 for one prototype (K4049); this was designated the Type 271, and was powered with Goshawks. However, by mid-1934 the Type 271 had been further revised to accept two 850 hp Pegasus 10 engines instead.

The prototype first flew on 15 June 1936 and a production order was placed in the same year, followed on 29 January 1937 with specification 29/36 to cover the production of 180 Wellington Mk Is. The name that was suggested by the manufacturer for the aircraft was 'Crecy', but this was not acceptable to the Air Ministry, who bestowed the name 'Wellington' on the production

Wellington Mk.II bomber powered by Merlin X. (RAF)

Wellington II T2545 powered by Merlin Mk 60 engines. (Rolls-Royce)

aircraft. In service it was nicknamed 'Wimpy', reputed to have been derived from the *Daily Mirror* comic strip cartoon 'Popeye', whose hamburger devouring friend was J. Wellington Wimpy — of rather portly outline!

Prototype K4049 was lost in April 1937 when it went out of control during diving tests, though by then a large amount of data had been accumulated and the design accepted as the basis for development.

The Wellington Mk I entered service in October 1938, having been modified considerably from the prototype; appearing more portly, but with a continual upsweep underneath the fuselage to the rear turret; it had an increased bomb-load, and was now powered by Pegasus 18 engines of 1,000 hp. This was followed by the Type 408 — the Wellington Ia — then the Type 415 Wellington Ic, on which was introduced the FN5 front turret and FN10 rear turret; followed later by the addition of beam guns. The Wellington when first introduced into service had a 'dustbin' under turret, but this was removed when it was found that in the lowered position excessive drag was induced.

With the Wellington Mk I in service, the Air Ministry became concerned over the effect that enemy bombing might have on engine supply, so decided that an alternative engine supply should be made available.

This resulted in the 38th Wellington I airframe (L4250) being re-powered with Merlin 10 engines, design work on it beginning in January 1938. Vickers allotted the Type 298 to this airframe, which first flew after conversion on 3 March 1939, followed by the second prototype R3221, which was a converted Mk Ic. The first production order for the Wellington Mk II — now designated Type 406 — was for a quantity of 200, all being built at Weybridge.

The weight of the Merlin installation was found to be 400 plus lb more than estimated, so alterations were made to the main undercarriage in the down position as it was found necessary to install ballast in the rear fuselage during trials. Then in production form the Mk II had a wider span tailplane, its all-up weight was then 33,000 lb and it carried a bomb-load of 4,000 lb. In this form its maximum speed was 254 mph with a service ceiling of 23,500 ft, and its normal range was 1,570 miles with an absolute range of 2,220 miles.

Early in 1940, when consideration was being given to carrying larger bombs, proposals were made to convert a Wellington to carrying a 4,000 lb bomb, a Mk II (W5389) was selected. The normal bomb beams and intermediate bomb doors were removed, and a special frame inserted for the carriage of a single large bomb. This installation went into service.

Top: Wellington L4250 modified to carry 40mm cannon in mid-upper position. (RAF)
Above: Wellington L4250 modified to twin fins and rudders and 40mm cannon turret. (RAF)

The following installation did *not* go into service, it was purely an experimental installation; this was the fitment into a Mk II (L4250) of a heavy mid-upper turret which mounted a 40mm Vickers gun; as the geodetic structure was so flexible, the airframe structure in the locality of the turret was replaced with stressed skin construction. With the size and operation of the gun turret affecting the aircraft's directional stability, twin fins and rudders were later fitted.

Construction of the airframe was based on the goedetic structure that was first introduced on the Wellesley, which consisted of closely pitched diagonal members of special lipped channel section arranged in diamond pattern. The Wellington fuselage comprised top, side and bottom panels of light alloy geodetic structure bordered by longerons to locate it; this was joined by a lower structure consisting of a floor panel, which formed the top of the bomb compartment, this being braced by two girders running the full length from Station 12½ to Station 55.

The tail unit was quite conventional and consisted of a tailplane, elevators, single fin and rudder. Both the elevator and rudder were shrouded and the elevator horn balanced. The tailplane was constructed around a main spar of unbraced tubular booms, root ribs, leading and trailing edge members with built-up ribs. The elevators were hinged to the trailing edge of the tailplane at four points, and comprised a light alloy riveted tube, ribs and trailing edge member, all fabric covered. The fin was similar in construction to the tailplane and the rudder similar in construction to the elevators, all fabric covered.

The mainplanes were similar to the fuselage, being of geodetic construction and fabric covered. The structure was constructed around a main spar of tubular booms joined by Warren-girder bracing, the spar extending from tip to tip; with the wing tapering in chord and thickness from root to tip, and comprising outer and inner sections. The wing also had leading and trailing edge members formed from 'C' section booms joined by plate webs. Fuel tanks were accommodated in the wings, plus a fuel tank and oil tank in each engine nacelle. The wings had ailerons constructed of a built-up channel spar and flanged plate ribs joining onto a trailing edge steel tube member; the ailerons were of the semi-Frise type. The flaps were of light alloy and built-up in three sections of 'Z' section ribs and intercostal stringers with ribs hinged to the trailing edge of the wings.

In 1938 Vickers-Armstrong were asked to investigate a possible high altitude development of the Wellington, and priority on it continued even after Beaverbrook took over as Minister of Aircraft Production. This was initially projected and produced in small numbers to be powered by Bristol Hercules engines; the first production order being placed at the end of May 1939, and the type designated the Mk V. As an alternative engine Rolls-Royce produced the Merlin 60 engine, (two-speed two-stage type), and with this powerplant fitted the type was designated the Mk VI. As a production model it went into production as the Type 442, the first prototype being W5795. The bomb-load was 1,000 lb, but in the production version the bomb-load was 4,000 lb.

The Mks V and VI used the same geodetic construction, but a pressure cabin was incorporated which was fitted with integral feet bolted into and nestling into the geodetic framework. The cabin was fitted forward of Station 12½ and provided accommodation for a crew of three. This cabin was a metal shell lagged internally, with entry being made through a circular door in the rear of the cabin. Observation windows were fitted as well as a projecting dome for the pilot, the pressure cabin being supplied with heated air from an engine-driven pump.

A Mk V airframe was also re-engined with Merlin 60 series engines and given a 12 ft extension to the wings. This was the Type 443 and was designated the Mk VIA. With the wing extension the aircraft reached 40,000 ft, while the Mk VI had a ceiling of 38,500 ft. All the Mk V and VI aircraft were produced at Weybridge.

The handling of the Mk II and Mk VI on take-off varied only slightly between the two, for on the Mk II the throttles were opened fully without hesitation, the tail was raised and the aircraft kept straight with the rudder; though at the heavy loading there was a tendency to swing left and the left throttle needed to lead the right-hand one. On the Mk VI there was always a tendency to swing left, which needed to be controlled by the throttles. Vision for the pilot was quite good from the dome, though in bad weather trying to 'fly in' using instruments was not very good, as the vision inwards to the instruments was far from ideal. On the early marks of Wellington an 'engine out' situation was one in which the chance of getting home was remote, for they had no feathering propellers. With the increase of power with the Merlins the situation was improved, though the liquid-cooled installation was more vulnerable to enemy action than the aircooled Pegasus engine. The Mk VI was in flight generally unstable and required flying all the time that it was not on autopilot, and on take-off its safety speed with one engine 'out' was 130 mph.

These pressurised Wellingtons were at one stage intended to operate with OBOE, and a few were on the establishment of 109 Squadron at Wyton, but finally the 'Wimpy' was rejected in favour of the Mosquito.

The Wellington Mk II was used in the experimental role for a number of installations, including being the test vehicle (BJ895) for the trials with the Barnes Wallis 'bouncing bomb' during its early development, as well as the flight test-bed for the early Whittle gas turbine units. One of the Mk IIs had late series Merlins to allow high altitude

testing of the gas turbines.

The last of the 'cloth bombers', as the Wimpy was affectionately known, in its pressurised form as the Mk V and VI got nicknamed the 'Flying Coffin', as it was considered impossible to escape from the pressure cabin in the case of a crash, and, in the case of an emergency exit in the air, it was necessary to get out of the cabin and walk to the rear exit! It is obvious from crew reports and test reports that the Mk V and VI were not viable weapons — certainly not for Bomber Command; and most finished their lives as experimental aircraft or stored in Maintenance Units. Which was a far cry from the lives of most of the other Wellingtons, which operated far and wide, and were remembered with affection by their crews.

Wellington Mk VI high-altitude bomber with pressure cabin and powered by Merlin Mk.60 engines. (RAF)

Vickers-Armstrong Wellington Mk.II

Wingspan	86 feet 2 inches	(26.26 metres)
Wing area	840 sq.feet	(78.04 sq.metres)
Length	64 feet 7 inches	(19.68 metres)
Empty weight	20,258 lb	(9,208 kg)
Maximum loaded weight	33,000 lb	(15,000 kg)
Maximum bombload	4000 lbs	(1,818 kg)
Maximum speed at height	254 mph at 17,500 feet	(410 kph at 5,334 metres)
Service ceiling	23,500 feet	(7,230 metres)
Range	1570 miles	(2,494 kilometres)
Engines	two 1145 hp Merlin Mk.X inline	
Standard armament	up to eight 0.303-inch machine-guns	

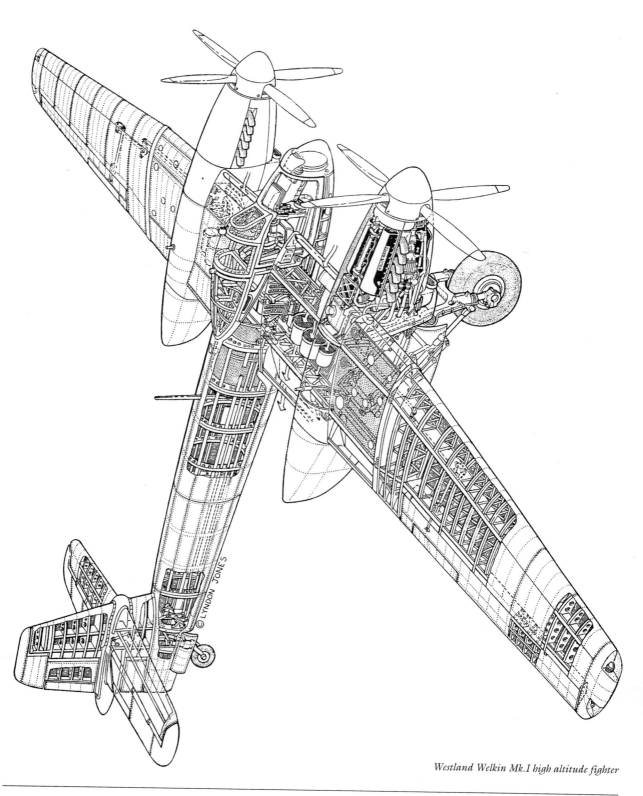

Westland Welkin Mk.I high altitude fighter

20

Westland Welkin

This aircraft could truly be called the forgotten fighter, for it must have been the only fighter that, though produced in quantity, never got past the Maintenance Units to operational units.

The origination of the Welkin began with the issue of specification F4/40, which called for a specially designed single-seat high altitude day- and night-fighter armed with 20mm cannon. The need for this aircraft arose when in the early months of the 1939–45 war, it became evident that enemy aircraft were operating over Great Britain at a height above the contemporary fighter's capabilities, and the Air Staff concluded that this could presage high altitude bombing attacks in the future. The enemy intruders were Junkers Ju 86P high altitude aircraft powered with Junkers Jumo 207 engines.

Westland Aircraft Ltd was selected to translate the requirements into hardware, and preliminary investigation determined that these could only be met by a high aspect-ratio mainplane and a pressure cabin. The Welkin was the first British aircraft design to incorporate a pressure cabin from its conception.

The Welkin in general appearance resembled the Westland Whirlwind, and its construction followed the same lines, having a planklike wing of high aspect-ratio, the wingspan being 70 ft and its wing area 460 sq ft. A project based on the Whirlwind powered by Merlin engines had been a paper exercise early on, but this never achieved acceptance, so the time expended on this possibly contributed to the Welkin design. The Welkin had its mainplane set in the mid-position, and its outline resembled an extended Whirlwind wing, such aspect-ratio giving the Welkin high lift characteristics at high altitude, reduced the possibility of high speed stalls in tight turns, and with its wing loading of 38lb/sq ft ensured it a satisfactory take-off and landing performance.

At the start of the P14 Welkin design, the design staff at Westland realised that to achieve an operational ceiling comparable to or higher than the Ju 89P, their design would require a large wing span, and if the strength was not to be excessive a somewhat greater thickness/chord ratio above

Welkin DX340 with 'beard' radiators as well as leading-edge radiators. Engines were a trial installation. (F. Ballam)

Merlin RM16SM engine as installed on Welkin DX340. (F. Ballam)

average would be required. As a result of this decision, the same section aerofoil (NACA 230 series) as the Whirlwind was used, but the thickness ratios at root and tip were increased from 17 and 8 to 20 and 12 per cent respectively.

Pressurisation was dictated by the operational requirements of the specification, and so Petter and his design team decided to go for a pressure cabin that would be continuously supplied by oxygen, with a differential of three and a half psi above that of the ambient atmosphere at around 40,000 ft. To relieve the pilot of any need to control this — which would be an unacceptable distraction for a combat pilot — it was decided to install a system that once selected 'on' would function autonomously in accordance with the actual height of the aircraft. At the same time it was decided that the system was to incorporate safety devices, and also regulate not only

the pressure but the temperature and humidity of the cabin air. This cabin pressure control valve was developed by a special department at Westland, which would later become Normalair Ltd. The intake of air was provided by a Rotol cabin supercharger and the exit of the air to atmosphere was controlled by the cabin pressure control valve.

Difficulties with the aerofoil and its thickness/chord ratio became apparent when model test results were received from the RAE high speed wind tunnel, for these indicated that not only did drag increase rapidly at near the predicted top speed, but the maximum lift decreased as quickly. Fortunately the actual figures produced when the prototype was test flown were not quite as bad as the wind tunnel tests, and with the power available with the Merlin 61 engines, the compressibility effects were only just beginning to affect the climb and level speed performance, though there was some deterioration in the Welkin's handling.

The requirements of the specification were revised in April 1942 and re-issued as F7/41, and this called for a single-seat fighter for high altitude and world-wide use. An aircraft was to provide a steady gun platform, have good all round visibility, and its maximum speed to be at least 415 mph at 33,000 ft with a service ceiling of 42,000 ft minimum.

The 1,290 hp Merlin 61 engines had initially been developed for the Wellington VI high altitude bomber, and when the first Welkin prototype DG558/G took the air for the first time on 1 November 1942 flown by Harald Penrose, they gave the Welkin a maximum speed of 387 mph at 26,000 ft and 358 mph at 40,000 ft. Its maximum climb rate was 3,850 ft/min and its climb to 40,000 ft took 20 minutes. While the take-off and climb were satisfactory the diving speed was restricted due to compressibility, ailerons were not very effective at any speed and particularly ineffective at high altitude. The angle of climb was steep but the rate of roll was slow. The single-engine performance was unacceptable owing to rudder oscillation but the general stability was good. As initially flown DG558/G had a rounded top to its rudder, but this was later removed; the suffix/G on the aircraft serial number indicated special equipment aboard and required an armed guard when the aircraft was parked.

On the second prototype and on subsequent aircraft the rudder top was square cut as produced, sixty-seven Welkins being eventually produced, as well as the two prototypes DG558 and DG562. Tests between two Welkins flying at between 38,000 and 40,000 ft, indicated that the Welkin was capable

Underneath view of nose showing AI radar dish and four 20mm Above: Hispano cannon under fuselage. (F. Ballam)

of dealing with high altitude reconnaissance or bomber aircraft, though the low diving speed was a handicap, as was the low rate of roll.

Engine cooling on the Welkin was similar in layout to the Whirlwind, with the radiators situated in the wing centre section between the nacelles and the fuselage. The first radiators supplied were not only an unacceptably tight fit, but susceptible to leakage, and their cooling capability was marginal; so at the Ministry's urgent recommendation, a request was made to Morris Radiators Ltd to supply an alternative design; this was delivered in quick time, gave adequate performance and occupied less space.

The armament requirements of F7/41 was for six 20mm cannon with 120 rpg, and this again followed the trend set by the Whirlwind, though not mounted in the extreme nose. In the Welkin four 20mm cannon were mounted under the fuselage centre section, the other two — one in each wing root — were cancelled during development.

The pressure cabin was built as a bolt-on separate unit and was complete with windscreen and hood, being removable from the centre plane. Due to experiments carried on at a Government armament establishment, it had been determined that aluminium plate could form an armoured surface for projectiles hitting at oblique angles. So Westland used this principle in building the pressure cabin, constructing it with a 9mm armour plate front end attached to an annular casting, with the cabin side panels of various thicknesses of aluminium plate curved to the shape of the fuselage, with the thickest panels at the front and tapering to the rear; with the rear end closed by a 4mm thick curved armoured bulkhead. The windscreen was built into the cabin structure with it sloping rearwards to the apex of a built-up arch. This and the sliding portion of the hood were sealed by inflatable gaskets. A detachable nose cowling set off the front of the cabin and also provided mountings for a camera gun and a cold air scoop.

The rear fuselage consisted of 'planks' of thick magnesium alloy in longitudinal lengths joined at the edges by buttstraps, with skin reinforcing supplied by 'T' section extrusions and channel section stringers. Scalloped doubling plates extended all the way around the front end where it joined the integral centre section mainplane and fuselage.

The mainplane consisted of a centre section and outer planes, port and starboard. The centre section was constructed in one piece across the fuselage,

and was built around two spars, which in the radiator ducts had oval section tubes interbracing the booms, with the spars in the area of the nacelles and outboard having plate webs. The inner ribs on each side next to the fuselage formed the main joint with the fuselage. The outer plane main spar was bolted to the centre section main spar with a false rear spar supporting the tail ribs with the nose ribs riveted and bolted to the skinning and spar. Fuel tanks were built up from two cast end ribs, duralumin front and rear plates, and top and bottom panels which were tapered in thickness. The whole was de Burgue riveted to the ribs, which acted as intermediate baffles in the tanks. The front tanks had an armour plate panel bolted to the front across the centre plane leading edge.

The nacelles carried the powerplants at the front and provided attachment points and housing for the main undercarriage units. The undercarriage doors were hinged along their top edge and were automatically operated by the undercarriage movements. The undercarriage legs housed oleos, to which were bolted at the base the axle and wheel, the whole retracting to the rear.

The flaps were in two portions, extending from the fuselage sides to the mainplane joint, the inner portion of the flap acting also as part of the radiator cooling duct. The flaps and the ailerons were of all metal construction and metal covered, with the ailerons being of the inset hinge and shielded nose type.

The tailplane was detachable from the fin and consisted of a main spar, ribs and stringers, covered by a dural stressed skin. The fin supported the tailplane and formed a detachable end to the rear fuselage. The fin spar extended downwards and spread through the lower portion to form attachment points for the tailwheel unit. The rudder and elevator were both divided into two sections, and were based on spars with angle section booms, flanged plate ribs with a metal skin riveted on.

All the control surfaces were operated by push-pull control rods from a conventionally jointed control column and rudder bar, but the rudder was fitted with a spring bias gear, electrically operated from the cockpit. Apart from the sixty-seven aircraft manufactured, a further amount of spares were also produced for at least the same number again; these were sent to Maintenance Units, but rumour has it that many were buried after the war.

First flights on the Welkin during contractor's

Welkin prototype DG558/G with modified fin and rudder. (R.K. Page)

trials determined that the aircraft was tail heavy, ailerons not very effective and overbalanced, and the rudder was heavy. When the rudder was applied and then released it tended to oscillate. Positive elevator angle of 5° was necessary to keep the aircraft level at cruising speed. The CSUs were a weak point on the engines and were the cause of a number of incidents and accidents; on one test flight on DG558 the port CSU failed and caused a forced landing at Zeals. Further CSU failures, during the testing period at the works, resulted in a forced landing at Yeovilton which then, due to circumstances, developed into a crash-landing. Apparently the MAP was not particularly worried about this, as the aircraft had flown ahead of schedule and was not particularly badly damaged, so DG558 was repaired and modified. The propellers were changed to 12 ft 6 in diameter DH Hydromatic type, and the tailplane was increased slightly by a new tip contour with the

elevator having a horn balance added.

Over a number of dives carried out by Penrose preliminary vibration set in, and when the dive angle was persisted in the outer wing sections began to flap. This resulted in correspondence between Westland and the RAE Farnborough, as Westland's aerodynamics department felt that they had shock stall conditions on the outer wing sections; nothing further came of this as the aircraft was Mach limited.

DG558 was despatched to A&AEE for trials, where it was tested at an all-up weight of 18,250 lb. The maximum speeds recorded there were 375 mph at 25,000 ft and 323 mph at 40,000 ft. During further tests at the A&AEE with DG558 an engine fire occurred and resulted in an emergency landing at Upavon with a burnt-through starboard aileron control. The A&AEE handling report on the second production Welkin (DX279), which was powered by a Merlin 72 (port) and Merlin 73 (starboard) and flown at Boscombe Down during October 1943, gave the following: taxying was easy; flew off in a three point attitude; climb was good with steep angle of climb; longitudinal and lateral stability were neutral and the directional stability positive; control harmonisation was good; landing the aircraft in a three point position was no problem and the undercarriage had little bounce. Items faulted were: ailerons were not very effective at any speed or altitude and rate of roll slow; *at low altitudes* the elevator was effective but extremely heavy for combat, and lateral control poor (it *was* designed for high altitude fighting!); and asymmetric flight with an engine shut off resulted in unacceptable features. Further to this, as foreseen, compressibility effects started to restrict the aircraft's performance in the dive, for at about 0.66 M the aircraft began to porpoise with nose-down pitch. In regard to the pressure cabin Westland had a winner, for the cockpit control and environment at 40,000 ft was comfortable without problems.

DX286 went to the Air Fighting Development Unit for assessment and comparative trials at high altitudes, as well as trials of equipment; while DX328 was allocated to RAE Farnborough for research into pressure cabins and equipment.

Later on in the war Westland received a contract for a trial installation of uprated Merlin RM16SM engines in Welkin DX340, these engines being later developed into the Merlin 113 and 114. The unusual feature with these power plants in the Welkin was that they had 'beard' radiators for increased cooling capacity. When flight tested in this condition DX340 had an increased top speed of 398 mph at 30,000 ft.

A further contract awarded to Westland was to develop and flight test an engine boosting system that had been conceived at RAE Farnborough, using liquid oxygen injected into the induction manifold. The aircraft in which the trial installation was mounted was the second prototype (DG562), and the liquid oxygen was carried in a 70-gallon light alloy tank insulated with glass wool, being led to the engine through a system of triple concentric pipes. At the flow rates eventually used at altitude, this gave approximately 200 shp, or equivalent to 50 per cent increase at 50,000 ft. This liquid oxygen system proved more effective than the nitreous oxide system tried in Mosquito night-fighters, which gave a far smaller power increase for a greater weight penalty of the installation.

Regarding the mainplane's thickness/chord ratio and its effect on performance, the decision was made to increase the chord, so as to give a lower aerodynamic ratio, and this was proposed to the Ministry. This proposal was quite simple as a modification, for it was intended to increase the chord forward of the front spar by about 12 per cent; this would have reduced the average T/C ratio outboard of the nacelles from 18 to about 16 per cent. The Ministry replied that this improvement was not required, more or less indicating that use of

Westland Welkin Mk II two-seat night-fighter. (K. Page)

the Welkin was limited. This was no doubt due to the Luftwaffe failing to exploit the tactical advantage gained with their high altitude bombers, for the flights ceased and so the countermeasure in the form of the Welkin was no longer required.

In 1945 a two-seat version was produced as a high altitude night-fighter; this was the Mk 2 serial numbered PF370, and was a conversion from a Mk 1. The Mk 2 was produced against specification F9/43, and was demonstrated at the 1946 SBAC Flying Display. Though basically similar to the Mk 1 it had a longer cabin, in which the pilot was

positioned further forward, with a radar observer seated behind facing aft. The windscreen was re-designed with a deeper sill and a longer nose to house the radar, making the fuselage 44 ft 1 in long. Also altered was the dihedral on the outer wings, which was increased from 3° to 4½°. Power was provided by two 1,250 hp Merlin 76 and 77 engines.

The Welkin never went operational, the threat had ceased; a few of them were used on research projects, but the majority and their spares rested in MUs.

Westland Welkin prototype DG558/G with original fin and rudder. (IWM)

Performance comparison of Welkin Mk 1 and 2

	Mk 1.	Mk 2.
Maximum speed at height	387 mph @ 26,000 ft	360 mph @ 30,000 ft
	358 mph @ 40,000 ft	330 mph @ 40,000 ft
Rate of climb	3,850 ft/min	2,650 ft/min
Service ceiling	42,500	41,000 ft
Take-off distance over 50 ft barrier	600 yards	1,115 yards
Landing distance over 50 ft barrier	680 yards	750 yards
Empty weight	14,420 lb	15,635 lb
All-up weight	19,840 lb	21,892 lb

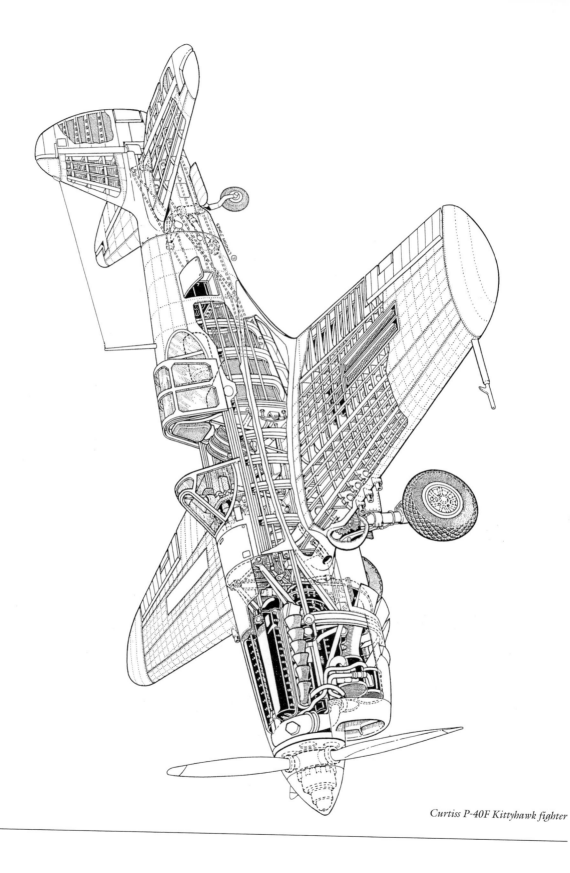

Curtiss P-40F Kittyhawk fighter

21

Curtiss P-40 Kittyhawk (Warhawk)

When the British Air Purchasing Commission was in the USA purchasing aircraft for the Royal Air Force, the P-40 was one of the aircraft types contracted for in quantity. To be fair, there were few American fighters in production comparable to their British or German counterparts, and the P-40 was about the nearest. Having said that, the RAF Army Co-operation Command got good practice in with them, and the type was well used in the North African desert campaign. The P-40 was a product of the Curtiss Airplane Division of the Curtiss Wright Corporation, and the aircraft dates back to early 1937; in fact, even farther than that if one accepts that it was a logical development of the Hawk 75 (P-36 in the USAAC). The Hawk 75 was a compact, manoeuvrable single-seat fighter, which could be powered either by the Pratt & Whitney Twin Wasp or Wright Cyclone engine. It was under-armed in comparison with the Hurricane or Spitfire, but was of fairly rugged construction. The USAAC pre-war viewed the fighter (or pursuit) as a ground attack or low altitude fighter, as opposed to the British point

Curtiss Hawk 75 (P-36) 'Mohawk', predecessor of the P-40 Tomahawk. (IWM)

of view, which was as an interceptor for medium or high altitudes. Yet during the 1941–45 period of the war, it would be the Americans who would clamber for the high altitudes with their bombers and fighters.

The P-36 (Hawk 75), after the 1937 USAAC pursuit competition, was awarded a contract for production aircraft; at the same time the Curtiss design team already had their eye on a further development; for Allison Motors were developing their Vee 12-cylinder liquid-cooled engine under USAAC funding. Curtiss development of the P-36 took two lines, one was a reworked P-36 powered with a turbo-blown Allison V-1710-C15 engine, this was the XP-37; the other was the XP-40 with the normal supercharged V-1710 engine. The XP-37 with its turbo-blower Allison had a power of 1150hp at 20,000ft. This was followed by thirteen YP-37s, which were powered by the Allison V-1710-21

engine, and were the Service test version of the XP-37, having a 25-in fuselage length increase aft of the cockpit. The XP-37 was easily identified in appearance, for it had the cockpit set behind the mainplane trailing edge, and thus a deep fuselage just forward of the fin. The turbo-blower proved too troublesome for immediate incorporation, so development went ahead on the XP-40, which had the manufacturer's designation of Hawk 81. The XP-40 was then awarded in April 1939 a contract for 540 aircraft, having won the USAAC's Pursuit Competition against much more advanced designs. With this a number of modifications were incorporated in the XP-40 design, and this became the P-40. The radiator was moved nearer to the nose, the armament was changed to two 0.5-in machine-guns synchronised to fire through the propeller, with provision for two 0.3-in machine-guns in the wings. Alterations were also made to

Curtiss P-40F Kittyhawk Mk.II (Warhawk) FL220 powered by Packard Merlin V-1650. (RAF)

Curtiss P-40B fighter of 33rd Pursuit Squadron that overshot Reykjavik runway – a frequent occurrence. (Author)

speed production and to reduce drag.

The French Armèe de l'Air had by that date purchased Hawk 75-A (RAF Mohawk) to supplement its inadequately equipped fighter arm; and had also placed orders for the export version of the P-40, the Hawk H-81-A model. These latter aircraft had not been delivered before the Armistice in June 1940 and were taken on charge by the RAF. The aircraft had metric calibrated instruments, no self-sealing fuel tanks and no armour, so were

relegated to the training role. The aircraft ordered by the RAF were known as P-40Bs and named Tomahawk II, the manufacturer's designation being Hawk H-81A-2. Deliveries of these began in September 1940, but it was not until June 1941 that they went into action in the North African desert. Next produced was the Mk IIB, which was the equivalent of the P-40C (Hawk H-81A-3) and was the last model powered with the Allison engine before the introduction of the Kittyhawk.

Although the Tomahawk had a rugged airframe and had been found capable of absorbing a large amount of damage, as a fighter it was not in the same league as the Bf 109E. While being successful in the ground attack-strafing role, it became the victim of enemy fighters due to its performance at altitude. In reviewing the situation, Curtiss proposed the use of the Packard-built two-speed single-stage Merlin 28, which could offer a higher power output at altitude. Permission was sought and granted to trial install one in a P-40, which was designated the XP-40F. This aircraft first flew on 30 June 1941, and was a P-40D airframe fitted with a Merlin 28: the P-40D being a Kittyhawk I (known in the USAAF as the Warhawk) with the works designation of Hawk H-87-B2, this latter model going into service with the USAAF in May 1941. 560 of the Kittyhawk Is were built for the RAF, serial numbers AK571 to AL230. A total of 1,311 P-40Fs were built and a number allocated to the RAF as Kittyhawk IIs, having the P-40E armament of six 0.5-in machine-guns; the P-40E being the Kittyhawk IA and powered with the Allison engine. Before the full number of contracted Kittyhawk IIs could be delivered, a number of them were re-possessed (!) by the USAAF for use in North Africa. The third P-40F was retained at the works for experiments with repositioning of the radiator to improve performance, but the original position was found to be the best.

The P-40F-5 models onwards had their fuselages extended by about 20 in, being inserted by the tailplane section; this was added to improve directional stability. The P-40F was the only Merlin-powered Kittyhawk to be assigned to the RAF, and were very small in number once the USAAF had acquired their share. The P-40Ls were similar to the Merlin-powered P-40Fs, but with minor equipment changes. This was a lightweight version having reduced armament, and was intended to be powered by the Packard Merlin engine, but due to a shortage of Merlins and spares a number of the P-40F and L models were refitted with the Allison. The Kittyhawk IV was also intended to be fitted with the Merlin engine, being the P-40P, but was then redesignated P-40N and fitted with Allison engines. These were the V-1710-99 or 81 rated at 1470 hp.

Construction of the airframe was quite conventional, with no advanced features of any sort; the mainplane was of the multi-spar type with seven spars and an aerofoil section of NACA series 2200. Flanged ribs and spanwise stringers were covered with flush riveted Alclad skin. The fuselage was built in two halves, which were joined together after the installation of equipment, the whole of metal construction and Alclad covered. The tail unit like the main wings were of multi-spar construction, with the control surfaces fabric covered. The undercarriage was retracted by hydraulic operation, with the main wheels retracting to the rear and pivoting about their axes, so that they lay flush with the undersurface. The flaps were of the split type and were hydraulically operated and metal constructed and covered.

Armament varied throughout the series of P-40s, in the end standardising on six 0.5-in machine-guns in the Kittyhawk series, except where already stated. The position of the tailplane was also changed on the later models, and a small dorsal addition made to the fin shape. A further change over the series was the difference in the windshield shape, with the later models having an unstrutted side glass. A 'bubble' type hood was also installed experimentally on one aircraft, but this never became standard.

By the time production of the P-40 had been terminated, 13,738 had been built of all series and models, and though outdated had still been employed on operational duties. The Kittyhawks in the North African desert campaign were carrying at the end, as fighter-bombers, the bomb-load that had been related to light bombers in 1940. In the Middle-East 112 Squadron became the first to adopt the 'Shark's teeth' markings on their Tomahawks, pre-dating the American Volunteer Group (The AVG) in China. This group were issued a quantity of P-40 aircraft from the British contract, so as to carry on their good work.

The P-40 was not an outstanding aircraft, but it was a rugged aircraft; it helped to achieve Allied victory in North Africa, Sicily, Italy and Burma. With the Merlin engine installed it became more competitive, and a number of World War Two aces gained that status on it.

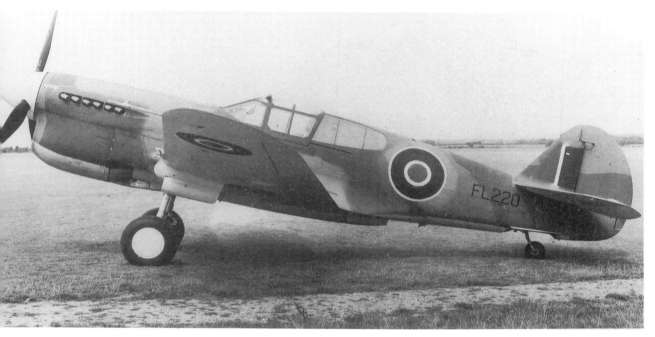

Curtiss P-40F Kittyhawk Mk.II (Warhawk) fighter of RAF. (RAF)

Comparison of Allison and Merlin-engined P-40

	P-40B	*P-40F*
Engine	Allison 1,150 hp	Merlin 1,240 hp
Wingspan	37 ft 3½ in	37 ft 3½ in
Wing area	236 sq ft	236 sq ft
Length	31 ft 8¾ in	31 ft 7⅔ in
Empty weight	5,622 lb	6,190 lb
Maximum weight	7,610 lb	8,674 lb
Maximum speed	351 mph at 15,000 ft	370 mph at 22,000 ft
Climbing rate	15,000 ft in 5.65 min	15,000 ft in 6.9 min
Service ceiling	30,000 ft	32,000 ft
Armament	Two 0.5-in mgs and two 0.3-in mgs	Six 0.5-in mgs.

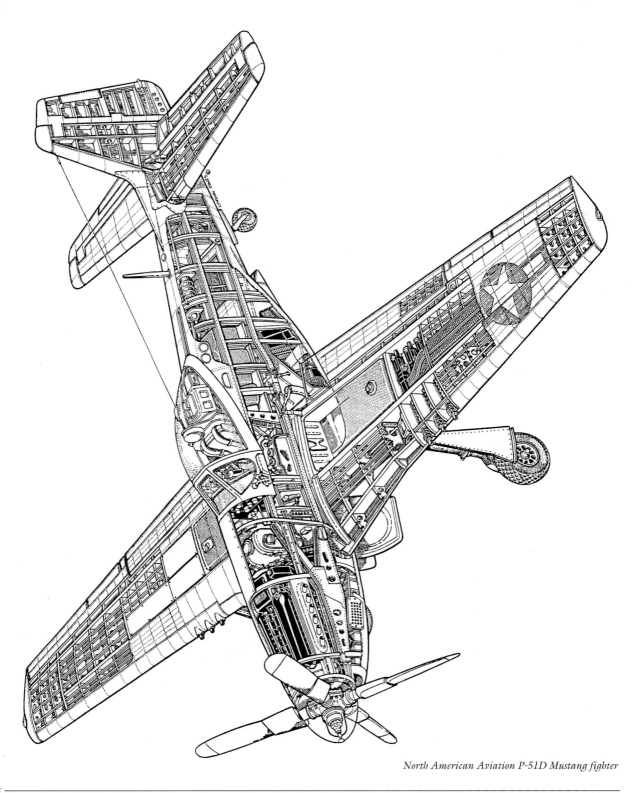

North American Aviation P-51D Mustang fighter

22

North American Aviation Mustang

In early 1940, the British Air Purchasing Commission was in the USA with the purpose of purchasing aircraft for the Royal Air Force. In the pursuit of purchasing aircraft, whether due to haste or lack of expertise, the RAF received a number of aircraft types for operational use that were so obsolete, that even in the training role, their use was marginal, aircraft such as the Chesapeake, Digby and Helldiver. The purchase of the P-39 and P-40 was a matter of course, as no other fighter aircraft was satisfactory, and neither of these were operationally comparable to the British aircraft in service in Europe. When it was found that the Curtiss Airplane Division were unable to supply sufficient P-40 aircraft, the Purchasing Commission made an approach to North American Aviation with a proposal that they licence-produce the Curtiss aircraft. Whilst the approach was welcomed by

NAA's President, J.H. Kindleberger, he counter-proposed that his company design an entirely new fighter, that would incorporate all the latest aerodynamic and constructional features of aircraft design. Not only was Kindleberger and his team against building what they considered a dated design, but they had their own ideas of a fighter aircraft for the European theatre of operations — and in hindsight, we can say thank goodness for that. The British accepted this proposal, but stipulated that the prototype must be completed within 120 days; they also laid down a number of requirements, mainly relating to equipment and armament, but also stipulated a liquid-cooled engine. Whether the time factor laid down was to deter the North American Aviation engineering staff, or panic to get more aircraft it would be hard to judge. Nevertheless, within 100 days the NAA team

NA P-51 Mustang Mk.IV powered by a Packard Merlin 68 engine. (RAF)

North American Mustang Mk.III fitted with Malcolm sliding hood and Packard Merlin engine. (RAF)

under R. Rice and E. Schmued (the latter an ex-Messerschmitt employee) had designed, built and prepared the airframe — known as the NA-73. The British were able to view the design prior to flight, as the promised Allison V-1710 delivery was delayed. This held back the NA-73X prototype's first flight until 26 October 1940.

In its project state the design was rejected by the USAAC, but NAA persisted with it and produced the NA-73. Basing their design on a laminar flow wing with a wingspan of fractionally over thirty-seven feet, with the whole aircraft shape and design geared to ease of production American style. They produced the NA-73 with a wing loading of 32.6lb/sq ft, a wing area of 235.95 sq ft, powered by an Allison engine that gave a power loading of 7.34 lb/bhp. Before any contract was signed with the British it was agreed that the 5th and 10th first

North American Mustang AL975-G at Rolls-Royce Hucknall modified with Merlin 60 engine. (Rolls-Royce)

series Model NA-73 should go to Wright Field for USAAC test evaluation, these aircraft being designated the XP-51. The test flights at Wright Field with the two aircraft determined that their recorded maximum speed was 382 mph. Unfortunately, the first prototype on its fifth test flight, being flown by NAA's Chief Test Pilot, Vance Breeze, had an engine cut on the approach, crashed in a ploughed field short of the runway and turned over and broke its back. This alone would have convinced many manufacturers to take the easy way out, but NAA had faith in their design and pressed on with it and produced the Mustang; which turned out to be one of the most outstanding fighter aircraft of World War II and certainly the finest long-range fighter. Very few modifications were required to the basic design of the XP-73 before it went into production.

The Mustang I was fitted with the Allison V-1710-F3R engine, which was rated at 1,150 hp at 11,700 ft. It had a mixed armament of two 0.5in machine-guns synchronised to fire through the propeller, and two more 0.5-in and four 0.3-in machine-guns in the wings. The Allison engine was soon found to have sufficient power low down, but not at the operational heights that the fighting was

now taking place at. The Mustang IA next appeared with the Allison rated at 1,125 hp at 15,000 ft and its armament changed to four 20mm Hispano-Suiza cannon; but even this engine power was failing to do justice to the airframe's capabilities. The next model was the Mustang II, or P-51A, which had an armament of four 0.5-in machine-guns in the wings, but this was considered weak against the eight of the P-47 Thunderbolt. A further point in the combat criticism of the Mustang, the name chosen by the British and accepted by the USAAF when they purchased the P-51, was its rearward vision, which although improved with retro-fitted Malcolm hoods, was still far from satisfactory. The first production Mustang (AG345) made its first flight on 16 April 1941, and the second production Mustang I (AG346) was shipped to the United Kingdom.

After tests at Boscombe Down, which determined that it was a very good fighter, except for its low-rated Allison engine, which lacked performance at altitude; a Mustang serial number AG422 was on test at AFDU Duxford, which soon determined that it was operationally unacceptable for Fighter Command. After this the Mustang in its then present form was relegated to Army Co-operation Command for low level sweeps and tactical photo-

NA Mustang Mk.IV post-war, owner Stephen Grey, at British Airways LHR 19. (Author)

reconnaissance. The handling characteristics on the other hand were exceptional, and so the Commanding Officer of the AFDU, I. Campbell-Orde, invited a member of Rolls-Royce test team, R. Harker, to carry out an evaluation of the aircraft's flight envelope and give his assessment. This was carried out on 29 April 1942, which resulted in Harker being very impressed with the aircraft's characteristics and handling; and in particular the light and effective aileron control and internal fuel tankage of 269 gallons — far in excess of British fighter aircraft. As has been told before, Harker immediately saw the possibilities of this aircraft as a long-range fighter if the airframe was re-engined with the RR. Merlin 60 series engine.

On return to Rolls-Royce, Harker asked the company's performance expert, Witold Challier, to carry out an estimate of the performance improvement with the Merlin engine installed. When Challier presented his report, this indicated that with the Merlin XX the top speed would be 400 mph at 18,600 ft and with the Merlin 60 the top speed would be 441 mph at 25,500 ft. With these figures Harker tried to convince the management of the viability of such a combination as the Merlin-Mustang, but to no avail. After a talk with Ray Dorey of the RR Hucknall team, Harker put his proposal to Hives and was persuasive enough to convince Hives to authorise a conversion. With that Hives contacted Air Marshal Sir Wilfrid Freeman at the Ministry, who despatched three Mustang airframes, AL963, AL975 and AM121 from the Lockheed handling unit in the UK to Hucknall. The first Mustang converted was AL975, which made its first flight on 13 October 1942, being powered by a Merlin 65 driving a 10ft 9in diameter propeller. The type was given the official designation of Mustang X, but was always known at Hucknall as the Merlin-Mustang. A great deal of experimental work was carried out on the three aircraft, with different engines, propellers and various radiator ductings. In the initial conversion the nose air-intake for the carburettor and supercharger-intercooler was quite large, but over a period of time this was changed until the final and more acceptable position and contour was found. On the seventh test flight of AL975 a 11 ft 4 in diameter propeller was fitted and the reduction gear ratio was changed to 0.42 to 1, and with this combination a top speed of 432 mph at 25,000 ft was recorded. The flight test data was passed to North American Aviation, as had the

original decision to convert to the Merlin. The conversion was also commenced by NAA at the same time, and a competition on who would finish first commenced; being won by the Hucknall team by six weeks. The NA-78 (XP-51B) having its first flight on 30 November 1942, this also had a different carburettor air intake/intercooler intake to the Hucknall Merlin-Mustang, and was fitted with the Packard Merlin V-1650-7 (Merlin 68) engine. The US Air Attaché in London had reported to Washington that the British were converting the Mustangs to Merlins, so that when the results of the flight tests of the conversions were known, production go-ahead was given by the USAAF. The Packard Merlin version of the Mustang became the P-51B in service with the USAAF and Mustang III in the RAF. Though similar in general outline to previous marks, it did differ around the engine and radiator installation; there was now no intake on top of the engine, but a small intake just below and behind the propeller spinner for the intercooler, and the radiator intake was separate from the fuselage, now having a pronounced projection. During delivery of a number of Merlin-Mustangs a number of engine mounting bolts failed; this was eventually traced to incorrect heat treatment. Meantime the Mustangs were grounded whilst the fault was traced and the bolts changed, and fortunately no aircraft were lost in flight due to this production failure.

The Mustang Is, used by Army Co-operation Command were fitted with single F24 or K24 cameras, and made their operational debut on the 10 May 1942. The Mustang also had the distinction of being the first single-seat fighter based in Britain to have penetrated the German heartland, when on 21 October 1942 an attack was made along the Dortmund-Ems Canal, covering between 600–700 miles on an out and return journey. By December 1943 the Mustangs were in action with their support of the 'big brothers' of the 8th Air Force in day raids into Germany. When the P-51D was introduced and drop tanks fitted under the wings, increasing their fuel capacity to 489 US gallons, Berlin was brought within their radius of action.

At the NAA plant at Inglewood, two P-51Bs were taken off the production line with a view to eradicating some of the faults found in combat. One of these modifications involved the cutting down of the fuselage aft of the cockpit and the strengthening of the area, then a 360° 'bubble-top' was fitted, wings strengthened to take heavier external loads and the airframe generally tidied up. This aircraft then went into production as the P-51D (RAF Mustang IV). This model was produced both at Inglewood and Dallas, the former factory fitting 11 ft diameter Hamilton-Standard propellers, and the Dallas factory fitting 11 ft 2 in diameter Aeroproducts propellers. The P-51D with its cut down rear fuselage and reduced keel surface was found to have reduced directional stability, so once production got underway, this was compensated for by the addition of a dorsal fin strake. A number of P-51D aircraft were converted to TP-51D trainers, whilst over one hundred were produced as F-6D and F-6K tactical-reconnaissance aircraft with cameras.

Pilots interviewed about the Mustang went into raptures over it and compliments became superfluous, one very experienced fighter pilot classified it as the finest fighter of World War Two. In the fighter scene the Luftwaffe viewed it with the same respect that they had for the Spitfire in the Battle of Britain; their test centre, Rechlin, also placed it on the top shelf, with words like handling and performance characteristics very good, control forces low, little trimming required. Having said that, how can one describe one of the finest fighting aircraft, its performance, its manoeuvrability? The Mustang had few vices, though the lack of pre-stall buffeting could mean that an over-confident 'sprog' pilot could get bitten. The Mk III's rate of roll was only slightly less than the Fw 190; its performance and handling at altitude had originally not been as good as the Spitfire V, and compressibility effects had showed up at a lower Mach Number than the Spitfire. Pilots found that the Merlin-Mustang was not quite so pleasant to fly as the Allison-powered version, and the combination not so smooth. With the Mk III the stalling characteristics were mild, but with the Mk IV the wing would drop sharply in high speed stalls. In general the landing approach left a lot to be desired regarding vision forward, but the tailwheel lock and good brakes stopped the type's desire to charge off course on touchdown. The cockpit was cramped for the distances that the aircraft was capable of flying; the Merlin, like all liquid cooled engines, was vulnerable with its plumbing to battle damage — having said that, one can only again return to the theme that the Merlin and Mustang were a fantastic combination.

The construction of the Mustang involved the laminar flow wing section, constructed around a two spar wing, with the spars of extruded booms joined by a plate web, pressed ribs with flanges and lightening holes, extruded spanwise stringers covered by an Alclad skin. The ailerons were of the single slot variety, based on a single spar and metal covered, being operated hydraulically. The fuselage was built in three sections, mainly constructed around aluminium alloy extrusions, with the engine mounted on two 'Vee' type cantilever engine bearers. The front section of the fuselage was based on two beams consisting of two longerons, with lateral vertical frames. Aft of the cockpit the second section is of semi monocoque construction, with the longerons extending into it with vertical transverse frames that are covered with Alclad skinning. This continued into the tail section. The fin and tailplane structure was conventional and similar, based on two spars, pressed ribs and extruded spanwise stringers, covered by Alclad skinning. The rudder and elevators were of metal construction and dynamically balanced. The undercarriage was of the inward-retracting type with cantilever air-oil shock absorbers, that had a track of 11 ft 10 in. Each main undercarriage leg was mounted on a large forging bolted into the reinforced wing area, and was hydraulically retracted. The tailwheel also retracted and was fitted with a lock for take-off and landing. Brake operation was by hydraulics also.

The Allison-engined models added a further role to its name, when it was designated the A-36 attack bomber; this had slat or grating type dive brakes installed above and below the mainplanes, and bomb-racks fitted underneath; these aircraft took part in the invasions of Sicily and Italy with the USAAF. With RAF Bomber Command, Group Captain Cheshire of 617 Squadron pioneered the use of the Mustang for specialist target marking. The Mustang also spread its wings in Australia, where the Commonwealth Aircraft Corporation produced Mustangs from imported components. Here in Great Britain an interesting 'one-off' came into being, when Alan Muntz and Co of Heston airport fitted a Maclaren drift undercarriage to a Mustang. So even though the Mustang was American designed and built, Britain can claim some credit for its conception, credit for the Merlin engine which powered it to fame, but we can thank the North American Aviation design team for a remarkable airframe, that made the Mustang an outstanding fighter — some would say *the greatest fighter*.

NA Mustang Mk.IV being refuelled at Blackbushe airport. (Author)

Comparison between Allison and Merlin-powered aircraft.

	P-51A	*P-51D*
Wingspan	37 ft	37 ft 0½ in
Wing area	233 sq ft	233 sq ft
Length	32 ft 1⅞ in	32 ft 3 in
Empty weight	5,990 lb	7,125 lb
Maximum loaded weight	7,708 lb	11,600 lb
Engine	Allison V 1710	Merlin 68
Armament	four 0.5-in mgs	six 0.5-in mgs
Maximum speed	390 mph at	437 mph at
	8,000 ft	25,000 ft
Initial rate of climb	2,000 ft/min	3,900 ft/min
Service ceiling	32,000 ft	41,900 ft
Maximum range	1,000 mile	2,080 mile

Abbreviations

A&AEE	Aeroplane and Armament Experimental Establishment.
AASF	Advanced Air Striking Force.
ABC	Automatic boost control.
ADAP	Acting Director Aircraft Production.
AFDU	Air Fighting Development Unit.
AID	Aircraft Inspection Department.
AMRD	Air Member for Research and Development.
AMSR	Air Member for Supply and Research.
ARB	Air Registration Board.
ASV	Air-to-surface-vessel radar.
AW	Armstrong-Whitworth.
BHP	Brake horse power.
Bf	Bayerische Flugzeugwerke AG, manufacturer of Messerschmitt aircraft.
BOAC	British Overseas Airways Corporation.
BSAA	British South American Airways.
CAM	Catapult armed merchantman.
CAS	Chief of Air Staff.
CO	Commanding Officer.
C of G	Centre of Gravity.
CSU	Constant speed unit.
D12	Curtiss D12 liquid-cooled aero-engine.
DB	Daimler-Benz aero-engine.
DC3	Douglas DC-3 transport, known in RAF as Dakota.
DD/DTD	Deputy Director of Directorate of Technical Development.
DD/RDA	Deputy Director of Research and Development.
DH	de Havilland.
DOR	Director of Operational Research.
DTD	Director, or Directorate, of Technical Development.
FAA	Fleet Air Arm of the Royal Navy.
FS gear	Refers to high gear of supercharging — fully supercharged.
FTH	Full throttle height.
FN	Frazer-Nash — gun turrets.
Fw	Focke-Wulf, prefix before the type number or name.
Glycol	Ethylene Glycol coolant.
HF	Prefix to Spitfire Mk indicating high altitude fighter; also high frequency in reference to radio telephony.
HMS	His Majesty's Ship.
HP	Handley Page, usually before type number, or 'HP' when referring to Sir Frederick Handley Page. Can also mean high pressure.
H2S	Refers to, and is the code name for, a radar navigational and bombing aid using the Magnetron valve and revolving scanner.
Ju	Junkers, prefix before the aircraft type number.
LF	Prefix to Spitfire Mk indicating low altitude version.
MAP	Ministry, or Minister, of Aircraft Production.
mph	Miles per hour.
MS gear	Refers to low gear of supercharging — moderately supercharged.
MU	Maintenance Unit, all of which are serialised.
NF	Night-fighter version.
NPL	National Physics Laboratory, Teddington.
OBOE	Radar bombing aid.
ORC	Operational Requirements Committee.
OTU	Operational Training Unit.
P12	Fairey 'Vee' 12-cylinder liquid-cooled engine, later named Prince.
P24	Fairey 24-cylinder engine with two halves of the engine driving contra-rotating propellers.
PR	Photographic Reconnaissance version.
PV	Private venture design.
PV12	Rolls-Royce private venture engine that became the Merlin.
RAE	Royal Aircraft Establishment.
RAF	Royal Air Force of Great Britain.
RATO	Rocket assisted take-off units.
RR	Rolls-Royce Ltd.
SAMM	Société d'Applications des Machines Motrices.
SBAC	Society of British Aircraft Constructors.
Schrage Musik	German name for the obliquely fixed guns installed in their night-fighters, allowing them to fire upwards at bombers.
TAG	Telegraphist air gunner, FAA equivalent of RAF wireless operator air gunner.
UK	United Kingdom.
USA	United States of America.
USAAC	United States Army Air Corps.
USAAF	United States Army Air Force.
VIP	Very Important Person.

Bibliography

This book is based mainly on reports from the A&AEE, RAE Farnborough and the Public Records Office Kew, Air Publications and personal archives, but for further reading on the subjects the following are recommended.

Adventure with Fate by H. Penrose, published by Airlife Publishing.

Hurricane by E. Bishop, published by Airlife Publishing.

Halifax – Second to None by V.F. Bingham, published by Airlife Publishing.

Not Much of An Engineer by Sir Stanley Hooker, published by Airlife Publishing.

Pathfinder by Air Vice-Marshal D. Bennett, published by Bennett.

Development of Aircraft Engines by E. Schlaifer, published by Harvard University Press.

History of World War 2, Design and development of weapons by M.D. Hay and J.D. Scott, published by HMSO.

British Aviation – Ominous Years 1935–39 by H. Penrose, published by HMSO.

Cooling of Aircraft Engines by F.W.Matthews. ARC R&M 1683, published by HMSO.

British Naval Aircraft since 1912 by Owen Thetford, published by Putnam.

Avro Aircraft Since 1908 by A.J. Jackson, published by Putnam.

Vickers Aircraft Since 1908 by C.F. Andrews, published by Putnam.

Rolls-Royce, Merlin at War by Ian Lloyd, published by McMillan.

The Merlin in Perspective, The Combat Years by Alec Harvey-Bailey, published by the Rolls-Royce Heritage Trust.

The Curtiss D12 Engine, published by the Smithsonian Institute.

Confound and Destroy by Martin Streetly, published by Jane's Publishing Co.

Mosquito by C. Martin Sharp and Michael J.F. Bowyer, published by Faber & Faber.

Birth of a Legend, the Spitfire by Jeffrey Quill, published by Quiller Press.

Bristol Beaufighter by V.F.Bingham, published by Airlife.

Index